The
Houseplant
Survival
Manual

The
Houseplant
Survival Manual

How to keep your houseplants healthy

William Davidson

Photography by Ian Howes

BOOK CLUB ASSOCIATES

London

A QED BOOK

This edition published 1982 by Book Club Associates by
arrangement with the copyright holder.

CN 3516
First printing 1982
Reprinted 1983

This book was conceived, designed and produced by
QED Publishing Limited, 32 Kingly Court, London W1.
Art director Alastair Campbell
Production director Edward Kinsey
Editorial director Jeremy Harwood
Senior editor Kathy Rooney
Project editor Nicola Thompson
Art editor Caroline Courtney
Editorial Louise Aylward , Carol Cormack, Victoria Funk,
Jane Kenrick, Judy Martin, Caroline Oulton
Designer Dennis Thompson
Illustrators Nigel Chamberlain, Chris Forsey, Edwina Keene,
Elly King, John Woodcock
Paste-up Chris Dickson

QED would like to thank the many houseplant experts who have
given so generously of their time and advice. In particular, they
would like to thank Valerie Day and all the staff of Thomas Rochford
& Sons Ltd., Turnford Hall Nurseries, Nr Broxbourne, Herts., without
whose help this book would have been impossible to compile.

Typeset in Great Britain by Oliver Burridge and Company Limited,
Crawley, Sussex and Flowery Typesetting, London.
Colour origination by Hong Kong Graphic Arts, Hong Kong.
Printed in Hong Kong by Leefung Asco Printers Ltd.

The photography for this book was specially commissioned from Ian
Howes, with the exceptions of p.79, p.88 (Harry Smith) and p.13,
pp.26-7, pp.36-9 (Thomas Rochford & Sons Ltd.).

Contents

	Page		Page
Foreword	6	Heptapleurum	124
Introduction	12	Hibiscus rosa-sinensis	126
Acalypha hispida	44	Hydrangea macrophylla	128
Aechmea	46	Impatiens	130
Aglaonema	48	Kalanchoe beharensis	132
Anthurium	50	Marantaceae	134
Aphelandra	52	Monstera deliciosa	138
Aralia elegantissima	54	Musa	140
Araucaria	56	Pachystachys lutea	141
Aspidistra lurida	58	Palms	142
Azalea indica	60	Passiflora	146
Begonia	62	Pelargonium	147
Beloperone guttata	66	Peperomia	150
Bougainvillea	68	Philodendron	152
Bromeliads	70	Pilea	156
Cacti and succulents	74	Pittosporum	158
Campanula isophylla	79	Primula	160
Chlorophytum comosum	80	Rhoicissus	162
Cineraria	82	Saintpaulia	164
Cissus	84	Sansevieria	166
Citrus mitis	86	Saxifraga sarmentosa	168
Clivia miniata	88	Schefflera	170
Codiaeum	90	Scindapsus	171
Columnea	92	Sinningia	172
Cyclamen persicum	94	Solanum capsicastrum	174
Cyperus	96	Sparmannia africana	175
Dieffenbachia	98	Spathiphyllum	176
Dracaena	102	Stephanotis floribunda	178
Euphorbia pulcherrima	104	Streptocarpus	179
Fatsia and Fatshedera	106	Tolmiea menziesii	180
Ferns	108	Tradescantia	181
Ficus	114	Yucca elephantipes	182
Fittonia	120	Zebrina pendula	183
Grevillea robusta	121	Glossary	184
Hedera	122	Index	186

Foreword

My introduction to the world of houseplants came in the late 1940s, when it became evident to my company that hederas, Ivies, were going to play a major part in houseplant development. As a consequence, it became my duty to care for what seemed millions of plants in a block of greenhouses stretching over a vast area. Some of the varieties I looked after then are still in demand today— *Hedera canariensis* is one of the most popular of all houseplants, if numbers sold are anything to judge by— while others seem to have totally disappeared, at least in their original guise. But, to this day, my affection for Ivies has remained. Some of this may be due to the fact that the first display of plants I ever put together was a collection of Ivies that won the Lindley Medal of Britain's Royal Horticultural Society. On display in the exhibit were specimens of *H. canariensis*, *H. maculata*, *H. helix 'Goldleaf'* (all larger-leaved forms), *H. helix 'Chicago'* (and its variegated form), *H. sagittaefolia*, *H. nielsen* and *H. heisse*.

All of these are still quite capable of holding their own against the many forms of Ivy that have appeared since then.

Though the houseplant world has been transformed in many ways since those early days, in this last respect things have remained virtually unaltered. As far as indoor plants are concerned, there have been few radical alterations in the number of plant varieties. The hederas, for instance, are still basically the same, while *Philodendron scandens*, *Rhoicissus rhomboidea*, *Sansevieria trifasciata*, *Monstera deliciosa* and *Ficus robusta* are only, if anything, more popular than ever. What has happened is that careful research and development has widened the available options in the existing varieties. The Rubber Plant, for example, has undergone numerous developments —so much so, indeed, that there is no comparison between *Ficus robusta*, the plant currently in favour, and *F. elastica*, the original version. Both are, of course, Rubber Plants, but the earlier one was a much poorer and thinner plant than its eventual successor. It was also much more difficult to grow successfully than the plant of today. Even the traditional favourite, rhoicissus, Grape Ivy, has had a new offspring in *R. rhomboidea Ellendanica*, which has indented lobes to its leaves and a more glossy appearance. *Ellendanica* indicates that the new plant originated in Denmark, the 'Ellen' being nothing more than the Christian name of the nurseryman on whose premises the common Grape Ivy decided to develop into a new variety!

Poinsettias, too, have improved almost out of all recognition over the last 30 years. The original plants, I recall, were tall and leggy. They were almost devoid of leaves and had thin bracts of washed-out red colouring. Research led to a more compact, shorter plant with many more leaves, which considerably improved its appearance. In addition, today's Poinsettia is easier to care for both in the nursery and the home. As a result of all these improvements, the quantity of Poinsettias sold has increased from practically none 25 years ago to the point where countless millions are sold throughout the world.

These few examples can only serve as an indication of how the houseplant world has changed since I first entered it. In addition to the developments in the plants themselves, there have been quite amazing improvements in the construction of greenhouses, automatic watering systems, ventilation and pest and disease control. Today, with the need to conserve energy as a priority, particular attention is being paid to the problems of heating and ventilation. The professional aim with every houseplant now grown is that it should occupy the minimum amount of space in the greenhouse for the minimum length of time and that heating requirements should be as minimal as possible. Yet, in spite of these somewhat limiting factors, high quality plants are still produced, since every professional knows that it is essential that standards be maintained, so that the optimum price can be commanded when the plant is offered for sale. Though growers are frequently taken to task for selling what the layman believes are inferior plants, in fact they go to much trouble and expense to ensure that the plants they produce are of the highest possible quality. Not only are inferior plants difficult to care for both in the nursery and the home; they also fetch far less and may not sell at all, if the standard falls below a certain level. It is invariably the better plants that are the easiest to sell, so there is everything to be said for putting all possible effort into producing plants of the best quality!

In case this sounds like special pleading, let me list some of the other improvements professionals have introduced, which can only benefit the amateur houseplant enthusiast. Though many traditionalists still cling to the old-fashioned clay pot, for instance, there is no doubt that plastic pots are more efficient, particularly for drainage. A clay pot is generally blessed with a single hole that can very easily become blocked for some reason or other while the numerous holes in the base of a plastic pot almost ensure good drainage which allows many plants to be watered by capillary action. Watering your plants slowly as a whole is more efficient and less time-consuming than dealing with them individually. You can also leave your plants with a clear conscience while you are on holiday! Of course, there are exceptions—*Cyperus alternifolius* and *Azalea indica*, for example, both need copious watering if they are to survive. But, in general, the capillary method works extremely well.

This book is intended to bring such professional expertise to the amateur in easy to follow, non-technical form. The majority of problems with houseplants can be avoided by a little common sense and remembering, in the words of the old saying, that prevention is better than cure. If you are on holiday in summer, for instance, it is only sensible to move your plants, with the exceptions of cacti and the sansevierias, out of direct sunlight, if possible; in winter, it is wise to make sure they will not become chilled. If a neighbour is caring for your plants, give them full instructions on how to look after them. Each plant is an individual, with its own characteristics and quirks.

Above all, remember that houseplants are fun. Despite all the advice I and other professionals can offer, there is always the exception—the broken rule that produces a completely contradictory result. But this element of unpredictability only proves that nothing is really impossible when it comes to the fascinating business of growing plants indoors.

How to use this book

Using this book This book is laid out so as to give the maximum amount of information in the clearest possible way. The introduction contains general hints and advice on plant care, which is amplified in the main part of the book. This deals individually with over 70 of the most popular houseplants. Arranged alphabetically, each section contains a picture of the healthy plant, advice on pests and diseases, illustrations to help identify problems, a plant care chart, and an easy care guide, as well as the plant's family or genus name and common names.

Avoiding problems This chart shows essential information at a glance. For ease of use, the symbols are explained here in detail. However, the chart also contains captions with detailed advice on treatment and care to help you avoid problems with your plants.

Crosses and ticks A tick indicates that the plant positively likes and a cross that it actively dislikes a treatment or condition.

Light and position This symbol indicates bright sunlight. A plant which likes bright sun could stand in a well-lit window, for example.

This symbol shows that the plant likes a bright position, but not direct sunlight, such as a position near but not directly in front of a window.

This symbol indicates partial shade. A position in a fairly light room, but away from a window, would suit a plant which likes this condition.

This symbol indicates full shade. Some plants such as ferns may thrive in a very shady position and can brighten dark corners of a room.

Care guide indicates how easy or difficult the plant is to care for.
- ● difficult
- ●● moderate
- ●●● easy

Family or genus

Name of plant

Common name(s)

General information about the plant

Varieties and purchasing – information on the best varieties available and what to look out for when buying

Close-up photograph of blooms

Names of specific varieties of the plant are abbreviated and given in italics

Picture of healthy plant showing colour, shape and so on

Temperatures and measurements are given in Imperial and metric forms, and, for ease of use, units have been rounded to the nearest convenient figure

---

ERICEACEAE

Florists' Azalea

Azalea

There is nothing that can compare with *A. indica* as a specimen plant in full flower. The oval-shaped leaves are small, coarse and evergreen; the flowers, which grow at the ends of branches, may be either single or double, with their colour ranging from pristine white to dull red. There are also splendid multicoloured varieties. Most of the better plants start their life in Belgium, from where they are shipped all over the world. Azaleas are always potted and grown on to flowering stage before being dispatched to the retailer.

Healthy plant One of the most beautiful of the winter flowering plants, many azaleas naturally flower in spring but are often forced into bloom for the Christmas season. They are very slow growing plants which is one reason why they are often expensive to purchase. Whether situated indoors in individual pots, or outside in large groups, azaleas always look attractive with their rich clusters of pastel or deeply-hued colours displayed against deep, green foliage.

VARIETIES AND PURCHASING

If carefully tended, the azalea can be one of the most rewarding of all the flowering houseplants. Because they are one of the few plants which flower in winter, they are usually seen in abundance in florists' shops from late autumn onwards. Selecting a healthy specimen is important if the plant is to survive. A healthy plant will be clean and bright in appearance. Some of its flowers should be open, but there should also be an abundance of buds. Tempting as it may be, avoid plants which have opened entirely. On the other hand, avoid those with small, underdeveloped buds, or no buds at all. When lifted, the pot should feel heavy and wet, which is how it should remain for the rest of the plant's life.

A. indica is the most common azalea and the one which is most easily available. It includes many variations of colour and is usually chosen for this quality and its general decorative appearance. *A. indica* needs a humid environment and should be sprayed with lime-free water every day. *A. obtusum* is commonly known as the Japanese Kurume. It is not as easy to force into bloom as *A. indica* and is thus not available in shops until its natural flowering period in late winter. *A. obtusum* has small flowers that nestle among the leaves of the plant. It makes a fine potted plant with its clear, pink flowers. It can be put in the garden following indoor flowering, whereas *A. indica* must be carefully guarded from frost.

Draughts Most plants abhor draughts, but a few will tolerate them. Pay particular attention to this symbol.

Temperature Always keep plants in temperatures they prefer as far as possible. Although they will not flourish, some plants may survive in temperatures other than those specified. The ideal temperature range is given for each plant. This may be cool (up to 60°F/15°C); intermediate or warm (over 65°F/18°C).

Watering The main methods of watering are applying it directly to the soil (**above left**), in the container under the plant pot (**above right**), spraying the plant

with a plant spray (**above left**), and immersing the pot (but not the whole plant) in water (**above right**).

Feeding There are three main ways of feeding houseplants. The three symbols (**above**) indicate that the plant should be given food in liquid form (**left**), as a spray on the leaves (**centre**) or as a solid applied to the soil as granules or in stick form (**right**). It is important to feed the plant as recommended. Most plants need food mainly during the growing season, but others require varying amounts of food all year round.

Seasonal care This chart shows when plants require watering and feeding. The pale blue colour on the watering chart (**above**) indicates when you should water, and the droplet symbol shows when

extra watering is essential. The feeding chart works in a similar way. The yellow area showing when you should feed, and the red dots indicating when more feeding is essential. In all cases the information is amplified in the captions.

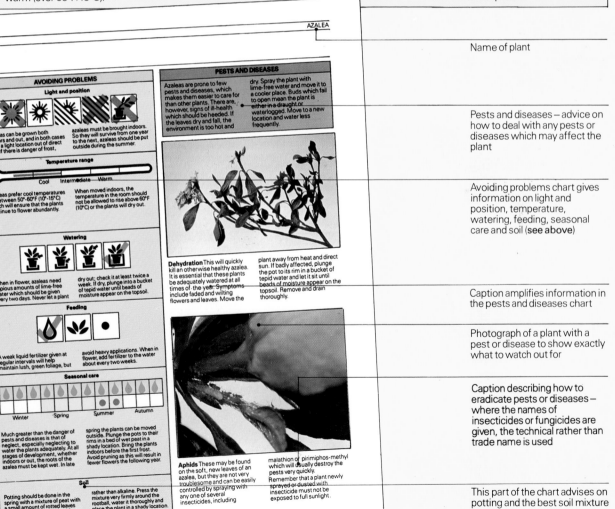

AZALEA

Name of plant

Pests and diseases – advice on how to deal with any pests or diseases which may affect the plant

Avoiding problems chart gives information on light and position, temperature, watering, feeding, seasonal care and soil (**see above**)

Caption amplifies information in the pests and diseases chart

Photograph of a plant with a pest or disease to show exactly what to watch out for

Caption describing how to eradicate pests or diseases – where the names of insecticides or fungicides are given, the technical rather than trade name is used

This part of the chart advises on potting and the best soil mixture

11

Buying your houseplants

The survival of all houseplants mainly depends on the person looking after them, and the general growing conditions which are provided. The better the grower and the conditions, then the healthier plants are likely to be, and the more aware the grower is of the problems that are likely to beset his or her plants, then the lesser the risks will be.

Some people are blessed with the gift of almost instinctively knowing what plants require if they are to do well, but, for the majority, getting to know what the various needs of a houseplant are or what pests and diseases it suffers from takes a little time. The houseplant grower with a trained mind and eye can usually diagnose plant problems at a glance—nearly every pest and disease gives a telltale sign of its presence. In fact, the ability to detect the presence of pests or disease at the earliest possible time is one of the most important qualities a houseplant grower can have.

In this context, the red spider mite can be taken as a perfect example of why pests should be detected and dealt with at the earliest opportunity. These minute mites are sucking insects that are found on the underside of plant leaves during the early stages of an attack. Early and repeated treatment with an insecticide is the best way of coping with red spider mites. If they are allowed to go about their business unchecked, the plant will soon be killed, and almost every other plant near it will become contaminated.

Frequently it is not enough to detect pests that may have appeared on a plant once it has been brought indoors. It is also necessary to look carefully at a plant before it is bought. Not that the commercial grower lacks diligence when it comes to pest control at the nursery, it is simply that pests will always be present where there is soft and succulent greenery for them to feed on. Therefore, all plants should always be inspected carefully before they are bought, and in particular the reverse side of leaves and the soft growing tips of plants should be keenly scrutinized.

When buying plants remember that very few homes are ideally suited to them and can provide the same growing conditions as a greenhouse. Inferior plants that have clearly not prospered during their maturing months in a greenhouse will find life even more difficult once the environment has changed to that of an average living room. So, if they are to do well indoors, only buy plants in a sparkingly fresh condition. As well as inspecting plants to see if they have any pests, check the foliage for discoloration, and note the condition of the margins and tips of leaves in particular. Brown margins or tips indicate poor culture, and leaves marked in this way will almost inevitably become discoloured all over before eventually falling off.

Flowering plants should never be too far advanced when they are bought, but do not be tempted into acquiring plants that are too backward, as there is a distinct possibility that in the limited light conditions that prevail indoors the flowers in fact will never be open. For example, the buds of immature potted chrysanthemums often rot and die before they have had the chance to flower. However, there are invariably exceptions in the plant world so, at the other end of the scale, always buy Poinsettias in full colour, making sure that the very small flowers in the centre of the coloured

Too dark A healthy Spider Plant has sharply defined variegations of green and white. Should these fade or disappear, it is usually a case of too little light (**above**). Move the plant to a lighter position.

Red spider mite Begonias are prone to red spider mite (**above**). In advanced cases, the spiders weave minute webs on the undersides of leaves. Treat by wiping or spraying with malathion.

Lack of food Any plant that appears drooping and lifeless could be suffering from a lack or excess of light, temperature, food or water. In a Croton (**above**), such symptoms usually mean underfeeding.

When to water Poinsettias should be watered only when the leaves begin to droop (**above**) or overwatering could easily ensue. However, do not let the plant dry out to a state of total dehydration. Water regularly and moderately.

Blackened Ivy If any houseplant is placed too near a window, there is always risk of scorching. If the ivy leaves turn brown or black (**above**), move the plant from its location to where it can absorb indirect light.

Proper environment A maidenhair fern reacts quickly if its environment is unsuitable. Discoloured, drooping leaves (**above**) are a sign of underwatering. Water thoroughly in regular, moderate amounts.

Plant buying Purchasing a plant requires patience and care. Time, money, and effort can be easily wasted if a plant is bought too hastily. A careful look at the general appearance of the plant will immediately reveal its condition. The leaves should be without blemishes, supple, and healthy in colour. In particular, the undersides of leaves should be checked (**left**) for signs of pests or disease. Also, check the stems of the plant near the soil for signs of rot. Few people can resist a group of healthy, flourishing plants (**right**), and plant shows can be a source of inspiration. Until plants are easily recognized, their name tags can be left in the pots. These also often provide useful information on watering, feeding, and general care.

13

EUPHORBIACEAE
CODIAEUM
(CROTON)
(JOSEPH'S COAT)

Store care Houseplants in
stores should be clean,
healthy-looking and well
displayed. Delicate plants such
as the Croton (**above**) ought not
to be left on the pavement
outside the shop, where they
will be exposed to draughts and
fluctuating temperatures, as
well as being more likely to get
knocked over. It is unwise to
accept wrapped plants without
first checking them. You can
legitimately remove a plant's
paper collar to check for
blemishes or leaf loss without
committing yourself to
purchasing it. Plants must be
wrapped carefully so that the
foliage and flowers do not get
damaged. The plant should have
a label that is clear, clean and
firmly attached. It is also helpful
if there are instructions on the
label regarding the plant's
cultivation requirements.
Sometimes a small colour
picture of a healthy plant in
flower is included, which will act
as a useful guide, particularly as
plants like the Croton come in a
wide range of colours and
varieties.

bract are still closed. When these small flowers are open it
is an indication that the plant has already given of its best
and is on the decline.

Crispness is a quality in potted plants that is often over-
looked, yet it is extremely important that the foliage is
checked for limpness. Often enough limp leaves are only an
indication that the plant needs watering. Whether this is
the case or not can be checked by placing a thumb on the
soil at the top of the pot. Limpness caused by dry conditions
can easily be remedied by adding water to the soil on getting
the plant home. However, limp foliage on plants that are
already wet at their roots is a sure sign that all is not well,
and that the plants are quite probably suffering from some
form of root rot. Should this be the case, it will be almost
impossible for the plants to prosper indoors. Roots often rot
and die either as a result of excessive watering, especially if
allied to cold conditions, or by being attacked by one of the
many pests that live in soil and eat plant tissue.

The general appearance of plants is something that is not
usually taken into sufficient account, but it is important
that plants should be well presented. A plant with a clean
pot, clean foliage and a ticket attached bearing directions on
how to look after that particular plant suggests that it has
been cared for and well grown. The premises of the retailer
from whom the plant is being bought are also important.
They should be clean, adequately heated and offer good
light, so that plants will not suffer unduly during the interim
period between leaving the grower and the time of purchase. For more tolerant plants, such as primulas and Ivies,
cooler conditions, even those outside the shop where plants
are so often placed, will not be harmful. But biting winter
winds around the foliage of Crotons and African Violets
among others will almost certainly mean that the plants
will die before long. Even a short time in the cold can be
harmful and unprotected plants being carried from shop to
home in cold weather will suffer irreparable damage.

When buying a plant it is usually better not to go for the
largest plant at the lowest price. Very often the case is that
large plants in smaller pots have exhausted the soil in the
container and have happily survived in the greenhouse
with regular feeding, the right humidity and so on. Not
surprisingly, the conditions become totally different for the
plant the moment it gets home, and survival is then not
such an easy matter. Younger and fresher plants may on
the face of it appear to be inferior, but in the end they will
generally do better. However, a large plant in a smaller pot
may seem to be too much of a bargain to pass over, and the
advice for anyone buying a plant that appears much too
large for its pot is that it should be transferred to a slightly
larger container without too much delay. If the temperature
and general conditions are favourable, the plant can be repotted at any time of the year. Spring and early summer are
the ideal times, but a large plant acquired at the end of the
summer should be repotted anyway as it could well be dead
or at least not very healthy by the time spring comes
around.

Frequently, the most difficult period in the life of a plant
before it is sold is the interval between the time it leaves the

Check that buds are firmly attached and almost ready to flower.

The foliage should be clean, well coloured and healthy-looking. Do not select a plant with limp or discoloured leaves.

Check carefully for pests and dead leaves. If leaves appear to have been lost from the lower part of the plant, it is probable that the plant is in bad condition.

Healthy hibiscus The Chinese Rose is a handsome plant that must be sold in good condition if it is to grow and flower satisfactorily. Healthy specimens should have plenty of unopened buds and dark glossy foliage. The plant should be bushy and compact in shape, with plenty of leaves round its base. It needs to be displayed in a substantial pot or container, with plenty of loosely packed soil or potting mixture around it.

Before buying, inspect the soil for quality and moisture content. The stem and leaves must be clean and crisp with no evidence of insects or sticky secretions. Inspect buds and flowers thoroughly before purchase. Buds, particularly those of the Chinese Rose, often drop off prematurely leaving bare stalks and depriving the plant of colour and interest. Any plant for sale should be clearly labelled and presented in a clean pot.

15

nursery where it has been grown and reaches the people who handle plants during their travels to various markets. So nearly every plant, unless it has been bought from the producer, will need some tender, loving care by the time it reaches home. The first thing to do is unwrap the plant, and then inspect it for dead leaves and dying flowers, both of which should be removed so that no pieces of stalk remain attached to the plant. Most dead leaves, particularly on cyclamen, will be in the area around the top of the pot where the canopy of leaves obscures them from view.

It is almost impossible to water plants in transit effectively so check the soil and, if it is dry, give the plant a thorough soaking. Surplus water should soak through the holes in the bottom of the pot after water has been poured onto the surface of the soil. Some plants, such as azaleas, might need a great deal more water and with these it is best to immerse the pot in a bucket of water, holding it below the surface until all the air bubbles in the soil have escaped. This will ensure that all the soil has been well saturated. Azaleas should always be watered in this way as they like plenty of water. They can wilt alarmingly, with their flowers going very limp, if they are deprived of water, but, if the drought period is short, a thorough soaking will quite quickly bring them back to life.

Quenching thirst The azalea (**above**) is extremely dehydrated, due to underwatering. In such cases, the best way to revive the plant is to immerse the pot in a bucket of water. Fill a bucket with water, immerse the pot — keeping the foliage and any flowers clear — and leave the pot submerged until no more bubbles appear on the surface. Plants like the azalea require a lot of water and can always be watered in this fashion. Remember, however, that it is far easier to overwater a plant than to underwater it.

Many of the foliage plants have their leaves cleaned by the grower with an oil which makes them look more attractive. However, if any plants have an unnaturally high glossy look to them, they will need a little attention. First, soak a sponge in soapy water—never use detergent—then wipe the leaves to get rid of some of the oil as it can be damaging if used in excess. Plants with an oily appearance should never be placed in direct sunlight as the effects of the sun's rays on leaves with an excessive covering of oil will result in rapid deterioration either from scorching or by the leaves becoming paper thin and lifeless. It is also unwise to place such plants in areas that are likely to be cold—somewhere in the region of 65°F (18°C) should be the aim for all newly acquired plants.

If plants are intended for rooms with lower temperatures, it is best to acclimatize them gradually to such conditions, as greenhouse-reared plants will not adapt satisfactorily to a sudden temperature change from, say, 60°F (15°C) to 45°F (7°C). But many plants can be persuaded to do reasonably well if the switch is not too dramatic. One warning that is frequently repeated by experts is that any indoor plants that are to be exposed to a low temperature, be it for long or short periods, will have little chance of survival if the soil in their pots is too wet.

Almost without exception, all plants that are despatched from reputable growers will probably have been fed at weekly intervals for several months before being sent on their journey to the retailer. Therefore, it is a good idea to feed all plants with one of the many proprietary fertilizers once they are at home. Even if the plant is to be potted on soon afterwards, it will not do it any harm if it has a feed.

There are many different brands of houseplant fertilizers available in liquid, tablet and powder form. Some can be inserted into the soil so that they provide nourishment for the plant over a long period, and others can be sprayed onto the foliage and for this reason are known as foliar feeds. The latter are fine for plants such as ferns that do not have a very vigorous root system. Extra fertilizer may be given to many of the houseplants that may have excellent foliage, but are reluctant to produce flowers—the African Violet is a prime offender in this respect. Although most flowering plants can be encouraged to do better by providing good light during the day and additional artificial light in the evening, it will also help considerably if the fertilizer being used has a high potash content. Experienced gardeners are always worth listening to, and they will usually grow flowering plants such as Gloxinias by applying a fertilizer that has a high nitrogen content while the plants are producing leaves, and then switch to one with extra potash when the plants have developed a full appearance and flower buds are about to form. The container in which the fertilizer is sold will indicate what the ingredients are, so compare different brands and if necessary seek the advice of the retailer when making a choice. The temptation to resort to the fertilizer pack every time a brown or dead leaf appears should be resisted, as such damage may well be the result of too much feeding in the first place. Always follow the directions given by the manufacturer closely.

Signs of insufficient feeding are a generally pale leaf colouring, an overall hardness in appearance, and the development of much smaller leaves. Plants that have had their soil changed as a result of potting on will not need feeding for at least three months.

Many plants fail not as a result of neglect, but because their owner is over eager to do everything possible for them. For example, a frequent mistake is potting plants into fresh soil much too often, or potting them into pots that are much too large for their needs. Vigorous plants that are obviously too big for their pots on purchase can be potted on right away, but once indoors growth tends to slow down considerably compared to the sort of progress that plants will make in a heated greenhouse, so too frequent potting on is not recommended. Once in a 5in (12·5cm) diameter pot the average houseplant will last for two years provided it is fed while actively growing, and once potted into 7in (17cm) diameter containers, most plants will thrive for a good three years before they need further potting on. Unless a plant is developing at a truly remarkable rate, 10in (25cm) diameter pots are the absolute maximum that are required indoors. In such pots plants can be sustained for many years by regular feeding.

The soil into which plants are potted can sometimes do more harm than good, and if the soil is simply something that has been dug up from the garden then there is every chance that the plant will decline rather than flourish. The mixture for potted plants has to be prepared carefully and much research is undertaken by growers over a period of many years before the right mixture is decided upon. Mixtures can vary considerably. Recently there has been a marked switch to soil-less mixtures that are made up almost entirely of peat. These are excellent for almost all plants in smaller pots if the medium is kept moist—any excessive drying out will present problems. Plants that are going into larger pots where they will remain for several years should have a mixture with a little more body to it and a loam-based mixture is more suitable. As it is advisable to go to a reliable supplier of houseplants, it is equally important to go to a reliable person when buying soil. Make sure that the contents of the bag are fresh when purchased, as soil deteriorates with age, and avoid thin mixtures that run like sand through the fingers, as these hold little moisture and would be suitable for only a very few potted plants.

Poorly drained soil will frequently result in failure, and a heavily compacted mixture will offer little in the way of drainage, as will soils that have become hard and encrusted on the top of the pot. In the latter situation, grey mould will grow on the surface of the soil, which is not only unsightly, but it will also harm the plant in time. The simple answer for encrusted soil, and soil that is generally slow to drain, is to disturb the top 1–2in (2·5–5cm) of soil on the top of the pot with a pencil or pointed stick and then throw it away. The pot can then be top-dressed with a fresh mixture that will help the drainage and considerably improve the overall appearance of the plant.

Worms are not often looked upon as a pest, but they will be harmful to potted plants if they get into the soil. A

Leaf care Dead leaves around the base of a cyclamen (**below**) should be pulled off regularly.

favourite time for worms to get into the soil is when plants are placed out-of-doors during the summer—either for a short time during a shower of rain or on a more permanent basis when placed in a sheltered corner throughout the summer months. The little heaps of soil that worms leave on a lawn are known as casts, and when worms are in plant pots the tendency is for these casts to block the drainage holes in the bottom of the pot, so restricting the free flow of water. If plants are slow to drain when watered, gently take them out of their pots. If any worms are present they should be removed and put back in the garden. When the worms are out of the way, any soil that has accumulated around the drainage holes should be cleaned away.

Water when given to plants in excess will invariably lead to disaster and overwatering is perhaps the most common reason for the failure of plants indoors. Yet it is extremely difficult to convince the inexperienced person that too much water can be damaging. There are one or two exceptions to the rule, but most potted plants prefer to be well watered and then allowed to dry out reasonably before the exercise is repeated. Plants can be watered by pouring the liquid over the soil and allowing it to drain through sufficiently for the surplus to be seen accumulating in the drip saucer in which the plant is standing, or they can be watered by placing the pot in a dish of water and allowing the plant to drink up the moisture by capillary action. Whatever the method, it is essential that the soil right through the pot should be wetted each time the plant is watered. Thin dribbles of water on the top of the soil will do little for the plant, as most plants have the greater number and the more active roots in the lowest third of the pot. If moisture does not reach this area then the plant will suffer. Capillary watering by drawing water up from a reservoir is ideal for plants such as the African Violet that have sensitive leaves, which can be damaged if cold water gets onto them. It is particularly harmful if plants are exposed to direct sunlight after their leaves have been wetted.

Plants that have their growing pots in decorative outer pots should have the outer pot checked about 30 minutes after watering to ensure that they are not actually sitting in water that has drained into the outer container. Allowing plant pots to stand in water for lengthy periods will almost certainly result in roots becoming damaged. Soil that remains sodden with water will be completely devoid of air with the result that roots will be deprived of essential oxygen. In such conditions the roots of most plants deteriorate alarmingly, and the condition is generally referred to as root rot. As roots break down the plant will inevitably begin to suffer, and will take on a weaker, less vigorous appearance. To check for this kind of root damage, remove the plant from its pot and tease away any brown and lifeless roots from the soil. Then, with a finger and thumb on either side of the root, gently pull its outer skin. If the skin comes away easily and leaves the core of the root attached to the plant, then lack of oxygen caused by overwatering has definitely been responsible for the failure.

Unfortunately, there is no magical concoction that can be bought to rectify this condition. The only thing to do is allow the soil to dry out thoroughly so that the roots have a chance of becoming re-established. One simple method of drying out the soil reasonably quickly is to remove the plant from its pot and expose the rootball to the atmosphere for a day or two. Then water it sparingly for several weeks while the roots are recovering from the ordeal. It is always much better to use water at room temperature rather than water that has come straight from the tap. It is a good idea to fill the can automatically after watering and leave it by a radiator so that water at room temperature is available next time. Some plants will benefit from rainwater if the tap water has a high lime content, especially dracaenas and azaleas. However, it is important that the water should be clean and not from a barrel that is alive with algae that will in time discolour pots and the surface of the soil.

Radiators can be a mixed blessing as far as plants indoors are concerned. When they are giving off too much heat the atmosphere becomes excessively dry with the result that many plants that prefer moister air conditions, such as philodendrons, will suffer. Also, any plants that are placed above or too close to radiators that are giving off an excessive amount of heat may dehydrate and shrivel up. The vast majority of plants like temperatures somewhere between 60°–70°F (15°–21°C) and many plants actually prefer to be cool rather than hot.

Root rot If your plant is starting to droop and look unhealthy, it may well be suffering from root rot. In order to inspect the roots, the plant must be taken out of its pot (**above**). Next, hold the plant firmly with one hand and gently tease any brown and unhealthy looking roots away from the central mass of roots. Then pull gently on the outer skin of these roots, to discover whether or not your plant has root rot. Root rot causes the leaves of a plant to become weak and faded (**right**). The condition is caused by overwatering, which is a very common mistake. If the drainage holes in the pot or container have become blocked, the roots will start to rot as a result of standing for long periods of time in the accumulated water. It is easier to prevent root rot than cure it. Plants tend to need less water in winter, and should always be watered carefully.

Potting your houseplants

Potting is a major area of indoor plant care where plants often suffer, not from neglect but from the fact that their owner is over-enthusiastic and repots them when they do not need it or else does not know how to pot plants properly.

The first sign of a dead leaf is sufficient reason for potting many plants, but the worst thing possible for a sick plant is to disturb its roots and put it into a mass of alien potting soil. If previously healthy plants lose some of their colouring and become less active they may well need potting on, but make sure that the deterioration is not caused by pests before potting on. To find out whether plants are genuinely in need of potting on, place a hand over the soil with the stem of the plant between the fingers, invert the pot and then tap sharply on its rim so that it comes clear of the rootball. Plants that need potting on will have a healthy mass of roots covering the soil, with most roots in the lowest third of the rootball. If plants do not need repotting, there will be much more soil showing than roots. The soil will also tend to break up so the rootball should be handled carefully when it is being removed from the pot.

It is quite impossible to say when all plants should be potted as the rate of growth, and therefore the amount of root, varies so much from plant to plant. The chlorophytum, for example, develops a great mass of roots in a very short space of time, and can probably be potted twice annually without being harmed in any way. Whereas, although they are in the same plant family, the sansevierias can last for several years without being potted on—in fact, they can remain until they actually break their pots. Some plants, such as ferns, have dark brown roots that will not vary much in colour from soil in which they are growing, so more careful inspection is needed to ensure whether they need repotting or not.

Newcomers to houseplant growing often ask why small, well-established plants should not be put into larger pots right away, so avoiding the process of potting from one sized pot to the next. The answer is that small plants placed in a large bulk of soil will be very much out of proportion to their pots, and more importantly the soil in the pot is likely to turn sour before the plants can become established in the mixture. There are various pots and pot sizes that may be used for growing indoor plants, but when it comes to potting on plants from one size to the next, it is best to be guided by the pot sizes used in commercial practice.

At the nursery, plants are started in propagating beds and are then put into pots of 3½in (9cm) in diameter. When they are well established, which usually takes at least a year, plants are potted on into 5in (12·5cm) pots. In normal circumstances, plants will go for a further year before transferred to pots of 7in (17cm) in diameter. Only the larger leaved and more robust plants, such as the monstera, will need potting on into 10in (25cm) sized pots. Surprisingly, although it may not seem likely, most houseplants will do very much better in pots that seem too small in relation to their growth, rather than pots that are too large. Once established in larger pots specimen type plants, such as philodendrons, monsteras and ficus, will usually last for several years if they are fed regularly.

Often enough plants do not actually need potting on in the conventional manner, but still require some sort of boost to retain their vigour. For these, instead of potting the plant, use a pointed stick to remove the top 1–2in (2·5–5cm) of soil from the pot and replace it with fresh mixture. Some roots will be damaged in the process, but the additional nourishment will outweigh this minor setback. The plant will also look better and the drainage of the soil will be slightly improved.

Drainage is important for all plants and before introducing any soil, place a layer of broken clay pots in the bottom of the new pot. These small broken pieces are normally referred to as 'crocks', and they prevent the soil from blocking the holes in the bottom of the pot.

When a plant is introduced to a new pot it should be at the same depth as it was in its previous container, so put enough soil in the bottom of the new pot to bring the plant to the right level. Holding the plant centrally, use your free hand to press the soil into position between the rootball and the pot. The mixture should be pressed firmly, so that it is neither too loose nor very tightly compressed. After potting, give the soil a good watering and no further water should be required for at least 10 days. Even then water should be given sparingly for several weeks until the plant is obviously growing more freely in the new soil. It will not be necessary to feed the plant for three to six months following potting on. The time varies with individual plants, and those that are vigorous growers will need feeding earlier rather than later. Soil for potting should be moist but not saturated, and the best time for potting most houseplants is late spring to early summer unless, of course, a plant needs repotting straight after it is bought.

Repotting When a plant has been newly potted, the base and roots should be firmly supported without being crushed. Use both hands to firm the soil into place without packing it down too tightly.

Pests and diseases

A hot and dry atmosphere will also encourage many pests, particularly red spider mites. This does not mean that, because it is hot, red spider mites will miraculously appear from nowhere, but if there are a few of these pests lurking among the leaves, they will breed much more prolifically in hot and dry conditions. In a dry atmosphere it will help most of the plants if their foliage can be sprayed periodically with a fine mist of water from one of the many types of hand-sprayers that are available. The plants that benefit most from this treatment are the ones with naturally glossy leaves, such as the philodendrons, and in particular the Swiss Cheese Plant which is probably the best known of the philodendron tribe, the *Araceae* family.

Of all the pests that are likely to attack houseplants, the minute red spider mites are the most troublesome, as in the first instance they are difficult to detect and so they often have a very firm hold on the plant before their devastating effect is noticed. Green leaves becoming a pale straw colour in patches indicate that red spider is in attendance, but this stage is in fact a firm assurance that the mites are very well established and will be difficult to eradicate. Minute webs that crisscross the veins on the reverse of the leaf and form in the area where the leaf meets the petiole are also signs that the red spider is active. But active is an understatement. When webs appear with mites trotting around from one part of the leaf to another it is a sign that the battle has been lost before any action has been taken. Any plant with mite webs clearly visible around the leaves, and forming a killing cocoon around the younger leaves, should be considered a liability. It poses a threat to all the other plants in a collection, as red spider mites spread quickly and will attack any available plant. Plants that are badly infested should be burned as this is the only answer. Insecticides will have little effect and plants rarely recover from very severe attacks.

These little pests must be caught at the earliest possible opportunity if there is to be a fighting chance of getting them under control. Some plants are more prone than others, and in the purely foliage range Crotons, *Hedera canariensis* and *Aralia sieboldii* are the most vulnerable, with mites having a deadly effect on both of these once they have got a firm foothold. Many of the flowering plants are also susceptible, particularly primulas and impatiens. To catch them young, inspect the undersides of leaves at frequent intervals, and with smaller leaves, such as those of the impatiens, remove a leaf at the top or near the top of the plant and inspect it under a magnifying glass. Some of the mites will be reddish in colour, but most will be flesh-coloured and will be most easily seen when they are moving.

As soon as red spider mites are spotted, the plant should be treated with insecticide. If the plant is small, one of the most effective ways of ensuring that the whole plant is dealt with is to immerse the foliage in a bucket filled with insecticide. When dealing with any sort of insecticide, always wear rubber gloves and follow the manufacturer's directions. The treatment should be given out-of-doors in the shade on a still day. If the bucket method is to be successful, put a piece of plastic over the top of the pot to stop

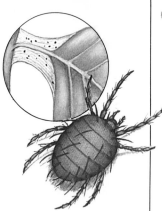

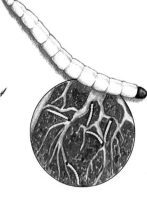

Red spider mite Adult insects are reddish-brown, but the young are flesh coloured and it is vital to eradicate both if the plant is to live. An infestation of spider mites is shown on the leaf of a *Chamaedorea elegans* (**top**). The insects make tiny webs on the undersides of the leaves, which may then fade and yellow. Inspect the plant frequently, with a magnifying glass if necessary, as mites are difficult to detect and must be dealt with at an early stage.

● Treat a small plant by immersing the foliage in a bucket of diazinon.

● Spray the plant thoroughly with malathion. Repeat the treatment at intervals to kill all the young insects.

Sciarid fly These insects, also known as fungus gnats, are encouraged by wet, dank conditions, such as when the plant is overwatered and the atmosphere is not warm enough to dry out the soil. In themselves they are more unsightly than harmful, but they lay eggs in the compost and the maggots which hatch will sometimes attack the roots of a plant. This undermines the health of the plant, causing it to droop like the *Calathea makoyana* shown here (**top**).

● Soak the potting mixture with endosulfan solution.

● Insert granules of lindane in the soil. Spray the plant with a solution of lindane or endosulfan.

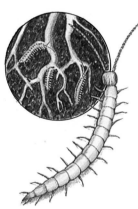
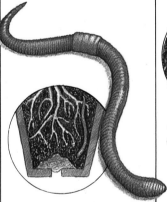
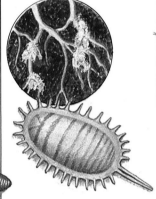
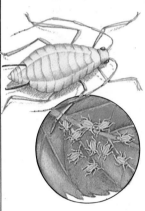

Symphalids These rarely occur in houseplants, but are extremely destructive when they do. Symphalids resemble small, cream-coloured centipedes. They gnaw into large roots and completely devour small ones. A plant such as the dieffenbachia (**top**) may suffer badly, but most potting mixtures are composed to prevent such problems. To find out whether symphalids are present in the soil, stir some into water and the insects should rise to the top.

● Soak the potting mixture with diazinon.

● Apply malathion granules to the potting mixture.

Earthworms A plant which is taken outside during warm weather may be troubled by the presence of an earthworm which has made its way into the soil. The problem here is that the worm will throw off casts as it moves through the soil, which can interfere with the drainage of water. This may cause the leaves of the plant to wilt or curl and become discoloured. The *Dracaena deremensis* (**top**) shows signs of this problem.

● Remove the plant from the pot and shake off the potting mixture from the rootball. Clear the drainage holes of the pot and repot the plant in fresh compost.

Root mealy bug These small, pale insects, often covered with a fuzzy white coating, infest the roots of plants, particularly cacti and succulents. As they suck sap from the roots, the plant itself becomes stunted in the new growth and cannot continue a healthy development.

● Soak the potting mixture thoroughly with malathion every two weeks. Repeat at least twice.

● If a small plant is affected, wash away the potting mixture with tepid water and cut out badly damaged roots. Soak the roots in pirimiphos-methyl or malathion and repot in clean compost.

Aphids Commonly called greenfly, these pests attack the soft tissue of plants, sucking the sap and depositing a sticky substance known as honeydew. The stems and leaves of the plant are weakened and distorted and in addition to their damaging activities, aphids can carry viruses and cause susceptibility to sooty mould. Despite the common name, aphids may be black, grey or yellow, as well as green. Prompt and repeated treatment is needed to eradicate the pest.

● Spray the plant very thoroughly with malathion and repeat the spraying at intervals of a few days.

● Treat the soil by inserting granules of a systemic insecticide such as disulfoton.

the soil falling out and then invert the pot, dunking the leaves in the liquid and ensuring that every part of the plant is wetted. As a precaution, the exercise can be repeated after one week to deal with any mites that remain. This will mean mixing a fresh lot of insecticide as few retain their more lethal properties for long after mixing. For the person who is not able to go to these lengths in order to control red spider, aerosol canisters of insecticide can be remarkably effective. When using one, spray mainly on the reverse sides of leaves as this is where most of the mites will be. Repeated treatment is usually necessary as it is extremely unlikely that all mites will be killed off by the first application.

Red spider mites can certainly have devastating effects on plants, but reputable plant growers will rarely supply plants that already have pests or disease in residence, as regular and thorough control programmes are carried through to ensure that problems are reduced to the minimum. Many of the problems are anticipated, even expected, so everything that the plant is likely to come into contact with is cleaned down between each crop going through the greenhouse, with particular attention being paid to the benching on which plants will stand. Most pots are now made of plastic and will be new when put into use, so few problems arise from this source. Nevertheless, the business of growing potted plants tends to be a little messy at some stages and sometimes the soil in which the plants will be grown may present problems.

There are many root diseases that affect potted plants and numerous insects that make their home in the soil. To counteract these, the soils that contain loam will have had the loam sterilized before it is mixed with peat and other ingredients, and insecticides are usually incorporated so as to minimize possible dangers. For example, the combination of diligence at nurseries and the use of more effective chemicals seems to have eliminated the problem of eel worms that at one time had a crippling effect on many potted plants. Better soil mixtures that have been more hygienically prepared have also considerably reduced the incidence of soil borne diseases, but not all problems around the roots of plants have yet been eliminated.

The sciarid fly is commonly named the fungus gnat. It is blackish grey in colour and, although provided with wings, it uses its long, slender legs to move around on the surface of the soil. Eggs are laid from which hatch almost transparent maggots that in time develop into fungus gnats. Maggots feed on the young roots of a plant and they can be harmful if present in large numbers. However, there are numerous effective insecticides that can be watered into the soil, with a repeat dose given after about 10 days to ensure the gnats have been completely eliminated. These pests are mostly found in very wet and dank conditions, and are therefore not often encountered indoors. Thrips, or thunder flies, are not very common either, although they may attack some flowering plants in hot conditions during the summer months. However, these are not particularly troublesome and can be controlled by using an insecticide as directed. A sign of their presence is silvery discoloration of the flowers

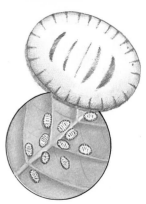

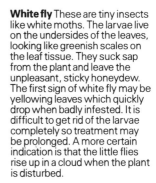

White fly These are tiny insects like white moths. The larvae live on the undersides of the leaves, looking like greenish scales on the leaf tissue. They suck sap from the plant and leave the unpleasant, sticky honeydew. The first sign of white fly may be yellowing leaves which quickly drop when badly infested. It is difficult to get rid of the larvae completely so treatment may be prolonged. A more certain indication is that the little flies rise up in a cloud when the plant is disturbed.

● Spray the leaves thoroughly, particularly the undersides, with malathion, repeating the spraying at three-day intervals.

● Place granules of disulfoton in the soil.

Scale insect Because these creatures are immobile, usually a yellow or brown colour, they are sometimes camouflaged on plants with woody stems, but are easier to detect among green foliage, for instance of a fern (**top**). The insects are protected by a waxy coating, and once in place suck the sap from the plant, causing it to wither.

● Wipe the insects away with a sponge soaked in malathion. Always use rubber gloves when handling insecticides.

● Spray stems and foliage thoroughly with diazinon.

● Insert granules of disulfoton in the soil.

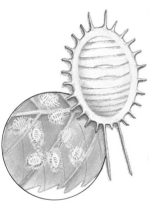

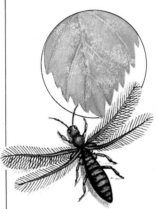

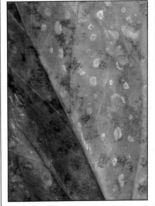

Mealy bug A visitation from mealy bugs is usually quite easy to see. The young are wrapped in a cottony coating which looks like a tiny piece of cotton wool clinging to the plant. They may build up into a thick cluster on the stem, as on the bougainvillea (**top**), or under the leaves. A light infestation can be dealt with quickly and easily, but if the problem is allowed to continue untreated, the plant will wilt, and the leaves yellow and fall.

● If there are few bugs, pick off those most noticeable and spray the plant with malathion. In a bad case of mealy bug, soak the foliage by spraying with malathion.

Thrips Although thrips are also known as thunderflies, they usually move by jumping, rather than by flying. They suck the sap of soft foliage and also attack flowers. Foliage and flowers will become streaked and spotted. Excretion from the flies turns black on the plant, speckling the leaves. The insects are less harmful than some, but the effect is extremely disfiguring to the plant and stunts the growth. Deal with thrips promptly at the first sign of attack.

● Spray the plant with pirimiphos-methyl.

● Remove seriously damaged foliage and place diazinon granules in the soil.

Mildew This is evident as a white powdery deposit on the leaves, which can also spread to stems and flowers. It is a fungus disease which particularly attacks plants with soft growth. Although not harmful, it is not very attractive and certainly does the plant no good. Fortunately it is not a common complaint in houseplants. When it occurs, as on the begonia (**top**), it is clearly visible.

● Cut away badly affected leaves and spray the plant with dichloran.

Botrytis This is another fungal disease, clearly distinguishable from mildew because of the fluffy, grey mould which forms on the plants. Again, plants with soft leaves such as the aglaonema (**top**) are the most likely to be affected but botrytis is quite common in all houseplants. It is usually a sign that the plant is being kept in the wrong conditions – too cold and damp, and also being overwatered.

● Cut away leaves with mould on them and spray the plant with dichloran. In addition, remove any sodden, mouldy compost and reduce watering or misting.

and sometimes the leaves. Thrips are very small, but can cause unsightly damage if not treated as soon as they are noticed.

Symphalids are small and white and they have the interesting common name of springtails—derived from the manner in which they dance about on the top of the soil when the plant is watered. These are not particularly harmful to plants, more of a nuisance than anything else, and can easily be controlled by saturating the soil with an insecticide. If this has an unpleasant odour, treat the plant out-of-doors in a sheltered and shady position and leave it outside until the smell has gone. Symphalids will be encouraged if the surroundings are damp and airless.

The only other common soil borne pest is the root mealy bug. This occurs mostly on older plants that have been standing around in the greenhouse for a long time. Besides the plant pots these pests will also make their home in the gravel on the staging in the greenhouse and will quickly move into plant pots that may be placed on the gravel. The bugs are very similar to the slightly larger mealy bug that gets onto the foliage and among the stems of the plant. The only way to detect them is by removing the plant from its pot so that the roots can be inspected. Bugs will usually be found nibbling away at the roots of the plant, and there will often be a covering of what looks like very fine snow on and around the roots in the lower part of the pot. Again, use an insecticide to soak the soil in the pot well. Make sure that the liquid drains right through the soil as most of these pests will be in the lower section of the pot. Further treatment will usually be necessary, but insecticides should not be used just for the sake of it, so inspect the plant for active bugs before repeating the dose.

Mildew is perhaps the most common of the diseases that affect potted plants, and will be found on the foliage of a wide range of victims. White powdery mildew spots will be more prevalent on plants that are growing in conditions offering poor hygiene, and where there is little change of air. For instance, begonia plants growing in greenhouses with conventional, but less effective, ridge ventilation have a much higher incidence of mildew compared to plants growing in houses that are provided with fan-extraction ventilation. In the former, the fungus spores present in the atmosphere are allowed to settle and become active on the plants, while with fan-extraction the spores are drawn through the greenhouse and away from the plants. In fact, almost all fungus diseases will thrive in damp locations that are unhygienic and where there is little change of air. Therefore, remove dead leaves and dead bits and pieces of leaf stalks and stems regularly. Any leaves that do become infected should be dealt with immediately by applying a fungicide, and very badly affected leaves should be removed from the plant and burned.

Botrytis is another fungal disease that can be dramatically fatal as far as many indoor plants are concerned. Small plants can become completely covered with the slimy mould that indicates botrytis in a surprisingly short space of time. This disease thrives in dank and airless conditions, and will quickly establish itself on any dead or rotting material that may be on the plant. A prime cause of botrytis can be the flowers that the plant produces. If dead flowers are allowed to fall onto leaves there is every chance that the brown and slimy blotches will begin to grow. Any leaves that may be affected should be removed from the plant without delay, as fungus spores that are produced will put other plants at risk. Meticulous removal of dead and dying bits of foliage and flowers should become a ritual if plants are to remain clean and unaffected.

Many of the begonias are susceptible to botrytis and they should be treated with a fungicide as soon as telltale signs of the disease appear. The cyclamen is another vulnerable plant, with botrytis attacking both flower and leaf stalks where they are attached to the corm. The danger very often goes unnoticed, as the corm is shielded by the plant's foliage, so it is important that the plant should be periodically inverted and the area around the corm thoroughly inspected. Mild attacks can usually be cleared up by removing all the affected parts of the plant and then treating the area with fungicide, but a severe attack is difficult to control and will often mean the end of the plant.

During the summer, aphids multiply at an alarming rate and can be found on many different plants, particularly those that produce soft and succulent growth at their tips. Luckily these are not difficult to kill with one of the many insecticides that are available. However, it is essential that these pests should be dealt with as soon as they are noticed. If there is any delay, the probing insects that live off the sap of the plant can cause damage to the leaves that will not be noticed until they mature. The chlorophytum is a plant that will have permanently marked leaves if aphids on young plants are not dealt with promptly.

White fly is another common pest that often mars the appearance of many potted plants and the undersides of a plant's leaves should always be inspected for signs of white fly before it is bought. If the attack on a plant is severe, white fly will dance around in all directions when the leaves are disturbed. If only because these pests are difficult to eliminate, avoid plants that are contaminated. There is also the added danger that these pests will quickly transfer to other plants in a collection. The only way to kill white fly is to be persistent. Treat the plant initially with a drenching

1

spray paying particular attention to the reverse side of the leaves. To ensure that young white fly are also killed, repeat the treatment a further three times with a four-day interval between each spraying.

Scale insects are the other common insect that may be found on some houseplants. Finding these pests can in fact be a problem, as they are often similar in colouring to the woody stems of plants, such as *Ficus benjamina*, and they cling very firmly to their anchorage. The mature pests are dark brown, almost black, while the maturing young are flesh-coloured. Occasionally scale insects may be seen on the upper surface of leaves, but they are found mainly on the undersides and along the stems and petioles. Where only a few plants and a few insects are involved, use a firm sponge to wipe the pests from their anchorage—it may be necessary to rub quite hard at times!

Like many of the sucking pests the scale insects will leave a visiting card in the form of sooty mould, a fungus that feeds on the excreta of the pests where it falls onto lower branches of a plant like *Ficus benjamina*. On detecting sooty mould, inspect areas of the plant above where the mould is forming. The mould clogs the pores of the leaves but is more unattractive than damaging to the plant. Use a soft sponge soaked in soapy water to wipe off the black mould and improve the appearance of the plant. Plants can often become badly infested with mould almost without detection as the pests are not very mobile and are well camouflaged against the brown or dark green background of many plants. *Ficus benjamina* suffers badly from scale and, rather than try to clean the worst affected branches, prune out the problem sections and burn them.

Another plant that attracts scale is *Asplenium nidus*, Bird's Nest Fern, which will usually have the scales along the midrib on the reverse side of the glossy green leaf. This plant's foliage is very delicate, so always handle the leaves with great care. Removal of scale insects is best done with a sponge that is used firmly but not harshly, as great damage be done by applying insecticides to fern foliage. Insecticides should never be used indiscriminately on potted plants as unsuitable chemicals will often do much more harm than good if the plant is at all sensitive. Many claims are made for pesticides, but it is always sensible to consider whether chemicals are likely to harm the plant before using them too freely. Therefore, before treating the asplenium with an insecticide for scale, for example, test the product on one of the lower leaves first to see what the reaction is. If the product damages the leaf then it can be easily removed while if the entire plant had been coated with something alien to its nature then the plant might well have died.

There are many other less common problem pests and diseases that might well attack plants, but if the total number were listed the would-be houseplant grower could well be completely discouraged. In fact, pests today are not quite as prevalent as they used to be, as houseplant growers at nurseries wage quite a war against all marauders. Most of the worst problems that afflict houseplants are brought on by the person who becomes responsible for plants once they are taken indoors and, surprisingly, neglect is well down the list! Many of the plants die from a surfeit of everything that the householder can lay hands on, when plants are really more inclined to respond to a little gentle neglect rather than being continually fussed over.

Houseplant essentials You will need all the following to care for your houseplants. Plant pots (1) can be either plastic or clay; potting soils and compost (2) for cuttings and potting. There is a wide assortment of insecticides (3) in either spray, liquid, or powder form. Garden gloves (4) will provide good protection. Plant foods (5) come in liquid, powder, stick, and pellet form. Twine (6) can be used for staking plants; shears (7) for pruning; and a sprayer and watering can (8) for watering.

Looking after your houseplants

In one way or another houseplants are invariably killed off —they are killed with kindness or from neglect, through having too much of this or not having enough of that, and there is no doubt that many succumb to the countless millions of pests and disease spores which feed off them. So keeping plants alive and healthy is always quite a challenge. Of course, the more that plants have their dead leaves removed or are inspected for pests, then the healthier they will be, so improving their many different aesthetic qualities.

Besides frequent inspection and coping with general hygiene there are numerous essential tasks that the keen houseplant grower must be expected to carry out during the year. These requirements take on a sort of running order that goes from the initial purchase to the day when pieces of the precious plants can be removed, cut up into various sized sections and with luck then new plants can be raised from the bits and pieces. The term used to cover all the methods of raising new plants is propagation. Propagators at nurseries which turn out millions of plants each year are some of the more important people in the houseplant world as their job involves many skills.

Initial purchase can make all the difference between success and failure, because it is unlikely that a half dead plant can be introduced to average room conditions and hope to be successful. After all, if the commercial grower who usually produces quality plants cannot get a plant to a sufficiently high standard in a heated greenhouse, then there is not much hope for it in a draughty hallway.

The answer is to choose all houseplants with care, as the better the original condition of a plant, the better its performance will be in the home. Other useful hints are never buy plants in cold weather from other than heated premises, and never accept plants wrapped in paper sleeves without inspecting the actual plants. Paper sleeves have a wonderful way of concealing plant defects and showing off only the top section that is in good order. If plants in sleeves are in a good condition, the retailer will have no objection to them being inspected.

If a plant is to be a present, consider the type of home that it is destined for. For accommodation tending to be cold and poorly lit the choice should lie in the range of hardier plants. Most well presented plants will have tags attached indicating whether or not they are difficult to care for. Highly coloured plants such as Crotons and variegated plants like dracaenas will have little chance of surviving in a low temperature and poor light. Also, flowering plants will shed both buds and flowers if the light is anything other than bright. When examining plants, remember that green plants should have bright green foliage and not hard and yellow leaves which indicate that they have not been given any food. Limp leaves that hang forlornly over the rim of the pot are a sign of poor culture. This means that plants have suffered probably from overwatering with the result that their roots have failed.

Any pests will usually be found on or under the topmost leaves of the plant, on the flower stalks of some varieties, and on young shoots of plants such as Ivies. Hard and crusty

Houseplants in a nursery The majority of houseplants for sale will have started their lives in a nursery (**left**). Here, plants can be kept in optimum conditions, with heating, watering, food and air conditioning all regulated to plants' requirements. Plants from nurseries should therefore be in peak condition, with clean healthy-looking foliage and no signs of pest, disease or discoloration. Plants should be thoroughly inspected prior to purchase.

Positioning plants The atmosphere in a bathroom (**right**) is often quite similar to that of a greenhouse, with diffuse light and high levels of warmth and humidity. It is often a good idea to keep new plants in the bathroom, for a short period immediately after they have been purchased, before exposing them to less congenial surroundings elsewhere. If the bathroom is not centrally heated however, this is not advisable as extremes of temperature may damage the plant.

scale insects will be clinging like small limpets to the undersides of leaves and to plant stems. They are dark brown when adult and flesh-coloured when young. Plants that are particularly susceptible are *Asplenium nidus*, Bird's Nest Fern, and *Ficus benjamina*, Weeping Fig, so these should be checked carefully before they are bought. Mealy bugs are similar to woodlice in appearance except they are powdery white. They wrap their young in waxy balls of what at first sight appears to be cotton wool on the plant. This makes mealy bugs easy to detect and plants suffering from this pest should be avoided at all costs. Minute red spider mites can be a major problem and they are just about the most difficult pest of all to see. Light brown discoloration is a sign of their presence, and in severe cases there will be small webs around the plant's leaf stalks and on the reverse side of leaves.

Flowering plants should not be in a very backward condition when they are bought, although some people wrongly believe that a plant in a backward condition will have a longer life in the home. The very opposite could be the result. For example, potted chrysanthemums bought during darker winter months in very backward condition might decide not to flower at all! Azaleas should not be too far advanced, but some flowers ought to be open and there should be lots of fat buds showing colour. Poinsettias must have colourful bracts in full colour, but keep a watchful eye for the flowers that are formed in the centre of the bract. If these are fully open rather than being tight, tiny buds it is an indication that the plant is beginning to lose its sparkle.

Having chosen a plant, make sure it is wrapped carefully. In winter, the wrapping will protect the plant from cold winds, and in summer the plant will be protected from the rays of the sun on the journey home. Plants that are fully exposed to the sun, in parked cars for instance, can be at considerable risk, particularly those with more tender leaves, so ensure that they are well protected.

Once you have got the new plant safely back home, carefully remove the wrapping and then consider where the plant should be placed. The final position of the plant will greatly influence its future performance, so this decision should be given a little thought. As already mentioned, flowering plants must have the lightest possible location, needing protection from only the strongest sunlight. Some plants will happily endure full sunlight, but problems arise when windowpanes act as magnifying agents. If this happens leaves can be scorched and any flowers will take on a papery and lifeless appearance. As a temporary measure, remove any plants which are near windows at the hottest time of the day, or simply place a sheet of newspaper between the plants and the glass. The colouring of variegated plants, such as Ivies and colourful Crotons, will remain sharper if they are put in the lightest possible place in the room. On the other hand, for areas that are not so well lit, green foliaged plants such as the philodendrons and rhoicissus, Grape Ivy, are much more suitable. The monstera, Swiss Cheese Plant, is also a good plant to use in darker places, and in the same family the yellow scindapsus is one of the few variegated plants that will retain its colouring in shade.

In fact, this is a most adaptable plant which will grow any-where except in very shady places and it can be either trained to a support or allowed to trail naturally downwards.

Draughts can be the cause of death for many indoor plants, so it is important that delicate plants should not be placed in hallways, or cold, draughty window spots. A disused summer fireplace is often used as a temporary home for houseplants, and it is an excellent place for those that are more durable. However, to give plants a better chance of survival reduce any draughts by blocking off the chimney vent with a piece of flexible material such as cardboard. Houseplants have come a long way since their early days, and they are now available in fairly large containers that will hold plants growing anything up to 20ft (6m) high. Not that such plants are suitable for the average home, but there are some slightly smaller plants that are being increasingly used as features in the home. Whenever possible, larger plants should be given a place of honour so that they can be admired from all angles.

Watering is the most difficult aspect of caring for house-plants. They will die if they are given too much water, yet they will also die if they are given too little, so it really can be quite difficult for the beginner to get it right. Plant growers are frequently confronted with what to the lay-man is the simple question of how often and how much water should be given. If someone buys a car, very detailed information is provided on how and when every little thing should be done. But plants are not cars, they are very much more like people and almost all their requirements will vary. Two similar plants in the same room will not necessarily want the same amount of water and may vary considerably once they have settled down. Like people, some plants are very vigorous by nature, while others tend to be slower and less active. Therefore, all plants should be treated as individuals. Some will be in large pots, some in small, while they will also be in different rooms offering varying temperatures. However, all of them will do better if tepid water is used, and if they are watered thoroughly at each watering session. To do this, pour sufficient water onto the top of the soil so that the surplus eventually accumulates in the dish, saucer or in whatever the pot is standing. To achieve this with larger pots it may be necessary to pour several lots of water onto the soil and allow it to soak through. Surplus water can be left to lie in the drainage receptacle for a few minutes so that plants can absorb a little more moisture by capillary action, but this will be fatal if plants are left for any length of time. Plants should only be watered again when they next need it. Do not water plants just for the sake of it, nor at set times, but only when the soil has dried reasonably as a result of the plant taking its fill, and through evaporation. The warmer the room the more evaporation there will be, and the better the performance of the plant the more water it will require.

Although it may seem old fashioned, one of the best methods of detecting when water is needed is by using a thumb! Press it into the soil to test the moisture content and do not repeat the watering exercise unless it feels dry. All

How to revive a parched plant
It is vitally important to give a plant the right amount of water – not too much and not too little. A plant that has not received a sufficient amount of water will quickly show signs of dehydration (**above**). The leaves wilt and, if the plant is not watered soon, may drop off. If a plant is suffering from dehydration, the first thing to do is to loosen the top layer of soil (**above**). This will allow the water to permeate to the roots. Then water the plant thoroughly, making sure that the water goes right through the soil. It is also a good idea, if the plant is very parched, to spray the leaves with tepid water (**above**). This will enable to the plant to absorb the water it needs as quickly as possible. The best way of ensuring that the plant has received enough water is to allow some water to accumulate in the tray or saucer on which the pot is standing. However, do not allow the plant to stand in water for more than a few minutes, as this may cause waterlogging, damage the roots and root rot may well develop. Always leave a plant to drain (**above**) after watering.

the same, never allow the soil to become so dry that it begins to shrink and loses touch with the sides of the container in which it is growing. Some plants, such as fittonias, will wilt through drought conditions and after watering will become perfectly normal again, without loss of leaves, provided the drought period is not prolonged. Other plants that become excessively dry, *Azalea indica* being the perfect example, will simply shed their foliage and never be the same again. *A. indica* is one of those plants that must be wet every day of the year if it is to succeed. When roots of a plant are deprived of oxygen through permanently sodden soil they begin to rot and are unable to support all the plant's leaves so these inevitably turn yellow and in time will fall. With a few exceptions, excessively wet soil is far more damaging to plants than soil that is on the dry side. In winter, when plants are either at a standstill or growth is very slow, the need for water will be much reduced.

Attractive plants deserve attractive containers in which to set them off, and there are now plenty of these available in either pottery or plastic. It is often wise to select both the plant and its decorative outer cover at the same time. Then there is a reasonable chance that a good match will be achieved, both in respect of pot colour to plant colour, and plant pot size to the decorative container size. Ideally, the outer container should be wider and deeper than the pot in which the plant is growing. This will make it possible for a handful of gravel to be put in the bottom of the outer pot on which the growing pot can rest, thus enabling excess moisture to drain through into the gravel. Totally saturated

soil conditions often come about when water that is poured over the soil drains into the outer pot so that the plant is actually standing in water to about half the depth of its pot. This is not desirable so it is wise to inspect the decorative pot from time to time to ensure that water is not accumulating there.

In rooms with a very dry atmosphere it is important that something should be done to create some humidity, even if it is only around the plant. For a houseplant on its own, this can be achieved by having a much larger outer pot than the pot in which the plant is growing. The spaces between the two pots should be filled with moistened peat and thereafter, as long as the peat is kept moist, the plant will benefit. Another way of providing humidity is to fill a gravel tray with about 2in (5cm) of wet pebbles or moist sand. A group of plants can then be arranged on the tray to make an attractive display. All the plants will grow better because of the additional humidity. Gravel windowledge trays can also be used for just a single row of plants.

Hanging plants are not as fashionable today as they once were, but there are still many planters and hangers of every description available. Quite tiny pots with many long strings attached are frequently offered for sale but unless the plants are going to be checked quite often, small pot hangers are not very practical. It is very much better to choose hangers that will take pots of around 5in (12·5cm) in diameter, as these will hold moisture for a much longer period. There are many suitable trailing plants for putting into hanging attachments, and ideally all these should never need too

Humidity Many plants require more humidity in the atmosphere than is provided in the average home. If the atmosphere becomes too dry, the plant's rate of water loss increases, which causes it to wilt. You can prevent this by standing the plant on damp pebbles or gravel, or filling the space between the inner and outer pot with damp peat.

much water. For example, the *Ficus pumila*, Creeping Fig, is a beautiful little green foliage plant that hangs very naturally, but it is hopeless as a hanging subject, as if it dries out on only one occasion that will be the end of it.

Feeding indoor plants is something that is frequently neglected, and occasionally overdone, and the plant is likely to suffer in both sets of circumstances. The commercial grower of potted plants usually feeds them every week once they have become established in their pots, with the food given at slightly longer intervals in winter. Therefore, all plants bought from a retailer are likely to have enjoyed a reasonably even programme of feeding for weeks, perhaps months, before they leave the nursery. For plants to get off to a good start indoors it is important that feeding begins some time during the first week of their arrival.

Plants that have been freshly potted will not require feeding until they have well filled their pots with active roots. A simple check can be made on the root condition by placing a hand over the soil with the plant stem between the fingers and inverting the pot before tapping it away from the plant. This operation should be done with care so that plants with only a little root will not have the soil broken away from around them. If the plant is well rooted, the soil will be held together by the intertwining roots and no harm will be done. However, it is not advisable to knock plants from their pots in this way any more than is absolutely necessary.

All fertilizers will have their ingredients marked somewhere on the container. By way of a simple guide, plant food that is bought for purely foliage plants should be high in nitrogen, which will be indicated on the container by the letter 'N'. Fertilizer that is high in potash, which will be abbreviated to 'K_2O', is much more suitable for flowering plants, so it is worth buying two different brands of fertilizer for a varied plant collection. It is also common practice to feed many flowering plants with a high nitrogen fertilizer while they are producing leaves only, and then to change to a high potash one when the plants are flowering.

Feeding plants with weak fertilizer with every watering makes good sense as it becomes a natural reaction to reach for the fertilizer each time that the watering can comes out. However, equally good results can be obtained by putting a plant food tablet in the soil that will last for several weeks and nourish the plant all the time. Fertilizer in a tablet form is excellent for hanging plants that can often be quite inconvenient and difficult to look after. The amount of food plants need varies considerably, depending on their size and variety but the larger and more vigorous the plant, the more feeding it will require. As well as feeding through their roots, plants will also absorb nutrients through their leaves and there are numerous foliar feeds available for this purpose. However, some of the concoctions that are on offer are not particularly effective, so experiment with a few foliar feeds on one or two less important plants before giving them to the whole plant collection.

Cleaning houseplants is a chore that is often neglected, yet they become just as dusty as all the other bits and pieces in a room. Many plants are cleaned before they leave the nursery on which they were grown but, because of the large

Mineral deficiency An under-nourished plant, such as this *Pittosporum tenuifolium* (above), grows sluggishly and the leaves fade and turn yellow.

numbers involved, the operation can never be very efficient. Some plants will miss the cleaning treatment entirely, while others will have a coating of cleaning oil on their leaves when they are sold.

Leaf cleaning chemicals can greatly improve the appearance of plants providing the directions that come with the bottle or packet are followed carefully. Too much can be very harmful and occasionally plants may suffer because they are sensitive to a chemical, so always test a new oil on a leaf before using it on the whole plant. In addition, chemical cleaners should not be used on most hairy leaved plants, such as platyceriums, and they will also damage many of the rex begonias. A further point to remember is that soft new leaves at the top of plants such as the monstera should not be cleaned or handled in any way. Also, when chemical leaf cleaners are being applied to plants the temperature should be above 60°F (15°C), as a combination of chemicals and low temperatures can be harmful. Equally, at the other end of the scale, never apply chemicals to plant leaves and then expose them to full sunlight. Strong rays of the sun shining onto plant leaves while they are still wet from cleaning can have a disastrous effect on some plants.

Many glossy leaves, those of the philodendron and ficus plants for example, can be effectively cleaned simply by using soapy water and a sponge to thoroughly wash them. Detergents should never be used nor should soft new leaves be touched. Leaves that need cleaning should have a supporting hand placed under them while the other hand is used to wipe the leaf clean firmly but not harshly. Pale water marks on foliage left over from the plant's days on the nursery, where water is normally splashed about very liberally, will not be removed by gently wiping the leaf. So for more persistent marks rub tougher leaves quite firmly.

Smaller plants, such as Ivies, with strong leaves that are difficult to deal with individually can have a piece of polythene wrapped around the pot and over the top of the soil so that the leaves can be immersed in a bucket of soapy water. While holding the plant under the water with one hand sponge down the leaves with the other. Many of the hairy leaved plants can be immersed in water to clean off loose dust, but it is important that they are allowed to dry thoroughly before being exposed to direct sunlight. Saintpaulias, however, do not like to have their leaves wetted at any time, use a soft brush to clean dust off their foliage.

Cleaning leaves Hardy plants with glossy leaves, such as the Rubber Plant (**above**) can be cleaned by sponging the leaves with soapy water. Never use detergent and wipe only well developed leaves, as soft new growth could be damaged when handled. The African Violet (**below**) has slightly hairy leaves which must be treated gently and never cleaned with liquid or chemicals. A soft brush is the best implement, lightly used to remove surface dust and any material collecting as flowers and leaves die off.

Types of food Liquid feeds (**above**) can be applied with the regular watering of the plant. Powdered food can also be added to the water. Note the plant's reaction to the feed, and adjust the dosage accordingly. Pellet feeds (**left**) do away with the necessity of accurate measuring and mixing. The pellets are pushed into the soil. When the plant is watered, the pellet releases the correct dosage of feed. Fertilizer sticks (**above left**) are even less time-consuming. The sticks are pushed into the soil at the pot's edge and, like pellets, release the correct amount of feed over a given period of time.

Staking of indoor plants is something that is frequently done very badly, both by plant growers at the nursery and by the eventual buyers. To cut costs, almost everything that is done to plants is done with maximum speed, so supports are pushed into the soil at all angles and are frequently too slender to support the plants properly. Stakes should be secure but not obvious. For example, stake a monstera by putting a stake at the back of the plant where it will look less clumsy, but still do its job of keeping the plant upright. Stakes do not have to be huge pieces of timber but they must be solid enough to support plants firmly. They should also be tall enough for new growth to be tied to them as the plants develop.

Many plants, especially those of the *Araceae* family that produce natural aerial roots, will benefit from a moss-covered support into which the roots can penetrate. These are not difficult to make. Use a piece of plastic tubing about $\frac{3}{4}$in (19mm) in diameter rather than timber which will rot in time. Bind moss firmly to the tubing with wire that has a plastic coating around it to prevent corrosion. If the moss is kept wet all the time, the aerial roots will develop much more freely. Taller climbing plants, cissus for example, will often do better if their growth is encouraged to fan out on a trellis, or even plastic netting support, and as most of the indoor climbers are green foliage plants they will usually look more attractive if the trellis is painted white in contrast with the greenery of the plants.

Staking plants It is important to use the right material when tying stems to a stake (**above**). String may rot in time; plain wire will corrode and may damage the plant. The best thing to use is plastic coated or cardboard-covered wire.

Types of staking There are many ways in which plants can be effectively and attractively staked, and there is no need to use an inadequate piece of dowling rammed into the soil at an awkward angle. Trellises (**above left**) are most effective methods of staking, both visually and practically. A stephanotis or a jasmine could be trained round a piece of plastic-covered wire (**above top**) Ordinary pieces of wood can be tied into interesting and functional shapes (**above**). Whatever the method of staking chosen, ensure that the stake is strong enough to support the plant. Bromeliads can be grown on mossy logs (**right**).

From time to time, nearly all houseplants need pruning. Most plants are pruned because they are growing too much and, particularly in the case of the Rubber Plant, because they have outgrown their allotted space and are trying to push their way through the ceiling. Non-flowering plants can be trimmed to shape whenever growth is getting in the way of something in the room. This type of pruning simply requires cutting the plant back to the desired shape. Natural climbers such as the cissus need not necessarily be pruned, as in most instances untidy growth can be doubled back and pinned in lower down on the plant. It is important, however, not to bend the stems too acutely.

Pruning a Rubber Plant can be quite a challenge for the inexperienced houseplant grower as it is a traumatic moment for both the plant and the owner when the time comes to chop the plant's head off. The operation takes a little courage and is best performed during the winter months when the plant is more or less dormant and will not have so much sap flowing in its stem. Use sharp and strong secateurs to cut through the main stem just above a leaf so that there is a space of about 2ft (60cm) between the ceiling and where the cut is made to allow for future growth. When new shoots start to grow there will be three or more branching ones rather than the single stem that was there before. Sap flowing from the stem can be checked by applying a little damp soil to the cut. There are more expensive ways of drying up the sap but they will be no more effective than this method. The severed top section should be cut up into individual leaves with a piece of stem attached so that other plants can be raised. If the severed ends of the cuttings are allowed to dry before they are inserted in a peaty mixture they will not be so difficult to manage. It is most important that the temperature remains somewhere in the region of 70°F (21°C) day and night until new growth appears, when it can be reduced by around five degrees.

Separating plants A plant that grows in clumps can be divided into two separate plants. Carefully remove the plant from its pot, shaking the soil off. Divide the root ball into two smaller clumps. Do not tear the roots more than is necessary. Each new plant can then be potted.

Pruning Plants are normally pruned when they have grown too large. If a plant has grown out of shape or too leggy, it can be cut back with a sharp pair of scissors or secateurs (**above**). Look for the growth buds on the stem and cut just above one of them. Pruning also encourages new growth and if this is what is required, cut the plant back well. Alternatively, you can pinch out a plant by removing the small growing tip. Pinch the growth with the finger and thumb just above the node (where the leaf joins the stem) and remove it. This will encourage dormant buds further down the stem to shoot. In this way, a plant can be made bushier and better-shaped without having to do any full-scale cutting back. Judicious pruning will produce vigorous plants.

Propagation is an aspect of houseplant growing that arouses the mother instinct in many enthusiasts as they carefully nurture and fuss over their seeds and cuttings. Indeed, it is quite exciting to lift the cover off the propagator and see that the once limp cuttings are actually sitting up and looking alive. Successful propagation requires certain conditions. Chief among these is that a temperature should be provided which is warm enough to encourage seeds to germinate and cuttings to take root. Although cooler conditions will do for some plants, it is wise to aim for something in the region of 70°F (21°C). In such a temperature, cuttings will root more quickly, and the sooner roots develop, the greater the chances are that the cuttings will do well.

Preventing transpiration is another important requirement. The best way to do this is by providing some kind of propagating unit. Many of these have built-in heaters, and obviously a unit containing a heater will have no temperature problems. Plants transpire naturally which means that they give off moisture into the atmosphere through their leaves. Usually, the root system of a plant replaces all the lost moisture, but, as they do not have a root system, cuttings will simply shrivel up and die once all the moisture in their leaves and stems has transpired. However, if cuttings are put in a sealed propagating case, they will give off sufficient moisture to saturate the atmosphere inside the propagator. Transpiration will then be much reduced and so the cuttings will survive. Polythene bags are inexpensive yet satisfactory alternatives to propagating cases. Pots of cuttings should be grouped together inside sealed bags and plants such as tradescantias and impatiens will generally root very easily by this method. Until cuttings have become well established, keep them in shade out of direct sunlight.

Cuttings should be put into clean, moist peat from which water can just be squeezed when a handful of it is compressed. Both pots and shallow boxes are suitable for growing cuttings in, but pots are usually better for a small number of them. Seed can either be sown in shallow pans or in boxes, and the directions on the seed packet will say what the depth and time of sowing should be. After sowing seed, place a sheet of glass over the seed box or pot until the seedlings have germinated when the glass can be removed. Most seedlings should be allowed to grow until they are large enough to handle when they should be spaced out in boxes filled with a peaty mixture. Seedlings should be kept moist but they should not be allowed to get too wet or they will tend to rot at soil level.

Whatever the plant being propagated, its cuttings should be of the best quality, if they are to have a good chance of succeeding. All cuttings should be removed with a sharp knife and any trimming should be done before they are inserted. Most cuttings will benefit if they are treated with a rooting hormone mixture, before they are planted. Smaller cuttings of plants like Ivies and tradescantias will develop into better plants when they mature if several cuttings are put into the pot at the outset. One cutting in a pot will probably produce a plant, but the finished product will be superior if about five to seven cuttings are used.

Plants can also be increased by propagating them from individual leaves, as well as stem cuttings, and the best plant for this is the saintpaulia, African Violet. Remove firm and healthy leaves from the plant and then dip the end of the leaf stalk in rooting powder. Put several of these into small pots containing a peaty mixture. Approximately five cuttings should go around the outer side of the pot with the centre left so that air can circulate. Saintpaulia cuttings must be provided with a temperature of at least 70°F (21°C) otherwise they will not grow. There are many other plants that can be successfully propagated so long as the basic essentials are remembered, these being a good temperature, sealed conditions, good quality cuttings and conditions which are moist but not sodden.

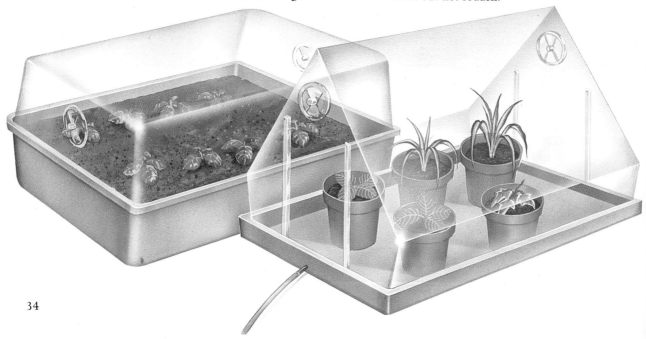

Taking cuttings When taking stem cuttings it is best to cut the stem just below a node. Some plants have aerial roots (**left top**) and these can be used to start off a new plant. It is important to make a clean cut, preferably with a razor blade, as if the plant tissue is damaged it may rot. The best length varies from plant to plant, but there should be at least three nodes between the tip and the cut end. Trim off the leaves attached to the bottom node. As plants lose water through their leaves in the process of transpiration, it is also a good idea to remove several other leaves in order to reduce this loss. The cutting should then be planted in a pot. As the cut end is very delicate, it is advisable to make holes in the rooting mixture with a small stick or pencil to avoid damaging the plant tissue. A single cutting can be rooted in a small pot or it may be more convenient to put two or three cuttings round the edge of a large pot (**left centre** and **bottom**). When the cuttings are planted, make firm the soil around them and add a little more soil if necessary.

Hormone rooting powder
This powder will encourage the production of roots, particularly in those plants which have woody stems. Some brands contain fungicide, which helps to prevent stem rot during the time roots are growing. Before inserting the cutting in the rooting mixture, dip the cut stem tip into the hormone rooting powder.

Propagators A simple propagator (**far left**) is basically a seed tray full of earth covered by a perspex or plastic lid with vents in it. The cuttings are planted in the box itself. A more sophisticated propagator (**left**) incorporates a heated element which helps cuttings become established more quickly. The cuttings can be planted in pots before they are put in the propagator.

Protection and humidity If they are to take root, cuttings need a high degree of humidity. This can be achieved quite easily by covering the cutting with a plastic bag tied firmly to the rim of the pot (**near right**). Alternatively, a jar can be used (**far right**). Its rim should rest on the potting mixture. This will also protect the plant. Whatever protection is chosen, it must not touch the cutting.

Positioning your houseplants

To grow plants successfully usually requires a combination of things—knowledge about houseplants, inherent ability (having greenfingers) and offering an agreeable environment. Having acquired rudimentary knowledge relating to plant problems, the next stage is to consider how to use plants to achieve the best effect indoors. For example, plants with green foliage, such as tough aspidistras, palms and nephrolepis ferns, will do much better in poor light than plants with variegated or highly coloured foliage, while nearly all flowering plants need good light if they are to do well. Inadequate light and heating facilities will always prove to be a taxing combination of problems for almost all indoor plants but generally improved methods of heating today mean that conditions can be provided which are like those in greenhouses at the turn of the century.

However, the one essential ingredient that is frequently missing in the indoor environment as opposed to the heated greenhouse is humidity. In greenhouses, the floor area and the areas of gravel on which plants are standing can always be damped down, with the result that the general growing conditions for plants are improved. Although plants may be regularly watered at their roots, a permanently dry atmosphere will have a weakening effect on them, resulting in a much greater incidence of red spider. A simple and effective method of counteracting dry atmospheric conditions is to invest in one of the many room humidifiers which are available. Also, although some plants will object to water being sprayed onto their foliage, saintpaulias being an example, many plants will also improve if they are sprayed with water. Lightly misting the leaves of plants such as philodendrons will help create a local moist atmosphere, which helps plants considerably as they adjust to room conditions.

For the odd few plants another simple way of creating humidity is to provide a plant pot that is a little larger than the one in which the plant is growing and to put some peat in the bottom. Then place the growing pot on the peat and fill in the area between the two pots with more moist peat. If kept moist, the peat will continually give off moisture into the atmosphere, so benefiting the plant. If a larger container is provided it will be possible to plunge a selection of plants into the pot so giving more agreeable conditions and an effective display at the same time. Houseplants in their pots can be surrounded with almost any moisture-retaining material in order to create more humid conditions. Wet newspaper is the cheapest, though not necessarily the most attractive, example.

When displaying all plants inside, it is important that they should be seen in order to be fully appreciated, which will perhaps mean using some form of pedestal to provide better elevation. Placed on the floor, many plants have little or no importance, but if they are raised they become a room feature commanding considerable attention. Of the purely foliage plants there are not many that are bold or distinguished enough to become room features when placed in isolation. For a cool room offering reasonable light, one of the best pedestal plants is *Aralia sieboldii* (which is also sold as *Fatsia japonica*), the green leaves of which

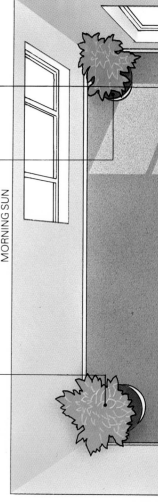

This large window will get plenty of light all day, but this includes the hot midday sun in summer and plants pressed against the windowpane may scorch. Flowering and variegated plants thrive in a well lit position.

Morning sunlight should not be too fierce, although the light is bright all day. Plants needing moderate conditions but good light are well placed here.

MORNING SUN

If a room is large and well supplied with light, a corner can provide a pleasant haven for a plant requiring moderate conditions of light and temperature. The Kangaroo Vine is a tolerant and long-lived plant which can attain quite luxurious growth. Many types of foliage plant will live happily here provided the corner is not too dark.

Measuring light intensity
A light meter can be useful if you are not sure how bright the light in a room is. Set a photographic light meter for film speed ASA 25. Hold a sheet of paper to the plant and the light meter to the paper. Adjust the dial of the meter according to the light reading obtained and check the f stop needed for a shutter speed of a quarter second. f64 or f32 indicates bright, direct sunlight, f16 bright light and f8 medium light.

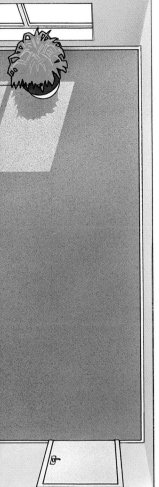

MIDDAY SUN

EVENING SUN

The corner of a room which gets no strong light is too dark for flowering plants. Ferns may appreciate the shade if the humidity and temperature are suitable.

A shady room has a low light level most of the day and is rather gloomy. The Rubber Plant is adaptable and hardy, and prefers to live in cool temperatures.

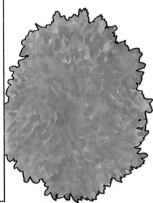

In this position the light in one window is obstructed by a tree outside, but there will be warm, evening light on most days. Philodendrons, although they thrive best in good light, can tolerate and adapt to the shade.

A light, airy kitchen (**left**) is an ideal location for many flowering and foliage plants which enjoy the warm, humid atmosphere. A Croton with brightly coloured leaves is a good choice for a warm window-sill. Plants placed on the work surfaces get plenty of light. A thin curtain across a large window (**right**) protects plants from the heat of direct sun and diffuses the light. Hanging and trailing plants are contrasted with the bold, unusual shape of the Swiss Cheese Plant.

The level and direction of the light available to an indoor plant considerably affect its growth. A plant placed near a window (**above**) against a white wall receives light directly through the window and also as it is

reflected from the wall, so the growth of the plant is healthy and straight. A plant placed against a dark wall obtains no reflected light and leans towards the window as the source of light.

radiate from a central stem so that the plant can be appreciated from all angles. For a warmer, lightly shaded place the Bird's Nest Fern, *Asplenium nidus avis*, can be especially beautiful when well grown. However, as this is one of the plants that are most pleasing when they are looked into rather than seen from the side, it is important that the plant should be placed at about waist level rather than shoulder level where only the reverse side of leaves would be seen.

Among the philodendrons there are many plants well suited for important individual locations, particularly those plants that produce a rosette of leaves, or leaves that radiate in all directions from a central stem. Some of the taller philodendrons, such as *P. hastatum*, can have their growing tips removed when they are young to encourage a more branching habit. If plants are left unstaked, growth will tumble over the sides of the container in which it is growing and this can look very attractive when the plants are placed on a low pedestal or table. The Grape Ivy, *Rhoicissus rhomboidea*, is usually thought of as a plant for climbing walls and pillars, but it too can be a very effective trailing subject if left unstaked and placed on a pedestal. Similarly, *Ficus benjamina*, the Weeping Fig, will develop into a most elegant indoor tree very naturally if the central stem of the plant is allowed to grow upwards unhindered. However, if the tips of young shoots are removed, the plant will branch out and the spreading, slightly weeping branches will present a very pleasing effect if the plant is given sufficient space in which to develop.

As an alternative to the more expensive larger plants that are likely to make features on their own, smaller plants can be placed in groups to provide a colourful and interesting arrangement. Although individual plants suspended in a wall bracket will not do so well because of the very dry surrounding conditions, reasonably sized wall mounted containers containing a group of plants can be most impressive. These wall mounted units for groups of plants can be very effective when set in a corner of the room. They should be placed at a higher level if trailing plants are being used, and at lower level if the plants are more attractive when looked down on. If the planter unit is placed in good light, then more colourful plants can be used, but in poor light the emphasis should again be on those with green foliage. One of the exceptions in respect of colour and light is the Devil's Ivy, *Scindapsus aureus*, which has pleasantly variegated golden yellow and green colouring that is retained even in poorly lit conditions. This plant is also very accommodating in that it will climb or trail depending on what is required. A support of some kind should always be used for climbing plants. Frequently it is more desirable and more attractive to fill wall or floor planters with plants of the same variety rather than have a clutter of all kinds, shapes and sizes. The scindapsus does very well in this situation and is seen at its best when it is trailing naturally from a wall-mounted container or reasonably large hanging pot. The rhoicissus and *Philodendron scandens*, the Sweetheart Plant, are two others that are trouble free and ideal as hanging subjects.

This is a very good position for many types of plants. As it is near the window the light is good but sunlight will not be too direct and glaring and it is also out of the line of draughts from the window and fireplace.

A window position is suitable for flowering and variegated plants, such as Busy Lizzie, Poinsettia or tradescantia, which all need plenty of light. However, they must be protected from full, hot sunlight, cold draughts or low winter temperatures.

If a plant is placed in a corner, away from the window but near a door, it will be subject to draughts of air and possibly inadequate and variable lighting. Very few plants could actively enjoy these conditions, but the hardy aspidistra, also known as the Cast Iron Plant, may adapt quite well and even flourish.

A few decorative plants make an attractive display in a hallway (**left**). A glass-panelled door or plenty of window space ensures bright, even light. However, the temperature and humidity change every time the door is opened, so plants of a fairly hardy nature are needed. Ivies, monsteras and the Spider Plant all adapt to cool conditions as do flowering plants such as chrysanthemums, cyclamens and certain types of begonia. Ferns flourish at the Chelsea Flower Show (**right**) but may be difficult at home, needing the warmth and humidity of a kitchen or bathroom.

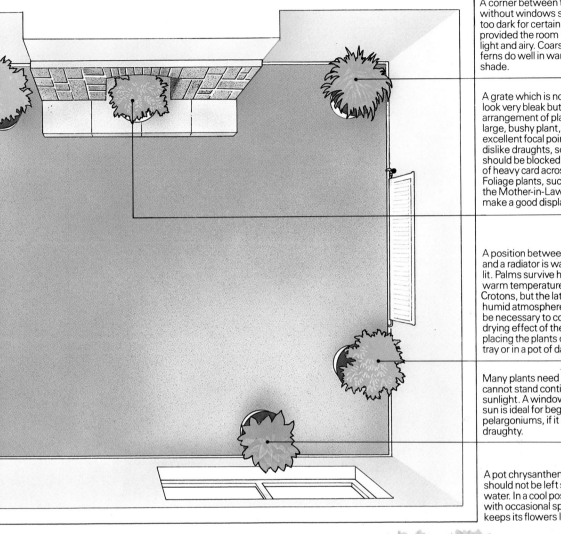

A corner between two walls without windows should not be too dark for certain plants provided the room is generally light and airy. Coarse foliage ferns do well in warmth and shade.

A grate which is not in use can look very bleak but an arrangement of plants, or one large, bushy plant, is an excellent focal point. All plants dislike draughts, so the chimney should be blocked with a sheet of heavy card across the vent. Foliage plants, such as Ivies or the Mother-in-Law's Tongue, make a good display.

A position between a window and a radiator is warm and well lit. Palms survive happily in warm temperatures as do Crotons, but the latter need a humid atmosphere and it would be necessary to counter the drying effect of the radiator by placing the plants on a gravel tray or in a pot of damp peat.

Many plants need good light but cannot stand continual strong sunlight. A window out of the sun is ideal for begonias and pelargoniums, if it is not too draughty.

A pot chrysanthemum (below) should not be left standing in water. In a cool position and with occasional spraying, it keeps its flowers longer.

Instant diagnosis chart

Symptom	Give the plant food	Water the plant	Repot in fresh soil or larger pot	Change the position of the plant	Reduce watering	Reduce feeding
Plant growing slowly	●		●		●	
Wilting leaves		●				
Mottled leaves						
Browning on the leaf margins				●	●	●
Flower heads dropping				●	●	
Leaves bruised or broken				●		
Leaves falling					●	
Rotting in the stems or leaves					●	
Leaf colour too pale	●			●		
Small leaves and spindly growth	●					
Leaves turning yellow						
Holes in the leaves					●	

Using the chart
To deal with common problems, check the symptoms (above) against the remedial actions along the top and down the right.

Symptom / Action	Check for damage to the roots	Look for pests in leaves or soil	Wipe the leaves	Examine the leaves for botrytis	Regulate humidity in the room	Allow for normal seasonal behaviour
The plant is probably in its dormant period	●	●				●
Check the quality of the soil						●
Watch for signs of virus infection		●	●			
Move the plant out of direct sun					●	
Handle plant gently when moving it						
Move the plant to a safer place						
Change the type of feed used		●				●
Remove dead flower heads				●		
Put the plant in better light						
Look under leaves for red spider						
Protect the plant from draughts		●			●	●
Look for caterpillars or earwigs		●				

41

The houseplants

43

Acalypha hispida

This woody tropical shrub originating from South-East Asia, can reach a maximum height of around 6ft (2m) when grown as a pot plant. Its coarse green leaves vary between 8–10in (20–25cm) in length, depending on how well the plant is cared for, but the principal attraction lies in the bright red 10–12in (25–30cm) drooping bracts that appear in profusion during the summer. However, well managed plants that are grown in good light in a reasonable temperature will oblige with at least a few bracts throughout the year. To improve the appearance of the plant, bracts should be removed the moment they have lost their sparkle.

New plants can be made by striking cuttings in warm, moist conditions in the spring. Top cuttings with about four leaves attached should be inserted singly in small pots filled with fresh peat. A temperature of 65°–70°F (18°–21°C) will be necessary, and the cuttings will root more readily if they are treated with rooting powder and then put in a sealed propagating case. These are hungry plants that must not be allowed to remain pot-bound for too long, so they should be removed from their pots occasionally so that the roots can be inspected. When potting becomes necessary, a loam-based potting mixture should be used, as thin peat mixtures will not sustain these plants.

Healthy leaf A healthy acalypha has shiny green leaves, varying in size according to age and degree of care.

Healthy plant The *Acalypha hispida*'s chief charm lies in its long red bracts. During the growth period, the plant requires heavy feeding; this takes place primarily in summer, though, given the right conditions, the plant will produce a few bracts throughout the year. Keep it in a good light, but away from full sun, at a temperature of around 65°F (18°C).

Diseased plant All acalyphas should be checked carefully before they are purchased. If the foliage has yellowed, it means the plant is suffering from starvation. The lower branches should not be denuded of leaves. Above all, check the upper leaves for red spider mites. As the infected plant (**right**) shows, these can play havoc with acalyphas. At home, keep plants away from hot radiators, which will encourage red spider to develop. The only treatment for an infected plant is to spray with an insecticide.

Red spider mite This is the chief pest which attacks the acalypha. Initially, the signs are dull green leaves with tiny spots.

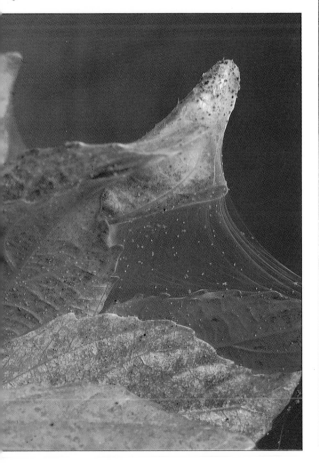

AVOIDING PROBLEMS

Light and position

The acalypha appreciates a bright position, but not one which is continually exposed to bright sun. On the other hand, it cannot tolerate too much shade. Keep it away from a hot radiator, as the dry heat will encourage red spider mites, and out of draughts.

Temperature range

Cool — Intermediate — Warm

A fairly warm temperature range is required, no lower than 60°F (15°C) and up to 70°F (21°C). Cuttings and young plants require the higher temperatures in the range. A high level of humidity is also required which can be achieved by standing the pot on a tray of damp pebbles and occasionally spraying the foliage.

Watering

The plant will flourish if the soil is kept quite moist at all times, which means extra water in summer when the soil dries out more quickly. The acalypha dislikes standing in water, so water from the top through the soil and discard the excess.

Feeding

This is a voracious plant during the active summer months and it will require plenty of food, but as it rests in the winter, it needs no food at all until signs of growth reappear.

Seasonal care

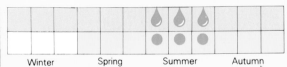

Winter — Spring — Summer — Autumn

The acalypha is difficult to grow unless the right conditions of warmth and humidity can be maintained. This may be a problem in the home, as in winter the plant will suffer from dry heat when gas or electric fires are used. However, there are steps which can be taken to ensure a moist atmosphere and if the plant flourishes it can be propagated from top cuttings taken in the spring.

Soil

Cuttings do well in small pots filled with fresh peat. When repotting becomes necessary, use a loam-based mixture which can sustain the plant during the growth periods. Remember that moisture is vital to the plant, in the soil and in a humid surrounding atmosphere.

Aechmea

Originating from tropical South America, this is not only one of the most exotic flowering houseplants, but also one of the most durable. Its foliage is very coarse and edged with quite vicious spines, and its colouring varies from light grey to dark red. The recurving and overlapping leaves form into a natural watertight urn shape, which gives the plant its common name of Urn Plant. In the plant's natural jungle habitat this urn fills with rainwater or heavy dew which can sustain the plant for many months in the event of drought.

Perhaps the most spectacular time in the life of the aechmea is when, after a number of years, it produces its fascinating bracts. These may vary in shape, but they all reach their high point when they become studded with tiny flowers that are mostly intense blue. Another characteristic of this plant is that it is epiphytic, which means that it grows on trees, by becoming lodged between branches, or around rotting stumps for example.

Although the commercial grower propagates aechmeas from seed in optimum conditions, this is generally not a very rewarding method for someone with limited indoor facilities. It is much better to remove offsets from the base of mature plants that have flowered and to pot these up individually in a very loose mixture composed almost entirely of peat and leaf mould.

VARIETIES AND PURCHASING

The greenhouse culture for aechmeas is highly specialized and it can take as long as five years to bring them to the flowering stage. Because the plants occupy space in the greenhouse for so long they are quite expensive to buy. Smaller, cheaper plants which are not in flower can be found but are less attractive. Choose a plant which has bracts showing above the urn shape formed by the leaves, but not one which is so advanced that it is flowering from the bract. The tough, leathery leaves are not easily damaged, so it should not be a problem to find a good looking specimen.

A. rhodocyanea This variety, also known as *A. fasciata,* is produced in the largest quantity by growers and is the most suitable for growing at home. It is extremely decorative, having grey-green foliage and, as its principal attraction, a fist-sized bract in a true, clear pink which is dotted with tiny flowers of an intense blue. The great benefit of this plant is that the bract remains colourful for a full six months from the time of

purchase. When the plant has flowered, the main rosette from which the bract emerged dies off naturally and smaller plants develop at the base of the main stem. These baby plants can eventually be removed and potted up individually, but it may be a year or even longer before a plant propagated in this way will flower. An attractive way of displaying an aechmea is to wrap the roots in damp sphagnum moss and wire it to a natural or chiselled hollow in a piece of bark.

A. fulgens discolor This is a much smaller plant than *A. rhodocyanea,* with a more open rosette and leaves with a dull green upper surface, but red underneath. The scarlet bract is also more open but if it is put in a group of plants, it produces an interesting contrast of colour, shape and texture. The flowers are purple, spread along the stem.

AVOIDING PROBLEMS

Light and position

The Urn Plant is a bromeliad and these usually object to a dark location. In good, strong light with partial sun it will be found that the leaf colouring is bright and

attractive. Although the plants are tough, do not place them in draughts or near heating appliances.

Temperature range

Cool	Intermediate	Warm

The plant is not especially fussy about temperature, and a moderate to warm range of 60°-70°F (15°-21°C) suits it very well. A slight change at either end of this scale will be tolerated but

do not subject the plant to extremes of heat or cold. It has no special requirements for humidity but the method of watering will tend to encourage a moist, rather than dry, atmosphere.

Watering

Leave about 1in (2.5cm) of water in the central rosette, changing it every three weeks. Rainwater can be used for this, as the plant is

kept moist in the wild by rain collecting in the leaves and running into the urn. Keep the soil just moist.

Feeding

It is not essential to feed this plant, but an occasional liquid feed added to the water will do it no harm. If something

seems wrong, do not resort to extra feeding. Check the temperature and look for pests.

Seasonal care

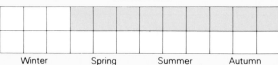

Winter	Spring	Summer	Autumn

Despite its exotically tropical appearance, the Urn Plant is quite easy to care for, requiring only regular, but not excessive, attention to watering. As the plant develops, the old flower bract can be cut away and in time the parent rosette can also be

discarded. New rosettes are put into small pots and may be repotted before flowering. The plants are usually trouble free throughout the year, but spotting may be caused by the use of household aerosols in the vicinity of the plant.

Soil

It is vital to provide free drainage through the soil so use an open mixture. Equal parts of fairly coarse leaf mould and peat,

worked together with a little fresh sphagnum moss, will be ideal. The plants should not need potting on more than every other year.

PESTS AND DISEASES

In keeping with the general tolerance and easy care of this plant, it is rarely visited by pests.
Mealy bug This may attack older bracts on a mature plant, but is uncommon. Gently remove the bugs with a small toothbrush dipped in methylated spirits.

The leaf texture of an aechmea (**left**) naturally varies. A mottled texture appearing to cut across the leaf is interwoven with broken stripey markings down the length. The heavy green marks, like scratches, which can be seen here are due to rough handling and may also be caused by a cat brushing past the plant and bruising the leaves. Never use a chemical leaf shine on this plant.

Discoloured bract After about seven weeks in flower the bract may darken slightly. Any bad discoloration may mean that the plant is too cold.

Healthy leaf This should be firm and even, arching gracefully from the central stem of the plant.

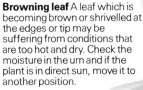

Browning leaf A leaf which is becoming brown or shrivelled at the edges or tip may be suffering from conditions that are too hot and dry. Check the moisture in the urn and if the plant is in direct sun, move it to another position.

Healthy plant The curving leaves should be tough, greyish green, and the bract a clear pink with no sign of browning. A fully grown leaf may be 12in (30cm) in length.

Aglaonema

Most aglaonema plants are compact and low-growing, with congested leaves borne on short stalks that are produced at soil level. *A. pseudobracteatum* has a more branching habit and is much less common, and therefore more difficult to acquire. An important quality of most aglaonemas is their ability to grow where there is very poor light.

New plants can be propagated at any time by splitting large clumps into smaller sections and potting them independently.

PESTS AND DISEASES

Mealy bug The congested leaves and stalks of the aglaonema provide ideal conditions for mealy bug. Rather than spraying with insecticide as normal, it is better to mix the insecticide (malathion) in a watering can and apply through a coarse rose.

Root mealy bug These small pests can only be found by removing the plant from its pot. Apply insecticide solution into the soil. Endosulfan is recommended.

Healthy plant *A. crispum 'Silver Queen'* (**above**) is an excellent plant for indoor use. It gains its name from the silvery markings of its foliage. Its leaves are usually between 5in (12.5cm) and 6in (15cm) long. The plant looks extremely attractive. Although it does require warm conditions, it will tolerate a very shady location. *'Silver Queen'* is one of the most popular aglaonemas, and is well suited to hydroculture.

Healthy plant *A. trewbii* (**above**) has mottled cream and green markings on its leaves. Although it is perhaps not so exciting to look at as *A. crispum 'Silver Queen'*, it is still relatively popular with house plant enthusiasts.

Types of leaf This leaf from *A. crispum 'Silver Queen'* (**below left**) shows the characteristic silver and green colouring on the foliage. The cream and green leaves of *A. trewbii* (**below**) should be densely packed on the healthy plant.

VARIETIES AND PURCHASING

When buying, avoid plants with brown leaf margins, as this shows that the plant has been raised in poor conditions and kept in too cold a temperature. It is best to select a young plant with firm leaves.

A. modestum This is the true Chinese Evergreen, but it is a rather dull plant.
A. crispum 'Silver Queen' This has blotched silver and green foliage.
A. trewbii This has cream and green mottled leaves.

Botrytis This leaf (left) showns signs of botrytis. Spray with an appropriate insecticide.

Leaf spot For leaf spot diseases (below) spray the plant with an appropriate insecticide.

Leaf damage The leaves of this plant (below) are damaged as the plant has been kept in too cold conditions. It is vital to keep aglaonemas warm.

AVOIDING PROBLEMS

Light and position

The aglaonema will tolerate poor light with no ill effects, but must not be exposed to direct sunlight as this may scorch the leaves. It is seen to best effect when grouped with other more colourful plants.

Temperature range

Cool   Intermediate   Warm

This plant must not be placed in cold conditions. A warm room anywhere between 60°-70°F (15°-21°C) is suitable, but an aglaonema will grow more vigorously if the temperature is even higher than this. Any slight chill may cause leaf discoloration. Humidity can be increased by placing trays of moist pebbles under the pots.

Watering

Aglaonemas should be watered regularly so that the potting mixture stays moist. Only the very surface should dry out between waterings. In the winter months the plants will require slightly less water. If the roots become too wet the leaves will begin to wilt.

Feeding

Established plants should be given a liquid feed each time they are watered if they are to flourish well. Again, less food is necessary during the dormant winter period. The fertilizer should be administered in a fairly weak solution.

Seasonal care

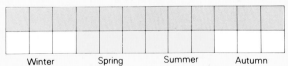

Winter   Spring   Summer   Autumn

If kept in suitable conditions, aglaonemas tend to stay healthy. They are susceptible to oil and gas fumes however, and should not be exposed to them. Unsuitable household aerosols used in the vicinity of the plant may cause spotting on the leaves but this can probably be removed by wiping the leaves gently with a damp sponge. Aglaonemas should be kept away from windows and draughts throughout the winter months, and whenever the weather is very cold.

Soil

A peaty mixture is needed for aglaonemas, and repotting should be avoided in winter if possible. The pots that are used should not be too large, as these plants grow best when their roots are confined in quite small containers.

Anthurium

Anthuriums belong to the same family as the philodendrons, which is a reasonably sure indication that they will enjoy moist, humid and warm conditions in preference to dry and cold. There are many different anthuriums, but only three that are really suitable for growing in room conditions. These three—*A. andreanum*, *A. scherzerianum* and *A. guatemala*—have broadly arrow-shaped leaves that are carried on slender stalks. They all have exotic flowers that remain colourful for many weeks, even when used as cut flowers.

The commercial grower raises new plants from seed. However this requires special skill and conditions and is not often within the scope of the amateur grower with only limited facilities.

Healthy plant A well tended anthurium makes a handsome houseplant. A white pot contrasts well with the dark leaves.

AVOIDING PROBLEMS

Light and position

Anthuriums require good, bright light, but if placed in a window they must be protected from the glare of direct sun. The plants are spectacular and one or two varieties become quite large when mature, so can be given a spacious, individual position.

Temperature range

| Cool | Intermediate | Warm |

Even, warm temperatures of 65°-70°F (18°-21°C) are necessary for a healthy plant and a radical change in the conditions, in winter or at night, will not contribute to its comfort. These are originally tropical plants, so they like high humidity as well as adequate warmth.

Watering

Keep the plant well watered in summer and during the main growing period. Less water is required in winter, but do not allow the soil either to dry out, or to become waterlogged as this will cause the plant to wilt.

Feeding

Give the plant a liquid feed weekly while it is active and reduce the feeding as the growth slows down towards winter. If the plant is dormant in winter, no nourishment is needed.

Seasonal care

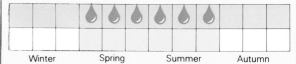

| Winter | Spring | Summer | Autumn |

Anthuriums are not easy plants to grow, and it is vital to maintain the correct temperature and humidity and to shield them from draughts. Provided these conditions are met, and the plant is neither overwatered nor allowed to thirst, it should do well. Rainwater is preferred when possible and may also be sprayed on the leaves. These may also be cleaned occasionally with a soft sponge, but do not handle soft, new leaves.

Soil

An open potting mixture is needed, composed of equal parts of peat, sphagnum moss and partly rotted leaf mould. To allow the soil to drain properly, place crocks in the pot before filling it.

VARIETIES AND PURCHASING

Only buy anthuriums from a houseplant specialist, as these plants are vulnerable, particularly to cold conditions, and need expert care at every stage of their development if they are to succeed. Ensure that the plants you choose are clean and that their foliage has lustre. It does not matter if there are no flowers present, except these are the only sure indication of the plant's colouring. The most important point to check is that the plant has a good number of fresh leaves that are clean and unblemished.

A. andraeanum This is probably the most demanding anthurium, needing a high temperature and humidity in order to flourish. It has long petioles and superb flowers, carried on long stalks.

A. guatemala This variety will flower practically throughout the year, given the right conditions.

A. scherzerianum This anthurium is well-suited to home conditions. The plant gets its common name, Flamingo Flower, from its curiously shaped red-pink spathe with its curling spadix. Controlled high humidity encourages flowering. The flower stalks may need staking as the plant grows.

Natural and unnatural deaths
The *A. churchurianus* (**above**) died naturally; the *A. scherzerianum* (**below**) is suffering from the fungus disease, botrytis, brought on by cold and damp. Though anthuriums love moisture, problems will soon arise if very wet conditions are allied to a low temperature.

Flower wilting The cause is possibly natural in this case, but this is often the result of poor conditions.

Leaves turning yellow The plant is too wet and cold so let it dry out and move it to a warmer place.

Brown patches These indicate the presence of fungus. Cut off infected growth, if possible, and spray with a recommended fungicide.

Aphelandra

Having greyish green foliage with silver markings, the aphelandra is one of the more attractive foliage plants. Its appearance is further enhanced when colourful yellow bracts are produced at the top of each growing stem. The small, yellow, tubular flowers are fairly insignificant, but the bracts remain colourful for many months making the aphelandra a spectacular, long-lasting plant. There are now two worthwhile varieties of the original plant which is indigenous to Mexico. *A. squarrosa Brockfeld* is the more robust plant, while *A. squarrosa Dania* is more compact and if anything flowers more prolifically.

New plants are propagated by removing the top section of the stem with two opposite pairs of leaves attached, or by removing a pair of lower leaves with about 1in (2·5cm) of stem above and below where the leaf stalk is attached. Use peat and sand mixture and ensure the temperature is not less than 70°F (21°C) and the atmosphere is humid.

Healthy plant Avoid buying plants which have a yellow look to their foliage (**right**). The bracts tend to attract greenfly and the leaves scale insects so both should be checked.

AVOIDING PROBLEMS

Light and position

The aphelandra is an exception among flowering plants in that it does not require full light in order to flourish successfully. Good light is needed, but not full sun. The plant should be given plenty of room in which to spread its leaves.

Temperature range

Cool   Intermediate   Warm

Warm temperatures of 65°-70°F (18°-21°C) are essential and this is a plant which is particularly vulnerable to a cool environment. A humid atmosphere is also appreciated and the pot can be packed with moist peat or left to stand on a tray of pebbles if the room is normally dry.

Watering

The aphelandra must be watered regularly, although overwatering may encourage botrytis and should be avoided. If the plant is allowed to dry out the leaves will rapidly fall. Less water can be given for a few weeks after flowering to allow a period of rest.

Feeding

This plant produces a mass of roots and is a heavy feeder. Liquid fertilizer should be supplied through the soil and it is possible to double the recommended strength of the feed without harming the plant.

Seasonal care

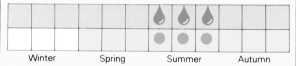

Winter   Spring   Summer   Autumn

The only real variation in the treatment of this plant is after the flowering, when it can be kept at the cooler range of its preferred temperatures and given less food and water while it rests. It is not a plant which can survive neglect but provided its basic needs are satisfied, it is not as difficult to keep as is sometimes imagined.

Soil

Pot on an aphelandra soon after purchasing, using a potting mixture with a high proportion of loam. The plant must be firmly potted and at a later stage can be potted on at any time of year other than the coldest winter months.

VARIETIES AND PURCHASING

A. squarrosa Dania This is the most readily available type of Zebra Plant. It is also the variety best suited to normal room conditions as it needs less care and growing space than some of the other kinds of aphelandra. It is quite difficult to make A. squarrosa Dania flower, but the dark green leaves have very pretty silvery markings.
A. squarrosa Louisae (see illustration left) The leaves of this plant are 8-12in (20-30cm) long and it has broad, conspicuous orange-yellow flower bracts. When buying this variety (which is also known as Saffron Spike) make sure that the flowers are not too far advanced. The actual flowers should not be visible along the edge of the bract.
A. squarrosa Brockfeld This is a compact plant with dark green leaves.
A. chamissoniana The variety has close-set leaves which are 4-5in (10-12.5cm) long. Its flower bracts are yellow, narrow and pointed.

Scale insects These pests (**below**) are encased in a white waxy coating. They suck the sap out of the plant.
Botrytis Aphelandras must not be kept in wet and airless conditions or they may contract this fungus (**bottom**). This can be controlled by improving the general conditions and applying a suitable fungicide.

Diseased leaves Mealy bugs (**right**) sometimes attack the stems and roots of aphelandras. They are distinctive for their white woolly looking coverings and can be removed with insecticide.

PESTS AND DISEASES

Despite its tough appearance, the aphelandra is vulnerable to a number of pests and should be examined regularly to make sure it is pest free.
Scale insect These look like miniature limpets and are skin-coloured when young and dark brown or yellow when mature. They attach themselves to the undersides of the plant's leaves and to its stem. Excreta falling on lower leaves encourages sooty mould fungus. This blocks the pores of the leaves and considerably weakens the plant. Scale insects can be removed by wiping the leaves with a firm sponge dipped in a pesticide solution. Alternatively, the plant can be sprayed with malathion. This should be done outdoors as malathion has an unpleasant smell.
Aphids These are frequently found on the bracts of the aphelandra. They can be removed fairly easily with one of the standard insecticides.
Sciarid fly These tiny insects are commonly known as fungus gnats. They tend to occur when the potting mixture becomes excessively wet and sour, depositing their larvae in the soil. Most of them are not harmful but one or two kinds may damage the roots of the plant. Dispose of them by drenching the soil with a liquid insecticide such as malathion. More than one application may be needed.
Springtails These pests are so-called because they jump about on the top of the soil. They are white, wingless insects, usually harmless but occasionally gnawing at the stems of young plants. They can be removed in the same way as fungus gnats.
Red spider mite This is not a common problem but red spiders will attack aphelandras that are growing in very hot and dry locations. They can be controlled by spraying the undersides of the leaves with insecticides.
Black leg This is a fungus that attacks cuttings at rooting stage. Affected plants should be thrown away.

Aralia elegantissima

This plant is also recognized by another name—*Dizygotheca elegantissima* which is often called the False Aralia. The common name is also confusing as it belongs to at least one other very popular indoor plant. However, despite the problems of its name, *A. elegantissima* is one of the most distinctive and attractive houseplants when it has been well grown. The foliage is very dark green, almost black, and it has a delicate 'filigree' appearance. The plant's leaf stalks are attached to stout central stems and the leaves appear evenly around the plant as it increases in height. It is quite possible for plants to reach a height of 10ft (3m) even though their roots are confined to pots that are little more than 10in (25cm) in diameter.

New plants are grown from seed that is easily germinated in a temperature of around 70°F (21°C). An odd characteristic of this plant is that delicately constructed leaves are produced at the seed stage and are retained by the plant until it reaches a height of about 7ft (2m). A complete change then takes place as each new leaf produced has a much coarser and less attractive appearance. This is the stage at which the plant develops its more tree-like habit. Nevertheless, due to the rather delicate nature of this plant, it rarely achieves tree proportions while confined to average room conditions.

PESTS AND DISEASES

Scale insect These are waxy, shell-like creatures, dark brown in colour. They are quite common and seem especially to like the *A. elegantissima*. The insects may be hard to spot as their colour blends with the woody stem of the plant, but it is important to treat them promptly as the plant may become very badly infested. They suck vital juices from the plant and it will eventually wither. The most effective method of treatment is to wipe the insects away firmly with a sponge soaked in malathion. Wear rubber gloves for protection when handling insecticides. Wiping ensures the leaves are saturated whereas efficient spraying is difficult on a plant with such an open arrangement of leaves.
Mealy bug These pests are white and similar in shape to small woodlice. They can be treated in the same way as scale insects (**see illustration right above**).
Root mealy bug These are also white bugs which, as the name implies, attack the roots of the plant within the soil. They may be unnoticed for some time but if the plant becomes mysteriously unwell

and there is no sign of a good reason, it is worth removing the plant from its pot to see whether root mealy bugs are the culprits. Soaking the soil thoroughly with malathion solution is the best remedy. The insecticide can also be sprayed directly onto the bugs, but this may not be quite as effective. A solution of pirimiphos-methyl could be used rather than malathion for soaking the soil.
Aphids These are small, soft insects, light green in colour. They cluster on the stems and new leaf growth of the plant, sucking out the sap. This undermines the vitality of the plant and will cause weak or distorted growth. To remove aphids, run a finger and thumb along the stem or leaf firmly enough to dislodge the insects but be careful not to damage the tender new growth of the plant.

AVOIDING PROBLEMS

Light and position

Small plants may be placed on a windowsill, provided they are not exposed to direct sunlight and the position is not subject to draughts. Larger, mature plants

may prefer a place on the floor or a table in a room which receives plenty of light and is fairly warm.

Temperature range

Cool   Intermediate   Warm

This plant generally prefers warm conditions and should be kept in a minimum temperature of 65°F (18°C). It may survive in cooler temperatures but will not maintain a continual healthy

growth. Neither does it enjoy dry surroundings so humidity must be maintained, by standing the pot in a tray of damp pebbles if extra moisture is needed.

Watering

Water the soil regularly but not to excess. The top two thirds of the soil can be allowed to dry out before more water is needed. The

watering may be evenly distributed throughout the year and occasional spraying of the leaves can be beneficial.

Feeding

Give the plant weak, liquid feeds at the same time as watering. It will need less food during the winter. The time when it needs

the most care in this respect is during the period of active growth in summer.

Seasonal care

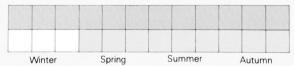

Winter   Spring   Summer   Autumn

There is very little seasonal variation in the treatment of an *Aralia elegantissima*. It should be kept moist all year round but should not be subjected to any

excessive conditions, whether wet or dry. A plant which is kept in a window should be moved during the hottest summer months to avoid direct sun.

Soil

Repot established plants in early summer, using a peaty mixture for the soil. This plant is slow growing and should be transferred to a larger pot about

once every two years. When it has reached a 10in (25cm) pot, simply top it up with peat mixture each spring.

Mealy bug This is a small, white pest which is common and persistent. The bugs appear like tiny lumps of cotton wool on stem joints and the undersides of leaves. Mealy bugs multiply quickly and must be dealt with thoroughly. Pick off as many of the bugs as you can. The plant can then be soaked with malathion. Because the aralia has an open framework of narrow leaves, it is best to wear rubber gloves and sponge the malathion onto the plant to ensure it gets to the right places.

Healthy plant The *A. elegantissima* is very attractive when it is well-grown. Each leaf has a delicate filigreed appearance (**inset**). When buying, choose a plant which has dark green foliage right down to the surface of the soil. This is a sign of careful cultivation.

Araucaria

In its natural home and throughout the tropics this coniferous tree can reach the majestic height of around 100ft (30m), and is one of the most handsome examples of plant life. With roots confined to a pot, a maximum height of 10ft (3m) can be expected after about 10 years if the plant is being grown indoors. The leaves, produced in layers at the top of the plant, are a bright green colour and they look like typical pine needles. All commercial plants are grown from seed that is exported from New Zealand.

PESTS AND DISEASES

Aphids The Norfolk Island Pine may suffer from these. They will settle on the soft top leaves of young plants, but can be easily eradicated with most insecticide sprays.
Mealy bug These are easy to spot on the araucaria's open foliage and can also be treated with insecticide spray. Alternatively, they can be wiped from their perches with a cotton wool swab that has been soaked in methylated spirits.

Healthy plant Also called the Norfolk Island Pine, this plant (**left**) was originally discovered in the South Pacific island of that name. It is an attractive evergreen conifer with fairly heavy branches that stick out horizontally from the central stem. Araucarias can be used as miniature Christmas trees but any decorations used should not be too heavy or they may damage the plant. The new foliage will be a glossy bright green that darkens slightly as the tree ages. Needles can grow to ¾in (19mm) long, forming groups that make up the tiers of each frond. In a healthy plant, the central stem should become tough enough to support the weight of all the branches, without the need for any artificial supports. Large araucarias are often displayed in porches, halls or on landings where they can look very striking. They tend to be less popular for mixed displays.

Unhealthy plant Araucarias tend to lose some lower leaves as they age. If the plant is drooping as well as dropping leaves (**right**), it is likely to be suffering from too much water, too much heat or lack of light. A plant in this condition should also be checked thoroughly for evidence of pest infestation.

VARIETIES AND PURCHASING

Araucaria plants are usually sold in small pots when they have reached a height of about 10in (25cm). Larger ones are sometimes available, but they tend to be much more expensive. Select plants that look fresh and free from blemishes. *A. excelsa* is the only variety that can be grown inside, but it has a very well-known cousin, the *A. araucana* or Monkey Puzzle Tree. This is often found in gardens and has more prickly foliage.

AVOIDING PROBLEMS

Light and position

Good light is essential to this plant, but take care to protect a young plant from direct sunlight. At an early stage an araucaria may enjoy the company of other plants, but it will grow to quite a size and a mature plant makes a feature if displayed alone.

Temperature range

Cool　　Intermediate　　Warm

The plant requires cool, though not draughty, conditions in a temperature range of 50°-60°F (10°-15°C). In a higher temperature the needle growth becomes thin and weak, whereas in a cool atmosphere they will look healthy and stand out proudly from the stem.

Watering

Araucarias prefer soil on the dry side so be careful not to overwater them. Let the soil almost dry out between waterings. Water at the top of the pot so the moisture drains freely through the soil.

Feeding

Feed the plant with weak fertilizer each time it is watered, rather than giving a heavy feed at less frequent intervals. If the plant continues to grow through the winter it can be fed continually, but leave it alone if it seems dormant.

Seasonal care

Winter　　Spring　　Summer　　Autumn

This is quite a hardy plant and provided it is not kept in an atmosphere which is too warm and dry it should not give problems. It follows the usual pattern of many plants in needing the most attention during a growing period in spring and summer, but minimal food and water in the winter. When the plant has grown to a height of about 4ft (1.3m) it will shed the lower branches. A leggy plant can be cut back and the cuttings used for propagation.

Soil

A loam-based potting mixture is essential at all stages of growth. The plant can be kept in a small pot for the first year, transferred to a 5in (12.5cm) pot for two years and so on up to a 10in (25cm) diameter pot, when it can be sustained by feeding.

Aspidistra lurida

In the business of houseplants, new varieties come along from time to time, eventually making the grade and being retained, but the aspidistra is a plant that, although popular in Victorian times, now appears to be out of favour. It is very easy to care for, but is slow to mature, and so is not a commercial proposition for plant suppliers. Luckily there are still many aspidistras around, a number of which have actually survived since the Victorian era.

New plants are made by dividing up established clumps and potting them individually. Either single pieces or clusters of leaves can be potted, the latter producing better plants more quickly.

VARIETIES AND PURCHASING

Choose a plant of full appearance with lots of stems and an elegant arching shape. Do not buy plants with split or speckled leaves or leaves that have been cut back.

A. lurida (or *A. eliator*) This is the only species in cultivation and is known as the Cast Iron Plant because it will survive in tough conditions.
A. l. 'Variegata' Very like the parent plant, this has white or cream stripes on some of the leaves.

Healthy plant Seen at their best, as lone specimens in an attractive china pot, aspidistras provide a fine display of dark green or green and white striped arching leaves. They need little care and in particular should never be polished with chemical leaf shine.

AVOIDING PROBLEMS

Light and position

Aspidistras will grow in very little light but will do best in a moderate light – in a window with not much sun, for example. The striped variety will need more light but neither type of plant should be placed in direct sunlight as this will soon scorch the leaves.

Temperature range

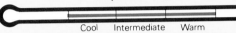

Cool   Intermediate   Warm

These plants will usually thrive in a wide range of temperatures – between 55°-70°F (13°-21°C) – and they can therefore be kept almost anywhere in the house. They will even survive below this range provided that they are kept free from frost.

Watering

Water these plants moderately throughout the year, allowing the top two-thirds of the soil to dry out before watering again. Water less in the winter months.

Feeding

These plants do not require much feeding. Apply liquid fertilizer once every two weeks in the growing period but stop feeding for the rest of the season if the leaves start to split.

Seasonal care

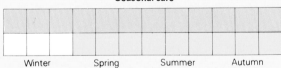

Winter   Spring   Summer   Autumn

One of the main advantages of the aspidistra is that it requires much less care than most other houseplants. Water it a little more frequently in the growing period and feed it occasionally. The plant will need less water in winter.

New plants can be grown by splitting off clumps of stems in the spring when the pot is overcrowded. Each section of the rhizome will need at least two leaves. Do not feed the new plants until the following spring.

Soil

Use a loam-based mixture. Aspidistras rarely need repotting and can be top-dressed once they reach the best size for the pot for several years. Very old plants are best left in their original pots. Remove new shoots and some roots if necessary.

PESTS AND DISEASES

These plants rarely suffer from pests, which normally find the leathery leaves too tough to penetrate.
Mealy bug These may occasionally attack this plant. If white woolly patches appear remove them one at a time with a piece of cotton wool dipped in methylated spirits or spray with a systemic insecticide.
Red spider mite These will cause the leaves to turn brown and will produce white webs on their undersides. Spray with systemic insecticide. Most leaf problems are caused by too much sunlight or overfeeding.

Damaged leaves The Cast Iron Plant's leaves will split if the plant is overfed. If this happens stop feeding for the rest of the season and start again the following year, cutting down the amount given to half that originally recommended.

The brown mark on the leaf, (**above**) is caused by direct heat from a radiator. Make sure that these plants are protected from heat sources and too high a temperature.

59

Azalea indica

There is nothing that can compare with *A. indica* as a specimen plant in full flower. The oval-shaped leaves are small, coarse and evergreen; the flowers, which grow at the ends of branches, may be either single or double, with their colour ranging from pristine white to dull red. There are also splendid multicoloured varieties. Most of the better plants start their life in Belgium, from where they are shipped all over the world. Azaleas are always potted and grown on to flowering stage before being despatched to the retailer.

Healthy plant One of the most beautiful of the winter flowering plants, many azaleas naturally flower in spring but are often forced into bloom for the Christmas season. They are very slow growing plants which is one reason why they are often expensive to purchase. Whether situated indoors in individual pots, or outside in large groups, azaleas always look attractive with their rich clusters of pastel or deeply-hued colours displayed against deep, green foliage.

VARIETIES AND PURCHASING

If carefully tended, the azalea can be one of the most rewarding of all the flowering houseplants. Because they are one of the few plants which flower in winter, they are usually seen in abundance in florists' shops from late autumn onwards. Selecting a healthy specimen is important if the plant is to survive. A healthy plant will be clean and bright in appearance. Some of its flowers should be open, but there should also be an abundance of buds. Tempting as it may be, avoid plants which have opened entirely. On the other hand, avoid those with small, underdeveloped buds, or no buds at all. When lifted, the pot should feel heavy and wet, which is how it should remain for the rest of the plant's life.

A. indica This is a common azalea and the one which is most easily available. It includes many variations of colour and is usually chosen for this quality and its general decorative appearance. *A. indica* needs a humid environment and should be sprayed with lime-free water every day.

A. obtusum This plant is known as the Japanese Kurume. It is not as easy to force into bloom as *A. indica* and is thus not available in shops until its natural flowering period in late winter. *A. obtusum* has small flowers that nestle among the leaves of the plant. It makes a fine potted plant with its clear, pink flowers. It can be put in the garden following indoor flowering, whereas *A. indica* must be carefully guarded from frost.

AVOIDING PROBLEMS

Light and position

Azaleas can be grown both indoors and out, and in both cases need a light location out of direct sun. If there is danger of frost, azaleas must be brought indoors.

So they will survive from one year to the next, azaleas should be put outside during the summer months.

Temperature range

Cool   Intermediate   Warm

Azaleas prefer cool temperatures of between 50°-60°F (10°-15°C) which will ensure that the plants continue to flower abundantly.

When moved indoors, the temperature in the room should not be allowed to rise above 60°F (10°C) or the plants will dry out.

Watering

When in flower, azaleas need copious amounts of lime-free water which should be given every two days. Never let a plant

dry out; check it at least twice a week. If dry, plunge into a bucket of tepid water until beads of moisture appear on the topsoil.

Feeding

A weak liquid fertilizer given at regular intervals will help maintain lush, green foliage, but

avoid heavy applications. When in flower, add fertilizer to the water about every two weeks.

Seasonal care

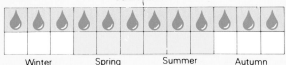

Winter   Spring   Summer   Autumn

Much greater than the danger of pests and diseases is that of neglect, especially neglecting to water the plants adequately. At all stages of development, whether indoors or out, the roots of the azalea must be kept wet. In late

spring the plants can be moved outside. Plunge the pots to their rims in a bed of wet peat in a shady location. Bring the plants indoors before the first frost. Avoid pruning as this will result in fewer flowers the following year.

Soil

Potting should be done in the spring with a mixture of peat with a small amount of rotted leaves which make the mixture acid

rather than alkaline. Press the mixture very firmly around the rootball, water it thoroughly and place the plant in a shady location.

PESTS AND DISEASES

Azaleas are prone to few pests and diseases, which makes them easier to care for than other plants. There are, however, signs of ill-health which should be heeded. If the leaves dry and fall, the environment is too hot and

dry. Spray the plant with lime-free water and move it to a cooler place. Buds which fail to open mean the plant is either in a draught or waterlogged. Move to a new location and water less frequently.

Dehydration This will quickly kill an otherwise healthy azalea. It is essential that these plants be adequately watered at all times of the year. Symptoms include faded and wilting flowers and leaves. Move the

plant away from heat and direct sun. If badly affected, plunge the pot to its rim in a bucket of tepid water and let it sit until beads of moisture appear on the topsoil. Remove the plant and allow it to drain.

Aphids These may be found on the soft, new leaves of an azalea, but they are not very troublesome and can be easily controlled by spraying with any one of several insecticides, including

malathion or pirimiphos-methyl which will usually destroy the pests very quickly.
Remember that a plant newly sprayed or dusted with insecticide must not be exposed to full sunlight.

Begonia

Among the most exotic of all foliage plants, the *B. rex* can have many colour combinations on the upper sides of its leaves, while the undersides are mainly reddish brown. Although mature plants can produce a few clusters of single pink flowers these are not their main attraction, as the *rex* type begonias are simply foliage plants. The leaves remain healthy for a reasonable time after they have been cut from the plant, making them useful material for inclusion in more colourful flower arrangements.

New plants can be raised from leaf cuttings, for which there are two methods of preparation. The first and simplest way is to remove a firm and unblemished leaf and cut the veins on its back in several places with a sharp knife, scalpel or razor blade. The leaf should then be placed, plain side down, on a bed of moist peat and sand in a shallow box or pan, with a few small pebbles on the leaf to hold it in position. The new plants will grow out of the knife cuttings. The other method is to cut up the mature leaf into sections about the size of a large postage stamp and place these about 1in (2·5cm) apart on a similar bed of peat and sand. From then on, the temperature must not fall below 70°F (21°C) and the atmosphere should be moist but not heavily saturated.

Healthy plant A *B. rex* (left) is kept for the beauty of its colourful leaves, and for these to show to best advantage, the plant should have a compact shape. The effect is undermined by straggling stems and untidy, formless growth. If the soil is kept too wet (**below**) the leaves droop and turn brown. This is more likely to happen in winter, when temperatures are low and the plant needs less water as it is not so active.

Botrytis (right) is a fungal disease which develops when conditions are generally too damp and stagnant. Cut away affected leaves and remove mouldy compost from the pot. Spray the plant with dichloran.

Foliage begonias These exist in such a variety of colour combinations and different leaf markings that with just a few plants, you can make a highly decorative display. The colours range through dark red to delicate pink, dark and light green and subtle silvery greys. They can be combined with other foliage plants to provide interest in a predominantly green arrangement, or with flowering plants which will complement the varied hues. Some of the common names given to these plants are descriptive of their festive appearance – Yuletide, Merry Christmas, Silver Queen – and although the individual plants are not long lasting, with the proper care they will give about two years of healthy growth and can be propagated quite easily from leaf cuttings. The common name of the *B. rex* is Fan Plant.

VARIETIES AND PURCHASING

When buying a begonia of any type – whether foliage, those with woody, trailing stems known as the cane types, or a flowering variety – always look for a clean, unblemished plant, making sure there is no sign of pests or root damage.

B. rex The varieties of these attractive foliage types are too numerous to mention. Visit a retailer with a good selection and choose the most pleasing. If the plant is quite large and crammed in a small pot, be sure to repot it as soon as possible or the plant will deteriorate through lack of nutrition from the soil.

B. glaucophylla This is one of the cane type begonias, a plant of natural trailing habit, with light green leaves. In late winter and early spring it produces clusters of orange flowers.

B. haageana Another cane variety, this plant has brownish leaves with a hairy texture and pale pink flowers. The plants are easy to manage, becoming very bushy and reaching a height of up to 6ft (2m) in time. The flowers appear almost continuously.

B. 'President Carnot' This is probably the best of the cane type begonias. It has brownish green leaves and during many months produces large clusters of pink flowers. Properly cared for, it can achieve a height of 6-8ft (2-2·5 m).

B. hiemalis Reiger This is a flowering begonia with soft and brittle growth which is easily damaged. Inspect the leaves to make sure there is no sign of botrytis and choose a plant with plenty of buds and only a few flowers fully open, so that the best is still to come.

B. tuberhybrid These can be bought as pot plants or as tubers to be potted. Select firm tubers which are clean and healthy. If choosing a growing plant, look for one with a few buds about to open so the colour of the flowers can be determined. A mixture of unnamed varieties can be bought quite cheaply in tuber form. The list of varieties of the tuberhybrid begonias is extremely lengthy, and new specimens are being added all the time. To take up serious cultivation of these plants, take advice from a specialist grower and go to see the plants at their best in a good, comprehensive flower show.

There is a large variety of begonias which creep or climb and almost all of them have decorative foliage and long-lasting, colourful flowers. Many can grow to a height of 6–8ft (2–2·5 m), while others are shrubby or trailing plants. These begonias are not popular with the commercial grower in spite of being easy to grow, probably because they are rather difficult plants to pack and transport.

Given proper care, there are few plants that can produce flowers quite as spectacular as the tuberous begonias when they are grown as pot plants. The best of these are invariably grown from tubers, and good quality, named varieties can be very expensive. Tubers are started into growth in early spring in boxes filled with moist peat, at a temperature around 65°F (18°C). When clusters on the shoots and a few leaves have formed, the young plants are transferred to 5in (12·5cm) pots filled with a peaty mixture in which they may be grown for the season, or more vigorous plants can be advanced when they are well rooted to pots of 7in (17cm) in diameter.

Healthy plant Flowering cane type begonias (**above left**) are beautiful plants, with their rich leaves and clustering, delicate flowers. The begonias need regular feeding and sufficient water or they may suffer from starvation. The leaves of a starved *B. tuberhybrid* (**above**) wither and become yellow, with brown, curling edges and the flowers also suffer from browning. Discoloration of the leaf tips and the deterioration of the flowers are also seen here in *B. solonanthea* (**left**). Mildew (**far left**) may form on plants in a badly ventilated environment. It is not too damaging but is unsightly on the plant. Remove badly affected parts and spray the plant with dinocap or dichloran.

Healthy plant *B. hiemalis Reiger* (**above right**) is an exotic, colourful variety which, given good care, will flower consistently during its life. The heavy green leaves give a rich contrast with the luxurious red flowers. Botrytis (**right**) attacks a plant which is kept in conditions which are too damp. It is an unpleasant grey mould which forms on leaves and stems. Cut away the most heavily affected leaves and spray the plant with dichloran. Also, remove any dank or mouldy compost and replace it with fresh. Flower petals which drop into the leaves and remain there to rot (**far right**) also cause this sort of disease in the plant, so they should be cleared away from leaves and soil regularly.

There is a completely new strain of begonia that goes variously under the names of *Reiger* or *Schwabenland*. As the names suggest, it originated in Europe. Initially, they were mostly red with single flowers, but now they are available in many colours with both single and double flowers. The foliage is glossy green and very dense, so that there are many branching stems, all of which bear flower clusters providing a rare wealth of colour. They are ideal room plants that can flower throughout the year, though fewer flowers are produced in winter.

New plants are raised from cuttings. These should be from the top of the stem with two or three leaves attached and all the flowers removed. A mixture of peat and sand and a temperature of around 70°F (21°C) are needed.

AVOIDING PROBLEMS

Light and position

Fibrous-rooted and rhizomatous begonias, grown primarily for their foliage, require bright light but not direct sunlight.

Windowsills which are not too cold are best. Tuberous begonias need bright, indirect light all the year round.

Temperature range

Cool   Intermediate   Warm

In active growth periods, fibrous-rooted, rhizomatous, and tuberous begonias all do well in normal room temperatures of around 60°F (15°C). Those with winter rest periods should be kept at the same level, but no lower. In winter, dormant

tuberous types should be kept at 55°F (13°C). In normal conditions, cane types should be kept at 55°F-70°C (13°-21°C); *B. hiemalis reiger* around 60°F (15°C); *B. rex*, 60°-70°F (15°-21°C), and *B. tuberhybrid* 55°-65°F (13°-18°C).

Watering

Begonias do not like dry air. The plants can be stood in their pots on moist pebbles, or, if hanging, saucers of water can be suspended beneath. During

active growth, water moderately allowing the top inch (2.5cm) of soil to dry out. Reduce watering as growth slows down.

Feeding

For actively growing plants, apply a standard liquid fertilizer every two weeks. Cane types should be liquid fed, erring on the side of too

much rather than too little. *B. hiemalis*, *B. rex*, and *B. tuberhybrid* should all be fed a weak mixture with each watering.

Seasonal care

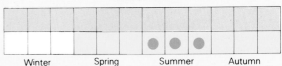

Winter   Spring   Summer   Autumn

In winter, *B. rex* requires limited watering. Cane types require year-round attention with dying petals and leaves removed to avoid fungus. *B. hiemalis reiger* needs less watering in winter, but avoid overwatering at all times. When older plants have passed their prime, trim them and use the

pieces for propagation. After flowering in late summer, *B. tuberhybrid* should have the foliage removed and the corm stored in a frost-free place in dry peat until early spring. When in leaf, the plant requires copious watering.

Soil

For *B. rex*, use peaty mixtures and keep the plants in pots large enough for new growth. *B hiemalis reiger* does best in

mixtures without soil; avoid repotting into pots too large. With cane types, use a loam-based mixture.

Beloperone guttata

The *B. guttata* has pale green, nondescript leaves attached to spindly stems, and is indigenous to Mexico. The plant is best known for its attractive reddish brown bracts that resemble shrimps and are produced in abundance for most of the year. Their white tubular flowers are comparatively insignificant.

New plants are propagated from firm top cuttings about 4in (10cm) long, with all bracts removed. They are put in a peat and sand mixture in temperature of around 70°F (21°C) and, like begonias, *B. guttata* requires moist but not saturated conditions.

Healthy plant The common name Shrimp Plant refers to the unusual bracts, dark red at the base and shading gradually to light green at the tips. These are produced during most of the year and in summer they contain small white tubular flowers. There is a quite rare variety, *Beloperone guttata Lutea*, which bears bright yellow bracts. In the common variety, however, yellowing bracts are a sign of ill health and when buying a plant, always make sure the bracts are a healthy red. Also avoid a plant which is leggy and has thinning foliage. The Shrimp Plant does thin out as it grows in height, but should not be bought in this condition as a new plant which has been well cared for will appear quite bushy. The Shrimp Plant is not very demanding and as long as it is given good light and sufficient water during its summer growing period, it will remain healthy and attractive.

AVOIDING PROBLEMS

Light and position

The Shrimp Plant needs plenty of light to maintain the colour of its bracts and encourage flowering but, in common with many plants, must be protected from direct, hot sunlight. It will not tolerate continual shade or a cold, draughty position.

Temperature range

Cool   Intermediate   Warm

The plant is fairly tolerant with regard to temperature, enjoying a range between 55°-70°F (13°-21°C). Extreme conditions of heat or cold are not usually good for any houseplant, and the Shrimp Plant is no exception. It will prefer the cooler end of the temperature range during winter.

Watering

Water can be added to the soil from the top of the pot. This is a plant which likes moist conditions, but not saturation. If the soil is allowed to become too dry, on the other hand, the leaves will quickly droop, so watering should be frequent in summer.

Feeding

Frequent, regular feeding is essential for a well-established plant. If the plant develops yellowing, curled foliage, it is probably suffering from chlorosis (iron deficiency) and should be treated by watering the soil with a special iron solution.

Seasonal care

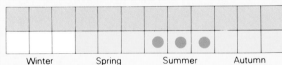

Winter   Spring   Summer   Autumn

Active plants require ample watering during summer months, and may need almost as much during the winter, since the soil must not be allowed to dry out. The Shrimp Plant has a tendency to become rather spindly, and this can be countered by pinching out the growing tips of a young plant to encourage bushiness. When the plant needs pruning, this can be done following the main summer flowering, or in the spring when it moves into a more active period of growth.

Soil

It may be necessary to repot a strong, young plant twice in its first year, and in general, frequent potting on is essential. Use a loam-based potting mixture and pot the plant firmly. For propagating top cuttings, use a peat and sand mixture.

A pot-bound plant (left) It may be possible to recognize a pot-bound plant simply when the roots emerge through the drainage holes of the pot. Even before this happens the growth of the plant will be sluggish, although it may have plenty of light, warmth and food, and the soil in the pot will dry out more quickly than usual. The plant must then be repotted to give it more room. The Shrimp Plant needs frequent feeding and signs of starvation appear in the leaves when it is undernourished. The leaf of a plant which has not been fed enough will look limp and go brown at the tip (**below**).

PESTS AND DISEASES

Aphids These greenfly are found on the softer top leaves of the plant. Their activity weakens the plant and in addition they secrete a sticky substance called honeydew which is unsightly and unpleasant. The flies should be easily disposed of by spraying the plant with malathion.

White fly This common and persistent pest attacks the undersides of leaves to suck sap from the plant. They multiply quickly and treatment must be repeated to be effective. Spray the plant with diazinon at least four times, with four-day intervals between each spraying. If white fly persist, change to another insecticide.

Red spider mite These flourish in warm, dry conditions. They must be treated at an early stage but they are difficult to see with the naked eye. Look out for mottled, drooping leaves which indicate the presence of mites on the plant. Isolate the plant to prevent the problem spreading and spray the undersides of the leaves with malathion or dichloran. Unfortunately, if the mites have really taken hold and formed small webs it is too late to treat the plant with any insecticide and it is better to remove and burn the badly affected areas or, indeed, the whole plant if necessary.

Mealy bug These little insects are like woodlice with a white, floury coating. On a Shrimp Plant the bugs are easily visible and accessible and can be removed with a sponge soaked in methylated spirits. Direct contact with this kills the bugs immediately. A malathion spray may be effective in killing the adult insects, but wiping should also remove the protected young, freeing the plant completely.

Black leg This is a fungus which may attack cuttings of this plant, if they are allowed to get too wet before roots have formed. The only sensible remedy is to remove and burn the affected cuttings and treat the surrounding soil with streptomycin.

Bougainvillea

In their natural tropical environment the brilliant flowers of the bougainvillea can outshine almost everything in sight. Its strong stems have vicious barbs and carry thin and insignificant foliage, but the defects of the plant are more than compensated for when it flowers throughout the summer. It would be misleading to suggest that the bougainvillea is the ideal houseplant. It can be most frustrating as it is very reluctant to produce flowers in a situation that offers only limited light. However, they can be grown successfully in a conservatory or bay window.

New plants are raised from cuttings taken in spring, using sections of 3in (7·5cm) stem, with a heel of older wood attached. A minimum temperature of 70°F (21°C) is essential if the cuttings are to survive.

Healthy plant (right and below) The decorative papery bracts of the bougainvillea make it a most attractive plant. If the plants receive plenty of light, they can make a very effective display, especially if trained to wind round a tall framework. Choose clean plants with some open flowers and clusters of flowers about to open.

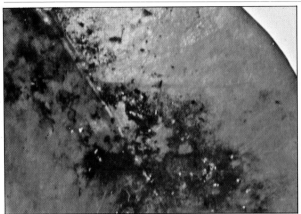

Diseased leaves Sooty mould (**above**), caused by aphids, is not only very unsightly but also harmful to the leaf. It blocks the pores and eventually the plant goes brown and dies. Mealy bug (**left**) can be identified by its grey-white woolly coat. The bugs can be removed by wiping with methylated spirits or spraying with insecticide. Bougainvilleas should be checked regularly for these pests.

PESTS AND DISEASES

Bougainvilleas are fairly tough plants and do not suffer a great deal from pests. However, it is as well to watch out for the following.

Aphids These can quite often be found on the tips of new growth. They suck the plant's sap, making the leaves go yellow and in extreme cases, causing distortion. They also secrete a sticky substance called honeydew upon which an ugly sooty mould may grow. Aphids also carry incurable viruses. They can be removed with an application of malathion or diazinon, sprayed on the leaves.

Mealy bug This often attacks older plants in the greenhouse but is less frequent indoors, unless it is actually brought in on the plant. The open leaves of the plant make detection of mealy bug an easy matter. The adults are a powdery-white and resemble woodlice. The young are wrapped in a protective waxy coat and tend to be attached to the more inaccessible parts of the plant where the branches intertwine.

VARIETIES AND PURCHASING

Bougainvilleas should be bought in flower . The mature ones will usually be wound round a frame but they can be unwound and put on a different frame if desired.

B.glabra This is the species most easily obtained in nurseries and shops. It has purple bracts which appear in summer and autumn. There are several variegated sorts, including *B.g. 'Harrisii'*, which has leaves streaked with cream, and *B.g. 'Sanderana Variegata'*, which has cream-bordered leaves.

B. buttiana This is the original parent of several hybrid bougainvilleas which are now very popular as it is easy to train them into shrub form. They can best be kept in 6-8in (25-30cm) pots. They are happy in most indoor locations and they are therefore more suitable as houseplants than the original species.

Light and position

Maximum light is vital to the bougainvillea, so place it in a sunny window, right against the windowpane. There is a chance that it will be scorched by the sun, so keep an eye on the leaves. However, it cannot flourish in poor light and scorching is a minor risk.

Temperature range

Cool Intermediate Warm

Temperature is not crucial during the plant's period of active growth, but should probably remain at 55°F (13°C) or above if possible. While the bougainvillea is dormant in the winter, a cooler temperature of 50°F (10°C) is preferred. Although it requires plenty of light and enjoys the sun, it will not be the better for being allowed to bake.

Watering

Water the plant from the top of the pot, but do not leave it standing in a full saucer. The soil should be moist while the plant is in active growth, but it will not require water during the winter until new growth begins to appear.

Feeding

Suitable feed for the bougainvillea is fertilizer containing a high proportion of potash. Again, this is not necessary during the winter dormancy, but is vital in spring to encourage new growth. Use a liquid feed when the plant is watered.

Seasonal care

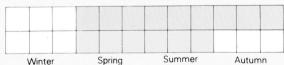

Winter   Spring   Summer   Autumn

The pattern of seasonal care to be observed is dictated by the summer growth period and winter dormancy, as explained above. Whereas many plants need less food and water in the winter, the bougainvillea may go for two or three months without any nourishment and then requires further attention when new growth starts in early spring. If the plant becomes straggly it can be gently pruned in the autumn, but flowering is better if growth is wound around established stems and tied back.

Soil

Potting mixtures without soil are useless to the bougainvillea. It requires a loam-based compost and can be potted on in spring once new growth has begun. A pot of 8in (20cm) diameter is ample and when the plant has reached this stage, sustain it by feeding.

Bromeliads

In this plant family there is a vast assortment of leaf formations, and an amazing diversity of colourful flowers and bracts, but only the pineapple has a commercial value that is other than decorative. However, the number of plants that are offered commercially for sale is lamentably few, principally because their slow rate of growth makes production expensive.

New plants can be raised from seed, but it is important that the seed should be very fresh. This in itself places a limiting factor on distribution, so seed is not easily available. By far the easiest method of reproducing plants is to remove offsets from the base of the parent rosette and plant them individually in small pots of peat to get them under way. Some of the clump-forming types, such as the fairly common billbergia, can be quite quickly increased simply by dividing the clumps into smaller sections and potting these individually into a mixture of equal parts of peat and rough leaf mould.

Healthy plant This billbergia (**above**) is a typical bromeliad displaying arching leaves and a central flower head. The tiny flowers of bromeliads are surrounded by bright pink, mauve or red bracts, and it is these, together with their coloured leaves and their unusual shape, that give them their exotic appearance.

Displaying bromeliads These plants grow in the wild clinging to the trunks or branches of trees, where they use their roots for anchorage. Only a greenhouse can recreate this habitat but plants can also be grown indoors on a mossy log provided that the moss is watered daily (**right**).

Cryptanthus

These are the smaller of the bromeliads and ideal for the houseplant grower who wants an interesting collection of unusual plants that are easy to care for and that will take up comparatively little space. Cryptanthus plants are also ideally suited for bottlegardens, as they are not invasive and seldom succumb to the usual bottlegarden problems of rotting foliage and the eventual paralyzing attack of botrytis.

Usually grown for their intricately patterned foliage and distinctive leaf formation, they do in fact produce a few flowers but these are never very interesting. Almost all these bromeliads are terrestial, growing among rocks and fallen trees on the floor of the jungle in their native environment.

New plants are propagated from offsets that develop around the base of the parent rosette. As the small rosettes have little or no stem, it is necessary to pin them carefully down on the propagating mixture with a piece of bent wire or a hairpin until the roots have developed.

Cryptanthus **plants** Also known as the Earth Star, these grow in rocky cracks and on tree stumps or roots in the wild. Their leaves are often edged with prickly spines and striped or barred in a broad range of colours from white and pale pink to purple and yellow. Healthy plants often have a whitish bloom called 'scurf' on their leaves which gives them a silvery look. *C. bromelioides* (**above**) the Rainbow Star, is one of the most beautiful with its white-edged leaves which take on a pink tinge in bright light. Unlike most of the genus it grows upright, sending out stems carrying plantlets which, if rooted, will become new plants.

VARIETIES AND PURCHASING

Bromeliads present a wide range of leaf and flower shapes of remarkable colour and will often grow during the whole year. Many types, though tree-growing in the wild, may be bought in pots but it is important to see that all small plants do have roots. Several types can also be grown on mossy logs and are ideal for a bottlegarden. The flowers are usually short-lived but the leaves often take on brilliant hues which last for several months.

Aechmea This is the best-known of the bromeliads (see page 46).

Ananas comosus The Pineapple Plant belongs to this group but is almost too large for growing indoors.

A. bractatus variegatus The most popular type, this is a far prettier plant than the common pineapple. It has green and cream striped leaves, which turn pink as the flower develops, and a rich reddish-pink pineapple.

Billbergia This is the easiest and most adaptable bromeliad. It has a rosette of leaves in a range of colours from red-bronze or grey-green to white or purple. The flowers, too, take on many shapes and display a wealth of brilliant colours.

B. nutans The Friendship Plant or Queen's Tears has an arching fountain of olive green leaves which may turn red if kept in sunlight. It produces flower heads with striking pink bracts rather like exotic ears of wheat.

Cryptanthus The Earth Star is one of the most popular bromeliads.

C. acaulis The Starfish Plant is small and easy to grow. Varieties have leaves suffused with pink.

Tillandsia These are available in a wide range and are particularly good for growing on branches.

Vriesea This is a genus with sword-shaped leaves and flower spikes standing on tall stems and composed of colourful bracts.

V. splendens The best-known species, called Flaming Sword, has 15in (45cm) long dark green leaves with purple and black bands and a tall flower spike of brilliant red bracts encasing the tiny yellow flowers.

Healthy plant The *Neoregelia carolinae 'Tricolor'* (above) is a plant which will grow to 2ft (60cm) in width. Its rosette of cream-striped leaves will turn brilliant red at flowering time and remain so for months if the centre is kept full of water.

Slug Bromeliads with their tough leaves are resistant to pests. Because of the need to keep the central funnel of many of these plants full of water, however, they will sometimes attract slugs (above). Empty the stale water regularly.

Plant care Most of these plants need a warm temperature and high humidity. Dryness and cold are the most common causes of damage. Only certain billbergias can withstand temperatures of below 55°F (13°C). The *Vriesea* (above) is suffering from lack of water and the banded leaves have lost their strength. Bromeliads are unique as a genus in that they require water round the growing point (in the centre of the plant). Many have a tube-like, watertight funnel formed by the rosette of leaves and take their food from it. For these types keep the central cup full of fresh water. Liquid fertilizer should also be placed in the central cup.

Dying plants The *Cryptanthus* (**left**) has been badly affected by root mealy bugs, which nest in the roots and stunt the growth of the plant. For a small plant, treat by washing the mixture from the roots, cut away the worst infected parts, and soak the rest of the roots in a solution of insecticide. Then repot in fresh mixture.
The *Tillandsia* plants are suited to bottlegardens. They have huge rosettes with colourful flower heads.
T. cyanea, the most popular species, has grey-green leaves 12-18in (30-45cm) long and a flower spike of delicate pink bracts from which small violet flowers emerge. As the flowers fade (**above**) the foliage still remains attractive.

AVOIDING PROBLEMS

Light and position

For neoregelias, good light is essential, even direct sunlight. With a selection of plants, a light location ensures bright colouring, but avoid direct sunlight.

All the other bromeliads need good light but it should not be too strong. Position them where they can be viewed from above as they are best seen from this angle.

Temperature range

Cool   Intermediate   Warm

Bromeliads thrive in warm room temperatures of between 60°-70°F (15°-21°C). Some types will not survive in temperatures lower than 60°F (15°C). A constant

level of warmth and humidity is necessary in the active growth period. When temperatures rise above 65° (18°C), spray the foliage daily with tepid water.

Watering

Water bromeliads moderately allowing the top inch (2.5cm) to dry out between waterings. During winter rest periods, water only enough to keep the top soil

slightly moist. Avoid using hard water which can leave deposits on the foliage. Rainwater or distilled water are preferable.

Feeding

When in active growth, apply fertilizer as recommended by the manufacturer. Liquid fertilizer can be splashed over the leaves. Plants grown in mixtures with

peat moss require extra feeding throughout the year. Those grown in soil should not be fed during winter rest periods.

Seasonal care

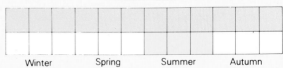

Winter   Spring   Summer   Autumn

Bromeliad selections should be watered twice a week in summer, once in winter. Cryptanthus should also be watered twice a week in summer and once a week at other times. When

watering neoregelias, the urn part of the plant should be topped up with tepid water and this should be changed regularly throughout the year.

Soil

All bromeliads require an airy compost. A recommended mixture is half sphagnum peat, half rough leaf mould, and a small amount of sand. Avoid potting

into large pots and pot on only when the plant seems out of proportion to its pot. Clay and plastic pots can both be used.

Cacti and succulents

For most people, the fascination with cacti begins at an early age. This is no doubt why more of them are sold during school holidays than at any other time of the year. Surprisingly, sales of these plants exceed those of any other kind of potted plant, much of their popularity being due to their interesting shapes, and the fact that they are easy to grow and never very large means that a considerable collection can be kept in a relatively small area.

There are two distinct groups of cacti—the desert cacti that come mainly from the desert regions of the American continent, and the forest cacti, all of which have smooth foliage, except for the Rat's Tail Cactus, *Aporocactus flagelliformis*.

A few of the desert cacti are extremely difficult to care for and quite beyond the scope of someone with little more to offer than a living room windowsill. But, in the main, they are very tolerant plants that will survive however badly they are treated. Unfortunately, the common belief is that cacti should be given minimal attention in order to get the best from them. Provided the temperature is reasonable during the winter months, spartan treatment will not do very much harm, but during the rest of the year all the plants will respond very much better if they are given that little extra attention.

Propagation of new plants is a comparatively simple task which no doubt also contributes to their popularity. To produce new plants in quantity the best propagation method is to raise them from seed. Ideally, the seed should be fresh and sown as soon as it becomes available. Shallow seed boxes filled with a well-drained mixture will give them a good start. Keeping the seeds in a temperature in the region of 65°F (18°C) will be enough to germinate them and they should have the lightest position available, with airy rather than stuffy conditions.

Succulents

Very varied, the succulents embrace a multitude of differing forms, and have among them plants with the most subtle colouring. The echeverias in particular offer a wide range of metallic colours, and make a fascinating collection of plants by themselves. Ranging in size from the tiny sedums to the giant aloes, succulents are excellent plants for the beginner. They will adapt to a wide range of conditions and even seem to thrive on periods of neglect, the main problems with succulents nearly always being due to overwatering.

Not all, but most succulents can be propagated with little difficulty. As well as the stems, the individual leaves of many can be removed and allowed to dry before being inserted in a sandy mixture in reasonable warmth. Wet soil conditions at any time can be damaging for succulents, but during the rooting stage of cuttings it can be positively diastrous.

Healthy plant This opuntia shows all the characteristics of its family, with its prominent ribs, long columnar stem and closely packed areoles. These are made up of small bristles, so take care in handling.

Two succulents The *Echeveria glauca* (top) and *Echeveria setosa* (bottom) are attractive representatives of one of the most popular succulent families. Succulents are good plants for beginners, as they require little attention. They are also among the easiest houseplants to propagate, as their cuttings root extremely easily. Take these in late spring or early summer. Seeds can be used as an alternative method.

AVOIDING PROBLEMS

Light and position

A sunny windowsill is ideal for most succulents, with the exceptions of the haworthias and gasterias, which like quite a shady position. Desert cacti need as much sun as possible, particularly in winter. Forest cacti like light, but need to be shaded from the sun.

Temperature range

Cool   Intermediate   Warm

Unlike most other houseplants, succulents thrive if the temperature varies between day and night. They do well at a modest average temperature of between 55°-65°F (13°-18°C). In general, desert cacti like the same basic temperature range, though they should be kept at the lower temperature in winter. It is a fallacy that cacti like excess heat; desert nights are often cold. Forest cacti thrive between 55°-60°F (13°-15°C).

Watering

Water succulents well from spring to autumn, letting them dry out between each watering. In winter, reduce to the absolute minimum. Desert and forest cacti should not be watered at all from late autumn to early spring. Then, water as succulents.

Feeding

Feed well-established succulents with weak liquid fertilizer every week, if necessary, but not in winter. Feeding is not essential for cacti, though a little will not hurt the plants. Feed weak liquid fertilizer every two weeks while watering, but, again, not in winter.

Seasonal care

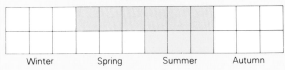

Winter   Spring   Summer   Autumn

Succulents need fresh air, especially in summer. Trim back overgrown non-flowering plants in autumn and flowering ones after they have flowered. Use a shallow pot, not a deep one, and repot only when essential. Desert cacti, too, require fresh air. Repot young plants annually into slightly larger pots to give roots space to spread. Broken pieces of pot at the bottom of each pot will improve drainage. Forest cacti need misting in summer. Repot annually after flowering, with the exception of epiphyllums which flower better if they are kept in quite small pots.

Soil

Most succulents like a cactus-type loam-based houseplant mixture, plus a little extra gravel and sand. Both types of cacti grow well in the same basic mixture, though some varieties need more specialized ones.

VARIETIES AND PURCHASING

With succulents, always look for fresh plants that are free of blemishes and pests. Large plants are frequently sold in smallish pots; in such a case, repot the plant as soon as you get it home. Cacti are particularly prone to pests – especially mealy bug – so always go to a reliable dealer and check the plant carefully before buying it. Dry brown marks on foliage are not harmful, but do not buy plants with wet brown areas at the base of their stems. Also check cacti carefully for stability. They are sometimes sold with very little root or incipient basal rot, both of which show up through a little gentle movement.

Astrophytum This is a globular desert cactus. There are two main varieties – *A. capricorne,* or Goat's Head, and *A. myriostigma,* Bishop's Hood. This keeps its globular shape for about two years, after which it begins to become cylindrical. From three years onwards, it flowers, each flower lasting a day or so.

Epiphyllum The two varieties generally available – *E. 'Ackermanni'* and *E. 'Cooperi'* – are both hybrids crossed with other jungle cacti. 'Ackermanni' produces flowers liberally through the year; 'Cooperi' is a plant which flowers at night.

Lithops These pebble-like succulents are given the common name Living Stones because of their appearance. Their shape is ideally suited to desert conditions. One of the chief characteristics of many succulents is their rosette shape, which acts as a water-conserving aid in nature.

Echinocereus The Hedgehog Cactus is a very popular houseplant because of its attractive flowers and spines. *E. pectinatus* is slow-growing, taking over five years before it reaches maturity.

Hamatocactus setispinus is a colourful single-stemmed desert cactus. It gets its common name, Strawberry Cactus, from the fruit it bears after flowering.

Three popular cacti The slender stem of *Cleistocactus strausii*(**far left**) is covered with fine white bristles. These give rise to the common name of the plant, the Silver Torch. The *Euphorbia pseudocactus* (**left**) is a succulent which looks very like a true cactus. It has spines along its ridges and it can grow up to 5ft (1.5m). *E. p. lyttonia* is a spineless form. The *Notocactus leninghausii* (**above**) is recognizable through its mass of dense yellow spines which tend to lie flat on the top of the plant facing the sun.

Astrophytum

Echinocereus

Epiphyllum

Hamatocactus

Lithops

More varieties The robust succulent *Echeveria gibbiflora* (**top right**) grows to a height of about 2 ft (60cm), its spoon-shaped leaves forming a closely-knit rosette at the top of its stem. These leaves are extremely delicate; they are covered with a wax bloom, which can be damaged easily, while drops of water left on the leaves after watering can cause scorch marks, or, in extreme cases, rot. They also provide perfect shelter for mealy bugs, whose presence can go undetected until real damage has been done. Check plants for bugs regularly and, if any are found, treat immediately. *E. gibbiflora* needs the brightest possible sunlight. It flowers in winter, producing attractive pale red blooms on stems about 1 ft (30cm) long. *Zygocactus truncatus* (**above**), the Christmas Cactus, benefits from being placed outdoors in a sheltered spot during the summer months. Bring it indoors again towards the end of the summer and place it in the light, ideally by a window. Keep the soil dry until buds appear. Then water more liberally. Flowers should appear in time for Christmas.
Trichocereus spachianus (**right**), or White Torch Cactus, can reach a height of 5 ft (1.5m), but is slow-growing. It takes eight to 10 years to reach 1 ft (30cm), at which stage the first flowers appear. As the plant ages, its stem can become disfigured with corky markings. These can be removed.

PESTS AND DISEASES

Both succulents and cacti are prone to various pests and diseases; cacti are more susceptible than succulents. In the former case there is an added problem; frequently cacti fail through too much attention. The commonest example is giving the soil too much water while the plant is dormant and unable to take up the moisture.

Mealy bug This affects both succulents and cacti. In the former, it can be controlled by spraying with insecticide, though always check suitability first. Cacti often need the individual bugs dabbed with a thin paint brush, moistened with methylated spirits. Alternatively, plants can be drenched with malathion or a systemic insecticide.

Root mealy bug This is almost always present on older succulents and forest cacti. Thoroughly drench the soil with malathion.

Scale insect On cacti, these resemble tiny shells, tightly clamped to the skin of the plant. Treat with insecticide.

Red spider mite Always treat this pest as soon as possible with insecticide. By the time its characteristic webs appear, it is very difficult to eradicate.

Botrytis Wet rotting patches around the base of the stem and, to a lesser extent, higher up the plant indicate this fatal fungus disease. If possible, cut out the infected area and treat with a fungicide. Otherwise, remove undamaged sections and use as cuttings for fresh plants.

Fungus disease The *Astrophytum myriostigma* (**left**) is suffering from botrytis, a severe fungus disease. Cut away any indications of rot as soon as they appear, cutting right back to healthy tissue. This will prevent the rot from spreading. Root rot is normally caused by over-wet potting mixture.

Watering problems The *Zygocactus* (**above**) is rotting and wilting through overwatering. One of the most common faults is to overwater a plant during its dormant season. The *Epiphyllum* (**below**) is dehydrated. During spring and summer, many cacti need as much water as conventional houseplants.

Campanula isophylla

The foliage of the campanula is insignificant, but its trailing bell-shaped flowers will cascade naturally for many months from spring into late summer. The white campanula is by far the best, but there are also attractive blue and lilac shades. The white form is much the easiest to manage, and is a fine plant for growing in a small hanging basket or a hanging pot. New plants can be raised from cuttings, but the stock should first be checked thoroughly to ensure that it is free from any pests or diseases.

VARIETIES AND PURCHASING

Choose a plant or plants for colour and ease of care or mix all three colours in a hanging pot. Buy young plants in the spring with many buds and some open flowers.
C. isophylla This will produce blue flowers between summer and autumn.
C. isophylla 'Alba' This white variety is the most prolific and the easiest to care for.
C. isophylla 'Mayi' This variety has mauve flowers.

PESTS AND DISEASES

These plants are easy to care for but may suffer from red spider and fungus.
Red spider mite If these appear, spray immediately with insecticide or immerse the pot in a dilute solution. Repeat after 10 days.
Systemic insecticides will not be very effective.
Botrytis This may affect the plants if they get too wet. Treat with fungicide, clean off the dead foliage and give the plants more air and space.

Healthy plant Seen at its best the *C. isophylla 'Alba'* presents a mass of star-shaped white flowers and bright green leaves on trailing stems ideal for display in a hanging basket.

AVOIDING PROBLEMS

Light and position

Campanulas prefer bright light, with or without direct sunlight at all times although they can thrive in a sunless window if they are placed on the sill. Remember, however, that too much heat will dry the plants out. Spray the plant or move it if necessary.

Temperature range

Cool   Intermediate   Warm

Campanula plants prefer cooler temperatures: 45°-65°F (7°-18°C) in summer and around 40°F (5°C) and not above 50°F (10°C) in winter. If the temperature rises above 65°F (18°C) in summer, spray the leaves and stand the pot in a plant tray on wet pebbles.

Watering

These plants may be watered in any way but do not let the roots get too damp. Water well in the flowering period, keeping the soil moist, but do not allow the pot to stand in a pool of water. In the rest period moisten the soil lightly every two weeks.

Feeding

Campanulas will not need a lot of feeding but it is best to give them some liquid fertilizer once every two weeks after the roots have filled out the pots and until the flowers have fallen.

Seasonal care

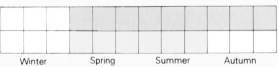

Winter   Spring   Summer   Autumn

To give a campanula the best care possible, spray the plant if the temperature rises above 65°F (18°C) and move it to a warmer spot if it drops below 45°F (7°C). Feed until the flowers fall and water less from that point onwards. To propagate new plants take 2in (5cm) long tip cuttings with three or four pairs of leaves each from old plants just as the growing period begins. Culture gently with the help of hormone rooting powder and potting mixture until they take root.

Soil

Take rooted cuttings and place three or four in a small pot in early spring. Move them to larger pots once the roots appear above the surface of the mixture. The largest pot size needed will probably be a 5in (12.5cm) one.

Chlorophytum comosum

The green and cream grassy foliage of the Spider Plant is extremely popular. This is largely because it grows so well, and the fact that new plants are so easy to raise from the natural plantlets that are produced on long stalks as the plants mature. When they have grown to a reasonable size, the plantlets begin to form roots at their base even though they are only suspended in the atmosphere. After these roots have developed, the plantlets can be removed from the parent and simply pushed direct into small pots filled with houseplant potting mixture. It is better to peg the small plantlets down in the potting soil while they are still attached to the parent plant and to cut them away when they have obviously rooted.

VARIETIES AND PURCHASING

Spider Plants are usually sold in small pots and they are cheap, cheerful and easy to grow. Selecting a plant is a question of looking for the cleanest and most fresh looking plant on display. It is sensible to check among the central leaves for pests, such as aphids, which have a particular fondness for the Spider Plant. The plant looks especially attractive in a hanging basket as the bright green and cream foliage spills over on all sides. For a really good display, put no less than three plants into the basket. They will grow quickly and beautifully in good light, although strong sunlight can be damaging. Also, it is easy to neglect the watering of hanging plants, so take care to treat them well.

C. comosum Variegatum is the only variety worth keeping. It is sometimes given the common name St Bernard's Lily, as well as the Spider Plant.

PESTS AND DISEASES

Aphids These are the main pests which bother the Spider Plant. Leaves that are attacked bear pit marks produced by the probing creatures (**see illustration**). Inspect the central leaves regularly and spray them with diazinon or malathion when aphids are found. Alternatively use a systemic insecticide such as disulfoton in granule form in the soil.
Symphalids Commonly named springtails, on account of their dancing motions on the surface of the soil when the plant is watered, symphalids are not harmful to the plant. They are often present on plants when the soil is musty and very wet. They can be killed if necessary by drenching the soil with malathion.
Mealy bug Spider Plants can suffer from these common little white pests. They are destructive and can cause the plant to wilt, shed leaves and eventually die if left untreated.

The bugs are easy to recognize, as tiny pale lumps with a cottony casing, sitting on the leaves (**see illustration**). Spraying is an effective treatment providing all the leaves are saturated with insecticide by this method. An even better remedy is to sponge the leaves with malathion, firmly enough to remove all the bugs, but not so heavily as to bruise the leaves.
Sciarid fly These pests, better known as fungus gnats, are found in the soil if it is very wet. Again, they are not at all harmful, though they may be irritating and unsightly. If you wish to get rid of them, this is easily done by soaking malathion into the soil.

AVOIDING PROBLEMS

Light and position

Good light is required if these plants are to retain their colouring and not become thin and wispy, but very strong light can damage the leaves. Protect the plants, too, from cold draughts, especially if they are placed on a windowsill.

Temperature range

| Cool | Intermediate | Warm |

These plants thrive at normal room temperatures in the range 50°-65°F (10°-18°C). They will not do well if the temperature is allowed to drop below 45°F (7°C). In winter, therefore, you may need to move them to a room which is always heated.

Watering

The Spider Plant is easy to water by any method and likes a lot of water in the growing period. In the rest period, water more moderately, allowing the top layer of soil to dry out between waterings.

Feeding

Feed fortnightly throughout the year with a good liquid fertilizer, especially once the plant has started to produce plantlets. Without feeding, the tops of the leaves will quickly turn brown, marring the appearance of the plant and retarding its growth.

Seasonal care

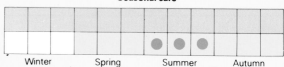

| Winter | Spring | Summer | Autumn |

In general this is an easy plant to care for but remember to water it less in the rest period and to protect it from direct sunlight and sudden drops in temperature. New plants can be grown at any time in one of two ways. Either cut off the plantlets when their leaves are 2-3in (5-7.5cm) long place them in a jar of water until the roots are 1in (2.5cm) long and then pot them. Alternatively, put the plantlets into soil and leave them attached to the mother plant until they take root.

Soil

Use a loam-based mixture for potting and make sure there is enough space around the plant for the growth of its thick fleshy roots. Place the root ball about 1in (2.5cm) below the rim of the pot. Repot in a larger pot whenever the roots force the soil to the rim.

Problems Aphids (**far left**) often attack the young leaves and leave scars which expand as the plant grows. This is why it is important to check the plant when you buy it. Mealy bugs (**centre**) are another common pest which can do a great deal of damage. Underwatering or insufficient nourishment cause the leaf tips to brown (**left**). This damage in the tips of young plants may indicate that they need potting on.

Healthy plant A Spider Plant grows well on its own, but also enjoys the company of many other plants and can be an attractive addition to a mixed display.

Cineraria

The cineraria is one of the many annual pot plants that are purchased in countless thousands each year. There are many other annual greenhouse plants that are sold for room decoration and most of them will respond to treatment similar to that required by the cineraria. The coarse green leaves of this plant radiate from a short central stem, and in season they are covered with a mass of brightly coloured daisy-like flowers. There are both compact and large-flowered types, the latter developing into impressive plants that will need plenty of space around them.

VARIETIES AND PURCHASING

The cineraria is really a member of the *Senecio* family – its full name is *Senecio cruentus cineraria*. They are peculiarly susceptible to almost every known pest, so it is extremely important to examine the leaves carefully for any signs of their presence.

S.c. cineraria grandiflora As its name suggests, this plant has large flowers, which come in a variety of vibrant colours.
S.c. cineraria nana This plant is much more compact and so is suitable for a windowsill where space is limited.

Healthy plants (above) Cinerarias come in a variety of brilliant colours – blue, purple, white, red and pink.

It is important to choose a plant with bright green foliage – hard yellow leaves indicate that the plant has been neglected.

Unhealthy plant If the cineraria is attacked by botrytis (**right**) the results can be disastrous – the plant can be reduced to a pulpy mass of rot. The fungus attacks when the air is too humid. First signs are usually wet brown patches on the lower leaves. Treat with fungicide immediately and remove and burn the worst affected leaves. This plant (**left**) has both botrytis and leaf miner and is a classic example of bad culture.

PESTS AND DISEASES

Cinerarias, like other soft-leaved houseplants, are vulnerable to sap sucking insects, and a careful look-out should be kept for aphids. Use a reliable insecticide.
White fly These are easily detected on the undersides of the leaves, but they are difficult to eradicate. Spray the undersides of the leaves with an insecticide such as pyrethrum or diazinon and repeat this treatment at least four times at four-day intervals.
Leaf miner and **botrytis (see illustration left below)** may also attack this plant.

Leaf miner (left) This is fairly easily detected. The grub leaves a white trail as it burrows through the upper and lower tissue of the leaf. When the pest is found, pierce its body with a pin. Badly affected leaves can be removed, but regular inspection will prevent a severe outbreak.

Unhealthy leaves Sometimes the foliage of a cineraria will turn brown at the edges (**right**). Possible causes are overwatering or an attack of root fungus gnats. Slugs can cause great damage to the soft delicate leaves of the cineraria (**below**).

AVOIDING PROBLEMS

Light and position

A cineraria appreciates a bright position but must be protected from the glare of direct sun. A light window is the best place providing the conditions are fairly cool and the plant should be placed well away from heating appliances of any kind.

Temperature range

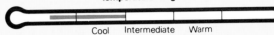

Cool   Intermediate   Warm

It is essential that the plant should be given cool, airy conditions, with a temperature range of 50°-60°F (10°-15°C). As is commonly the rule with houseplants, the cineraria abhors draughts and should not be subject to sudden dramatic changes in temperature, at either end of the scale.

Watering

Regular watering is needed but the plant must never be overwatered or the roots will rot, causing yellowing of the leaves. If this persists the plant will die. Immersion of the pot is a quite unsuitable method of watering and the cineraria dislikes foliar feeds.

Feeding

The cineraria often fails through lack of food. The plant has many roots when first bought and must be fed right away. A few drops of feed are not enough and the amount recommended by the manufacturer of the feed can easily be doubled without harming the plant.

Seasonal care

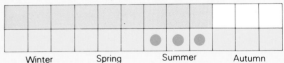

Winter   Spring   Summer   Autumn

The plant flowers in spring and, being treated as an annual, is thrown away when it has flowered. If it is properly fed and watered, and kept in a cool, bright position it should remain fresh and attractive. It is, however, a prey to many pests so it is as well to watch out for any signs of infestation or disease. Less water can be given in the autumn, before the active period leading up to flowering.

Soil

Since the plant has a brief pot life, repotting is not a problem, but a young plant may thrive for being potted on soon after it is acquired. Use a loam-based potting mixture and water the plant after potting.

Cissus

C. antarctica, which is better known as the Kangaroo Vine, has glossy green leaves with toothed edges. Recently it has lost much of its popularity, even though it is easy to grow. By contrast, *C. discolor*, the Begonia Vine, is quite tricky to grow; it is a delicate, much more colourful plant, with a similar climbing habit to the Kangaroo Vine.

Both these plants can be propagated from cuttings that are not too difficult to root in a peaty mixture in a temperature of around 70°F (21°C).

Healthy plant *C. discolor* (right) is quite difficult to care for but will repay the effort it demands many times. A natural climber, it has large heart-shaped leaves decorated with a profusion of coloured markings — metallic green, crimson, peach, white and even purple among them.

VARIETIES AND PURCHASING

Most varieties of cissus are easy to grow and will create a pleasant splash of green in a well-lit room. The most spectacular, however, is the Begonia Vine.

C. antarctica The Kangaroo Vine will reach a height of 10ft (3m) indoors. To grow well it will need some support, such as bamboo canes, and will provide a feature in a plant group or serve as a screen of bright, shiny leaves. It is quite an easy plant to grow.

C. discolor This plant has the common name of the Begonia Vine and it looks quite like *Begonia rex* varieties. The long heart-shaped leaves are patterned with silver and light purple on the upper surface and are a deep red colour on the underside. Ideally, this plant should be grown in a window where the temperature and humidity are closely controlled. This plant is a challenge, but one well worth taking on.

C. rhombifolia This is still called *Rhoicissus rhomboidea* by many growers. It has shiny green leaves growing in triplets. It too can reach 10ft (3m) if it is not pruned too harshly.

PESTS AND DISEASES

Although cissus plants, with the exception of *C. discolor*, do not require too much attention it is important to check them for red spider, mealy bugs and root mealy bugs.

Red spider mite This may attack all types but especially *C. discolor*. It is very difficult to detect on its brilliant variegated leaves. It is wise, therefore, to make a periodic inspection of this plant, since once the pest has taken a grip it is difficult to shake off. Red spider is best treated by saturation spraying of the foliage with a recommended insecticide. Treat immediately the pests are noticed and repeat at ten-day intervals until the plant is clear.

Mealy bug These powdery white pests are more easily detected on all varieties than the red spider. The young of these creatures are encased in a waxy substance which resembles cotton wool and protects them from insecticide. For this reason spray repeatedly.

Root mealy bug This pest will attach itself to the roots of these plants. Smaller than mealy bugs, they can only be seen by knocking the rootball from the pot. To treat a plant infected with these, spray the rootball with insecticide or immerse the whole pot in an insecticide solution.

AVOIDING PROBLEMS

Light and position

The cissus varieties in general need a good light without direct sunlight but the Begonia Vine is more delicate and needs the controlled conditions often found only in a plant window. Protect all varieties from direct sun and from draughts.

Temperature range

Cool   Intermediate   Warm

All these plants like a moderate atmosphere. The Kangaroo Vine needs 50°-60°F (10°-15°C). The Begonia Vine needs temperatures between 60°-70°F (15°-21°C) and will shed many of its leaves if the temperature drops below 65°F (18°C) in its growing period. It also needs a humid atmosphere. All types like a short rest period with the temperature at about 55°F (13°C).

Watering

Water most varieties well during the growing period so that the whole pot is moist but allow the top layer of soil to dry out between waterings. For the Begonia Vine wait until the top half of the pot is dry before rewatering and mist-spray to keep it moist.

Feeding

Once they are established all varieties should be fed regularly while in active growth. Feed at every watering with weak liquid fertilizer from early spring to early autumn.

Seasonal care

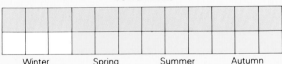

Winter   Spring   Summer   Autumn

All cissus plants should be given a cool rest period, with only just enough water to prevent the mixture from drying out. The Begonia Vine may well lose all its leaves in winter. To grow new plants, root tip cuttings, shorn of their lower leaves and dipped in hormone rooting powder, in a potting mixture. Enclose the pots in plastic bags in a warm, not too light place until the cuttings take root. It is also possible to root trailing stems by pegging them in small pots until they take root.

Soil

Small plants will do well in a soil-less mixture but when the plants take up 5in (12·5cm) pots use a loam-based mixture. Pot on in spring or summer. Plants of a height of 6 ft (2m) will need a pot of 8-10in (20-25cm). At this size they may be top-dressed with fresh potting mixture instead of being repotted.

Leaves Brown marks appear on an otherwise healthy leaf as a result of a sudden chill or too much light (**top**). When whole leaves start to wither and turn brown at the edges overwatering or lack of humidity may be the cause (**bottom**).

Citrus mitis

The citrus is one of the most fascinating of all the many houseplants that may be grown in a pot indoors, or in the conservatory, and when in fruit one of the most admired. The plants are compact with many branches carrying shiny dark green oval shaped leaves. Its heavily scented white flowers usually appear in late summer and a percentage of them become small green fruits that, given careful culture, will eventually develop into miniature oranges. When ripe these taste bitter but they are ideal for making marmalade if there are enough of them.

Healthy plant The Calamondin Orange is an expensive plant and should be chosen with care. The mature plant has an abundance of glossy, unblemished leaves and will grow in a bushy and pleasing shape, whether straight and tall or slightly branching. The exotic little oranges are unusual and make an exciting change if you already have a number of flowering plants.

AVOIDING PROBLEMS

Light and position

Full light is essential to this plant, and it will benefit from a period out-of-doors in the summer months. Place it in a sunny, sheltered corner, preferably on a stone base, and remember to keep up the necessary watering and feeding. Indoors or out, it will not stand draughts or too much shade.

Temperature range

Cool   Intermediate   Warm

The Calamondin Orange prefers cool temperatures and will survive comfortably in temperatures of 50°-60°F (10°-15°C). However, if it becomes too cold, this may contribute to browning of leaf tips which can spread across the whole leaf, and this is aggravated if the plant is overwatered.

Watering

This plant requires ample watering, especially in summer and if it is outdoors. Less water is required in winter, but the soil must never be allowed to dry out completely. If the plant is watered too lavishly in cold conditions, this may cause discoloration of leaves and root failure.

Feeding

It is recommended that the Calamondin Orange is fed at each watering, but it will require less food in winter. Soil deficiency will result in yellowing of the leaves, which can be rectified by watering with a solution containing iron, as directed by the manufacturer.

Seasonal care

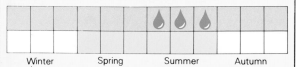

Winter	Spring	Summer	Autumn

The plant requires plenty of water all year round, through rather less in winter than in summer. The plant may be placed out-of-doors in late spring and can remain there until the nights become too chilly. Regular feeding during spring and summer will be beneficial and the plant does require food through the winter, although rather less than needed in the growing season.

Soil

Pot the plant in loam-based mixture, preferably in a clay pot, which is crocked at the bottom before the soil is put in. The soil should be free-draining and a properly fed plant should not need frequent potting on unless the growth is extremely vigorous.

PESTS AND DISEASES

Aphids These small insects are also known as greenfly, but may in fact be grey, black or yellow as well as green. They suck the sap of the plant, preferring new growth such as small top shoots and flower buds. The plant gradually becomes stunted, with distortion of stems, leaves and flowers. In addition, the aphids deposit a sticky honeydew on the plant which causes it further damage and makes it very susceptible to sooty mould. Thorough and repeated spraying with malathion will get rid of aphids, or a systemic insecticide can be used as granules in the soil.

Mealy bug This pest may be a nuisance to older plants but fortunately it is easily spotted and treated.

Scale insect This could be the worst problem for a citrus mitis. The young flesh-coloured insects and dark brown adults attach themselves to the stems of the plant and the undersides of the leaves. A large plant may benefit from a thorough spraying with malathion, but it is probably more effective to soak a sponge in the insecticide and firmly wipe the plant clean and free of pests. At the same time, it is a wise precaution to clean the upper side of the leaves as well.

Red spider mite If the signs of infestation by red spider mites occur in the plant (**see illustration left**), prompt action must be taken. A steady stream of lukewarm water run over the foliage may dislodge the mites and their webs, as may a thorough spraying with malathion. However, if the problem is widespread, treatment with insecticide is unlikely to be effective and the insects will move to other plants if left. In this case, there is nothing to be done but to remove and burn the infected areas, or burn the entire plant.

Sooty mould This is a mould which lives on the excreta of the above pests. It is not harmful, but is very unsightly. A sponge soaked in malathion will clean away the mould and no other treatment will then be necessary.

VARIETIES

C. mitis This compact and decorative variety is the only one which reliably fruits indoors and retains a good shape.

Mealy bug (top) The white, cottony bugs show up clearly on the plant and can be easily treated. Wipe them away with a swab soaked in malathion or methylated spirits.

Red spider mite (above) It is difficult to detect this tiny pest but the plant will become stunted, the leaves brown and discoloured and minute webs can be seen on growing tips.

Clivia miniata

As its common name suggests, the clivia is indigenous to South Africa where its native state is Natal. The clivia's rich green glossy leaves are broad and strap-like, sprouting from the thick bulbous base of the plant. Although a reasonably attractive plant when simply in leaf, it is at its best when clusters of bell-shaped flowers appear on strong stems. By far the greatest number of plants that are offered for sale are bright orange but there are yellow and apricot-coloured varieties as well. Clivias not only have stocky leaf growth, but they also develop an incredible amount of root that quickly fills the pots in which they are growing.

When propagating, new plants the clumps of growth are divided into individual sections and potted separately. However, due to the thick intertwining roots which can become difficult to divide, it is best to consider propagation before the plants become too large and unwieldy.

VARIETIES AND PURCHASING

Clivias, which make splendid free-standing showpieces when in flower, now come in a range of colours from pale yellow to deep orange. Although plants are seen at their best in flower they can be bought more cheaply when only in leaf.
C. miniata This is most commonly available and has dark green leaves.
C. miniata 'Variegata' This has a cream stripe along the length of the leaves.

Healthy plant The wealth of crocus-or trumpet-shaped flowers usually have a lighter centre. Here a cluster of brilliant red-orange blooms with yellow centres stand out from a mass of glossy leaves. Plants bloom in spring every one to four years.

AVOIDING PROBLEMS

Light and position

Clivias require good light if they are to flower successfully but they should be protected from bright sunlight. A shaded window is ideal but remember that these plants are also vulnerable to draughts.

Temperature range

Cool   Intermediate   Warm

When the flower buds appear clivias need a temperature of 60°-70°F (15°-21°C) and should be kept within this range throughout the growing period. In winter they need to be kept cool while the plant is resting. Choose a place with a temperature of 45°-50°F (7°-10°C).

Watering

Water these plants well in the growing period. This will probably mean once a week. In the rest period water less so that the soil remains almost dry. Increase again gradually once the flower stalks appear.

Feeding

Clivias develop very sturdy root systems and for this reason require regular weekly feeding once the flower stalks are well established. Use liquid fertilizer but reduce the feeding in the rest period to one feed every two weeks or even less.

Seasonal care

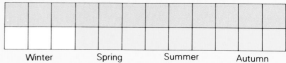

Winter   Spring   Summer   Autumn

Water and feed well in the flowering and growing period and keep in a warm position. Reduce watering, feeding and temperature in the rest period. Keep in a good but not too strong light and protect from draughts. Remove the flower stalks once they wither and cut off the fruits that develop with a sharp knife. To grow new plants separate the young groups of new shoots from the main plant after flowering has ended and pot in small pots. Left on the plants these offsets will ensure several heads of flowers.

Soil

Use a loam-based mixture and firm the plants into position with your hands to avoid damaging the fleshy roots. Well-established plants are best top-dressed for two or three years. Then repot just before the flower stalks appear.

PESTS AND DISEASES

Few pests attack clivias but it is important to guard against leaf rot caused by too wet roots. If the leaf margins turn brown check that the pot is well drained and that the drainage holes are not blocked by earthworm casts.
Earthworms These can be cleared by inverting the pot and holding the rootball in your hand to clear the drainage holes and remove the worms.
Mealy bug These may also attack this plant. Remove the white patches they cause with a piece of cotton wool dipped in methylated spirits or spray with an insecticide.

An unhealthy plant A good specimen of this plant will have glossy dark green or striped leaves. If the leaves turn brown or look scorched this may be the result of direct sunlight on wet leaves. It is important to avoid watering this plant while in sunlight. If the leaves start to wither, give the plant more water and spray immediately. If new shoots are fragile and there are no flowers move the plant to a cooler position. If there is no new growth at all in spring, however, the plant needs more warmth. Discoloured yellow foliage means that the plant needs more feeding, particularly in the summer months. The most common cause of rot at the base of the plant is overwatering.

Codiaeum

One common name of the codiaeum refers to Joseph's coat of many colours, for the plant's leaves are also many coloured —yellow, orange, red and green. Mottled and general mixtures of these colours make the Croton the most brilliant of all the foliage plants that are grown indoors. Indigenous to Ceylon, codiaeums are temperamental and require a degree of skill if they are to survive in room conditions.

Almost all these plants are raised from cuttings about 4in (10cm) long taken from the top section of main stems. The cuttings should be put in a peat and sand mixture and kept humid in a temperature of not less than 70°F (21°C).

VARIETIES AND PURCHASING

Whichever of the numerous varieties you choose, inspect it carefully for browning or dull leaves which may be a sign of root rot, or the invasion of red spider mite. The following are popular among the many codiaeums.
C. reidii This has broad leaves, mottled in rich pink and orange and with proper care may grow to 6ft (2m).
C. 'Eugene Drapps' This plant has predominantly yellow foliage and is the best variety with this colouring.
C. holufiana This is a variety which is easy to manage and is one of the most commonly available.

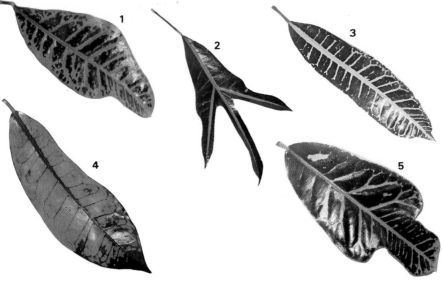

Healthy plant Many varieties of codiaeum are grown with all sorts of leaf shapes and colours. *C. 'Mrs Iceton'* (**above left**) has oval leaves in rich red and green while the leaves of *C. holufiana* (**above centre**) are larger, elongated and more yellow. *C. craigii* (**above**) is a taller plant with sharply indented, elongated leaves.

Foliage variation Examples of different leaves show the intriguing range of the codiaeums. The broad red and green leaf of *'Mrs Iceton'* (1) contrasts with the elongated yellow fingers of *C. craigii* (2). *'Eugene Drapps'* (3) and *C. holufiana* (4) have simple, oval leaves while the rich, pink-tinged *C. reidii* (5) has a more generous, undulating shape.

PESTS AND DISEASES

Red spider mite These share the codiaeums' preference for warmth and are likely to be found (**see illustration below**). They are difficult to detect on the bright foliage. Spray the plants with malathion once a month as a precaution. If the mites get a firm hold, the plant must be destroyed.
Scale insect This is a less common pest but it may attack older plants. Spraying with malathion should get rid of it.
Botrytis This is a disease which is not usually found in sturdy plants, but may attack soft, damp foliage. Remove the damaged leaves and spray the plant with dichloran.

Damaged leaves Codiaeums like warm temperatures and some humidity, but excessive moisture in a cold position discolours and shrivels the leaf (**above**). Damage from red spider mites (**below**) is clearly seen in the starved, curling leaf of the weakened plant.

AVOIDING PROBLEMS

Light and position

The codiaeum requires good light and plenty of sun to retain the beauty of its multi-coloured leaves, but take care that it is not scorched or parched during a hot summer. In poor light, the leaves will revert to green and the plant cannot flourish as it should.

Temperature range

Cool · Intermediate · Warm

Warm, moist conditions are essential to this plant and the minimum temperature at which it is kept should be 60°F (15°C) but it will benefit from more warmth and may prefer a temperature nearer 70°F (21°C). These are the conditions which would prevail in its native country of Sri Lanka.

Watering

The codiaeum requires plenty of water in summer and regular watering during mild weather and the winter months. Water should be supplied to the soil from the top of the pot and the plant may prefer that the water is tepid. Do not spray the leaves of a codiaeum.

Feeding

Established plants are rather greedy, requiring nourishment with every watering, except possibly during the winter months. The food may be introduced through the soil as a liquid, but never try to use a foliar feed.

Seasonal care

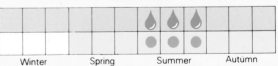

Winter · Spring · Summer · Autumn

The plant requires a good deal of attention throughout the year and will need more water the better its health and growing conditions. In winter it will require slightly less water, but overwatering at any time may encourage disease which will damage the leaves, especially in older plants. Periodic cleaning of the foliage will improve the appearance of the plant, but cleaning chemicals should not be used too frequently.

Soil

Loam-based soil must be used and the plant should be potted with reasonable firmness. Regular repotting is advisable, annually in summer, until the plant is in a 10in (25cm) pot. Thereafter it can be sustained by careful attention and regular feeding.

Columnea

The strange common name of the columnea must surely relate to the open flower which could be compared to the open mouth of a goldfish. The flowers are spectacular with glorious orange, red or yellow colouring. The plant's leaves are oval and small, attached to wiry stems that in all varieties other than *C. crassifolia* have a natural drooping habit, so they are good for hanging baskets and pots. By far the best variety is *C. banksii* which produces masses of orange flowers from early spring onwards. The secret of successful flowering is to keep the soil as dry as possible during late winter without causing defoliation. Many columneas are much tougher plants than they are usually thought to be.

The flowers of the Goldfish Plant are highly coloured and exotic. The common name of the plant probably derives from the open, fluted shape, resembling the mouth of a fish. The flowers grow separately from the stems but hang in rich clusters on the whole plant.

Healthy plant The Goldfish Plant is extremely striking, with its dark foliage and very bright flowers. It hangs in a luxuriant mass of straight heavily laden stems.

AVOIDING PROBLEMS

Light and position

The columnea requires a position with good light, to encourage flowering, but shaded from direct sunlight. It is best seen as a hanging plant, so it could be placed near the window in a bright room. However, it will not tolerate draughts.

Temperature range

Cool   Intermediate   Warm

Few plants care for a large temperature range or periods of excessive heat or cold. A suitable range for the columnea is 60°-70°F (15°-21°C) and it may not do well in a centrally heated house as it does not like dry air. If, however, it is possible to keep up a good level of humidity, the plant may exist comfortably, but it will prefer a slight coolness around the winter flowering period.

Watering

Water the plant regularly during the summer growth period, giving slightly less in winter. Water the soil from the top of the pot or pour it into the saucer, always avoiding the foliage. Keeping the soil almost dry during mid-winter will encourage better flowering.

Feeding

The plant is not too fussy in its feeding habits, but established plants should be fed about once a week in summer when they are active, once a month during winter. Cease feeding towards the end of winter when the watering is cut to a minimum. Introduce the food through the soil.

Seasonal care

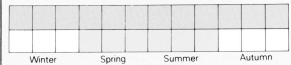

Winter   Spring   Summer   Autumn

The columnea is quite easy to care for and if the period of near starvation is adhered to in winter, the plant will flower more freely. The foliage can be trimmed to shape at any time when the plant is not in flower, but this is not essential to its health. The autumn is the time to tidy the plant and cut out any dead material. Beware of overwatering at all times, as this can ruin the leaves and ultimately whole branches.

Soil

Cuttings from the plant will root quite well in moist conditions and a temperature of 70°F (21°C). When transferring them to a hanging basket, use a loam-based potting mixture and include at least five cuttings, to ensure full and impressive growth.

VARIETIES

Finding a Goldfish Plant to buy can be a problem as they are grown in limited numbers. On finding a supplier, choose a plant with several cuttings in the pot so that it has a full appearance and is firm and healthy. The plant may be bought already in flower but this need not be a condition of purchase.

C. banksii This is the finest variety and forms a full hanging plant with evergreen foliage and bright orange flowers. It is easily propagated from cuttings.

C. gloriosa The slender, less rigid stems of this variety carry soft, hairy leaves and can grow to 3ft (1m). The tubular flowers are a vivid red with yellow throats.

C. microphylla The leaves of this plant are very small and abundant but the orange flowers are produced rather spasmodically and this variety may be rather less attractive than the others.

White fly This common pest is noticeable when the plant is disturbed as the flies rise up in a cloud. Persistent spraying with dichloran, at four-day intervals over about two weeks should kill both adult insects and young flies. If they should seem to become immune to the spray, change to a different type of insecticide.

PESTS AND DISEASES

Columneas seem generally to have a natural resistance to many common pests, but they are sometimes affected.

Mealy bug This small, white pest will be found only on older plants and can be removed with cotton wool soaked in methylated spirits.

White fly These suck sap from the undersides of the leaves (**see illustration above**).

Botrytis This is rarely seen but may attack a plant which is cramped and overwatered.

Cyclamen persicum

Cyclamen are among the most beautiful of all flowering plants, whether they are grown in pots or not, but they are no longer simply seasonal flowers that only appeared in the autumn. Hybridists have made it possible for plants to be in flower throughout the year, although the plants still tend to be more popular during the winter months. Over the years, however, the development of *C. persicum* has been quite an achievement, as the plants today bear little resemblance to those initially collected in the eastern Mediterranean. The commercial grower raises fresh plants from seed each year, and for the main crop these are sown in mid autumn in a temperature of around 70°F (21°C). The only time that plants need to be so warm is when they are germinating.

VARIETIES AND PURCHASING

The main quality to look out for when buying a cyclamen is that the stems, leaves and flowers are all fresh and upright. Avoid a plant with leaves drooping over the side of the pot. Look among the leaves to make sure there are plenty of healthy flower buds and inspect the whole plant for signs of botrytis, which will only become more and more troublesome. If the ends of leaves and flower stalks seem to be rotting, choose another plant. There are numerous strains and types among the many varieties of cyclamen. They are also available in many beautiful colours, so it is largely a matter of personal preference as to which should be bought, providing all the plants are equally healthy.

Healthy plant A plant which is kept in the right cool, airy conditions will thrive and flower longer than one which is in too stuffy or hot a place. Cyclamen with rich, pink flowers (**above left**) are often favoured for their decorative appearance, but the cool white flowers on their long, reddish stalks (**above right**) have a particular elegance. The cyclamen originally came from the Mediterranean area. Modern varieties have been developed which bear flowers in all shades of pink, red and purple and, although the original plants had plain green leaves, the newer strains have attractive borders of pale green, delicately drawn into the centre of the leaf by the light coloured veins (**right**). Cyclamen are very popular as gift plants, and in this case it is even more vital to ensure the plant is absoutely healthy when it is bought, as no-one will be pleased to be left with a present which rots or grows mould.

AVOIDING PROBLEMS

Light and position

Given cool, light and airy conditions, these plants remain in flower for a longer period and have a bright, healthy appearance. A kitchen windowsill might be a suitable location, but avoid subjecting them to hot sunshine through the glass on very sunny days.

Temperature range

Cool   Intermediate   Warm

A temperature range between 55°-65°F (13°-18°C) suits a cyclamen very well and it will not live happily in warmer temperatures or in a stuffy atmosphere. If the surrounding environment is too hot and dry the leaves of the plant will yellow. In common with many other plants, the cyclamen abhors cold draughts or sudden changes of temperature.

Watering

A cyclamen will be damaged if the soil becomes sodden. Water from below to moisten the compost, but never leave the plant standing in water. The plant will come to no harm if it gets to a stage where the leaves droop slightly before watering is repeated.

Feeding

A weak liquid feed given through the soil with each watering is required while the plant is in leaf. As with the watering, any excess should be avoided. The plant must be given the most attention during winter and spring.

Seasonal care

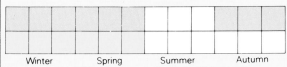

Winter   Spring   Summer   Autumn

The flowering season of the cyclamen is autumn to spring and the growth dies down after the flowering. The plant can then be allowed to dry out slightly and rest in a cool, but frost-free position until new growth starts in the summer. At this stage the corm can be divided and the sections repotted for propagation of the plant.

Soil

A good loam-based compost mixture is suitable for potting at any stage and can also be used to raise plants from seed. Cyclamen flower well if slightly pot bound so a pot of 5in (12.5cm) is the largest needed. Crock the pot and pot the plant firmly.

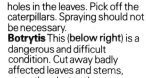

Aphids These (**above**) are damaging and unsightly but not particularly troublesome to cyclamen. Spray the plant with diazinon and repeat the treatment as necessary.
Caterpillars These (**below left**) are not often found on plants kept indoors, but may find their way in, especially to a conservatory. You will notice holes in the leaves. Pick off the caterpillars. Spraying should not be necessary.
Botrytis This (**below right**) is a dangerous and difficult condition. Cut away badly affected leaves and stems, move the plant to dryer conditions and spray it thoroughly with dichloran.

PESTS AND DISEASES

Cyclamen mite These tiny insects appear almost as dust on the reverse sides of leaves, which become stunted and very hard. Unfortunately there is no cure and the plant must be destroyed.
Red spider mite Check the leaves regularly if you have any suspicion that the plant has red spider. It is difficult to see and almost impossible to control. Spray the plant repeatedly with malathion.

Aphids These flies (**see illustration above top**) do occur on the cyclamen but are quite easily controlled.
Botrytis This disease (**see illustration above**) can quickly kill a plant so deal with it as soon as it appears.
Vine weevil The beetles attack the leaves of the plant, but the larvae in the soil cause the real damage. Water the soil with malathion regularly at fortnightly intervals.

Cyperus

The cyperus is one of the few water plants that can be recommended for indoor culture as, with reasonable care, it will do well. The plants grow in clumps and have rather thin, pale green, grassy leaves that are not in themselves attractive, but the 3ft (1m) tall umbrella-like flower adds much to the general appearance. The simple way of producing new plants is to allow clumps to develop to a reasonable size, then to remove the plant from its pot and, with a large sharp knife, simply cut the clumps into sections. These can then be potted individually using a houseplant potting mixture.

VARIETIES AND PURCHASING

Umbrella plants can be quite difficult to obtain but in the summer, two varieties may be available in the shops.
C. diffusus This variety may reach a height of 3ft (1m). It is a striking plant with a wide spread of leaves.
C. alternifolius (see below left) This is a much smaller plant, usually growing to around 12-18in (30-46cm). It has narrow sparse leaves.
C.a. 'Albo Variegata' (below) This is a variegated attractive houseplant which has white-striped leaves.

Healthy plant Umbrella Plants grow wild all over the tropical and subtropical regions of the world. Their natural habitat is swamp-land and the shores of sluggish rivers and lakes. The two species most commonly found as houseplants in this country (*C. diffusus* and *C. alternifolius*) both originate in Madagascar. Water is therefore essential to their healthy growth, and if they are allowed to dry out, their foliage will very quickly turn a yellowish-brown. When looking for a healthy Umbrella Plant in a shop, choose one with fresh green lush looking leaves. The necessity of keeping them moist makes Umbrella Plants ideal for the beginner, as they can never be overwatered! The other point to check when buying one of these plants is that the umbrella growths are free of signs of mealy bug and other pests.

PESTS AND DISEASES

As long as the Umbrella Plant is well-watered, it should remain quite healthy.
Mealy bug To check for these, look into the green flowers at the top of the plant. They can be removed with an insecticide.
Green and **white fly** These may attack young leaves.

Diseased plants If the leaves turn brown at the edges and develop brown patches (**bottom**), the cause may be insufficient watering. It could also be that the plant needs more light so it should be moved. Other danger signs are split leaves or holes in leaves (**below**). Check for pests if this occurs.

AVOIDING PROBLEMS

Light and position

The Umbrella Plant can be grown equally well in full, bright sunlight or slight shade. Highly adaptable, it will, with time, adapt itself to almost any location. If few stems are produced, however, the plant is getting too little light.

Temperature range

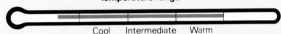

Cool   Intermediate   Warm

The Umbrella Plant will tolerate most temperatures between 50°-70°F (10°-21°C), provided there are no extreme fluctuations. In winter the temperature should not go below 50°F (10°C). *Cyperus papyrus* will need a minimum temperature of between 60°-65°F (15°-18°C).

Watering

Being aquatic, the Umbrella Plant must be grown in pots placed in a shallow pan of water. The water should be changed daily. During growth periods the plant will require more water than at times of rest. Do not totally immerse the pots which can cause the stems to rot.

Feeding

Because the plants sit in water, the best way to feed is with fertilizing tablets pushed well into the soil, Otherwise, a standard liquid fertilizer can be applied at monthly intervals during the active growth period.

Seasonal care

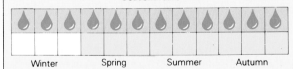

Winter   Spring   Summer   Autumn

Throughout the year, the Umbrella Plant needs a constant source of water to keep the roots saturated. If kept in dry, heated environments, the water level should be checked frequently. Feed at regular intervals except in winter. The plants can be propagated by division in spring. As the green plants die, cut them off at intervals throughout the year to allow for new growth.

Soil

The soil should have a high loam content to prevent it from disintegrating in the water. Pieces of charcoal can be added to the soil to keep it fresh and lessen unpleasant odours caused by souring compost. As they grow, the plants will require larger pots.

Dieffenbachia

Although these plants do produce insignificant spathe flowers, they are grown entirely as foliage plants—the vast quantities produced each year are a testimony to their popularity. Some of the more robust forms can grow to a height of about 6ft (2m) in only six years, but they are grown principally as compact plants that seldom get out of hand if confined to reasonably sized pots.

New plants can be raised from pieces of stem cut into sections and placed in a peat and sand mixture at a high temperature, or by removing the small plantlets that cluster around their parents, potting them individually in smaller pots.

Healthy plant *D. amoena* *'Tropic Snow'* (**below**) is a variety of *D. amoena*. It is highly attractive, its dark green foliage being relieved by interesting white blotches. The detail (**right**) shows new growth after the plant has been cut back for propagation. Always wash your hands thoroughly after taking cuttings or removing old leaves. Dieffenbachia sap is poisonous.

Two varieties *D. exotica* (**near right**) and *D. camilla* (**far right**) are two popular varieties. The former is extremely compact, with blotched green and white leaves. The latter is a more recent introduction. Its attraction is the creamy white centres of its leaves. Both plants need warmth and high humidity.

D. amoena This detail of the leaf of *'Tropic Snow'* shows the sturdy, fleshy quality and the spread of pale markings from the centre.

VARIETIES AND PURCHASING

D. exotica The blotchy leaf markings of this variety are less regular than those of 'Tropic Snow', although the colouring is similar.

D. camilla The creamy colour of the leaf, edged with green, is particularly striking, making D. camilla an unusual plant for display.

These highly attractive houseplants can produce flowers, but these are of little interest. Their main appeal is their attractive shape and their striking foliage. This is usually green, but it is often intermixed with shades of white or yellow. When you buy these plants, remember that dieffenbachias love heat. They originally came from Brazil and were given their name by Dieffenbach, the gardener to the Hapsburg rulers of Austria, in 1830.
D. amoena A vigorous-growing plant, this is popular since it is relatively easy to care for.
D. camilla This plant is a fairly recent introduction, noted for its combination of pattern and colour.
D. exotica Striking blotched white and green foliage, with leaves spreading outwards and arching downwards make this an attractive plant.

D. bausei This has lance-shaped yellow green leaves, up to 1ft (30cm) long, and marked with white spots and dark green patches and margins.
D. bowmannii This dieffenbachia has oval leaves 2ft (60 cm) long and 1½ft (45cm) wide on long stalks. The colouring is less striking than that of some varieties, being chiefly a mixture of pale and dark green.
D. imperialis This has leathery, oval leaves, splattered with yellow.
D. maculata Spotted Dumb Cane has many varieties, most with elegant pointed lance-shaped leaves, coloured dark green, with irregular off-white markings.

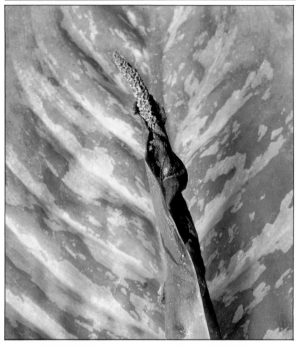

Leaves dying naturally It is common for the leaves of this plant to die back naturally (**above**). This happens first with the lower leaves. Plants should last at least three or four years with proper care.

Scorch This problem is caused by placing the plant either too near a radiator or too close to a sunny window (**below**). The best remedy is to move the plant to a more suitable location, although the damaged leaves will not recover.

Aphids This common houseplant pest will sometimes attack the dieffenbachia (**above**). It is best to treat aphids with a systemic insecticide in the form of either a spray or granules added to the soil.

Overwatering Brown patches on the edges of the leaves can indicate overwatering (**below**). Although this plant requires watering all the year round, water sparingly in winter.

Stem rot Plants kept in conditions which are too wet and cold may well develop rotting problems either on the stem (**above**) or foliage. Try not to overwater, and keep the plant in a temperature of at least 60°F (15°C).

Physical damage It is important to protect plants from damage by household pets (**below**). This leaf shows signs of scorch and of being eaten. There is no cure for such damage, but ensure that the plants cannot be attacked again.

AVOIDING PROBLEMS

Light and position

Place a dieffenbachia in a fairly light position, but shaded from direct sun. It should not be within range of heat from a radiator or cold draughts from a door or window. The colour of a variegated plant will suffer if it has poor light.

Temperature range

Cool   Intermediate   Warm

A dieffenbachia will live in a temperature of 60°F (15°C) but would probably prefer nearer 70°F (21°C). In higher temperatures it is important to keep up a good level of humidity. A cool, moist atmosphere can be tolerated for a short period, but may cause some falling of the leaves.

Watering

Moisture is required all year round, but the plant can be watered less in winter than in summer, when tepid water should be used. During spring and summer growth, watering should be generous and frequent.

Feeding

While the dieffenbachia is producing new leaf growth it should be fed with every watering, using weak, liquid fertilizer introduced through the soil. Feeding with every other watering is sufficient at other times.

Seasonal care

Winter   Spring   Summer   Autumn

Light and moisture all year round are vital to the health of this plant. A dark location or cold draughts will result in general decline, spindly growth and loss of leaves. In cold and wet conditions the leaves will brown at the edges. Propagation is most successful from stem cuttings, placed in peat and sand and kept moist and in a high temperature of 70°-75°F (21°-23°C). The plant requires the most attention, receiving plenty of food and water, during the summer months.

Soil

If the plant seems too large for its pot when purchased, it can be repotted immediately. Otherwise, wait until the plant is well established and repot in summer, using an open potting mixture containing loam and peat.

Dracaena

This is a diverse group of plants that look as though they should be growing on a tropical island. Many are stately plants that grow on slender stems, but there are also those with a more prostrate habit, such as *D. godseffiana*, and the more colourful ones such as *D. terminalis*. Almost all dracaenas are a little difficult to care for in rooms where the light and temperature are inadequate.

Propagation methods vary; some plants can be raised from stem cuttings and others from rooting fleshy roots that develop as the plants age. Both these methods need temperatures in the region of 70°F (21°C).

VARIETIES AND PURCHASING

D. deremensis This variety may grow to 10ft (3m) but can be contained by pruning.
D. marginata 'Tricolor' (below) At the top of this plant's stout stem is a cluster of narrow green leaves, edged with red.
D. souvenir de Schriever (below left) This plant has bold green leaves which have a margin of yellow.
D. terminalis (bottom left) This attractive plant may reach a height of 30in (75cm). Young plants have green leaves but as they mature they turn a brilliant red.
D. godseffiana This has yellow mottled foliage on wiry stems and may, in ideal conditions, grow to 6ft (2m).

Healthy plant Healthy dracaenas are most attractive plants. When buying a dracaena, check that the leaves are not discoloured and that their tips have not gone brown. The topmost leaves should also be examined, as the white, powdery mealy bug could be present. Although many species do grow to a great height in their natural environment, they can be kept to a reasonable size and pleasing shape by judicious pruning. All varieties like light and will not achieve their best colour and contrast unless given the maximum amount of light possible. Homes which have central heating provide ideal environments for these often exotic-looking plants. A group of dracaenas of different heights and colours, arranged artistically in a large window, can make a most attractive display.

D. terminalis – a healthy leaf.

D. terminalis – leaf with bacterial spot.

D. marginata – a healthy leaf.

D. marginata – a scorch-damaged leaf.

D. souvenir de Schriever – a rotting leaf

AVOIDING PROBLEMS

Light and position

All dracaenas need good light but care should be taken to avoid putting them in very bright sunlight as there is then a possibility of scorching. They should also be protected from cold draughts. Taller plants can be placed on the floor.

Temperature range

| | Cool | Intermediate | Warm |

Dracaenas can survive quite low temperatures in the region of 50°F (10°C), although their leaves will droop in such conditions and eventually fall off. However, a couple of weeks in such temperatures will do no harm.

The ideal temperature is somewhere between 60°-70°F (15°-21°C). They also need a humid atmosphere, so stand the plants on trays of damp pebbles or moss.

Watering

The plant needs plenty of water, especially during the growing period, throughout which the potting mixture should be kept very moist. Be careful, however, not to stand the pot in water, and in the winter months, keep the soil fairly dry.

Feeding

Fertilizer should be given to the plant during the growing period but it should not be fed during the winter. Either use a liquid fertilizer or place a slow-release pellet in the soil. Do not use a foliar feed as dracaenas do not do well if their leaves become wet.

Seasonal care

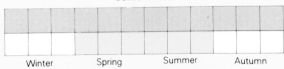

| Winter | Spring | Summer | Autumn |

During the summer months, when the plant is growing, water is the most important thing to remember. Making the roots excessively wet should be avoided, so allow the plant to dry out to some extent between each watering. Do not allow it to get bone dry in winter. Many of the taller growing plants will need cutting back, and this can be done at any time of the year. The cuttings can be used for propagating new plants.

PESTS AND DISEASES

Mealy bug Young bugs wrapped in a tell-tale substance like cotton wool are a sign that there are adult bugs in the foliage of the plant. They are normally found among the topmost leaves and can be eradicated by repeated use of malathion insecticide or by cleaning the bugs from the foliage with a sponge soaked in methylated spirits.
Root mealy bug If these are found in the roots, immerse the rootball in malathion.
Red spider mite This is quite common. The pest will be found on the underside of the leaf and brown patches may develop. Treat with insecticide.

Damaged leaves The effects of mealy bug can be seen in this D. deremensis leaf (**above left**). Dracaenas can be watered freely in summer. However, care must be taken not to overwater them and they should be kept rather dry in winter. The effects of overwatering can be seen in the picture of a D. godseffiana (**above**).

Soil

Use loam-based potting mixture and pot on the plants during the summer months, ensuring that the new pots are not too large. It is a good idea with some plants to remove the top layer of old soil and replace it with fresh mixture. Pot on only when the plant is nearly pot-bound.

Euphorbia pulcherrima

●●●

In the past 25 years, Poinsettias have come from virtually nothing to being far and away the most popular Christmas flowering plant. This is due to the development of greatly improved strains and growth retarding chemicals which control the eventual height of plants.

There are varieties with pink, creamy white and bi-coloured bracts, but the important colour is the brilliant red of the Christmas Star. The plant's leaves are pale green and the flowers uninteresting, but the brilliantly coloured bracts are a magnificent attraction. The bracts are, in fact, coloured leaves that begin to develop in the topmost branches of the plant in autumn.

Cuttings about 4–6in (10–15cm) long are taken in mid-summer from top sections of the stem. These are rooted in moist peat and sand in humid conditions at a temperature of around 70°F (21°C).

Healthy plant A Poinsettia will always be striking because of its colour, and is usually displayed alone (**below**) to considerable effect. The coloured bracts that cluster round the plant's flowers (**right**) can grow up to 10in (25cm) long.

AVOIDING PROBLEMS

Light and position

The Poinsettia, like other flowering plants, especially winter varieties, must have plenty of light to maintain the colour of its bracts. It will not be harmed by weak, winter sunshine once established, but young plants should be protected from direct sun and cold draughts.

Temperature range

Cool   Intermediate   Warm

Keep the plant in intermediate temperatures. Room temperatures of 60°-70°F (15°-21°C) are fine. When the Poinsettia is not in colour it will survive in a cooler atmosphere, but should on no account be exposed to frost. The plant appreciates a moist atmosphere and may be adversely affected if there is a gas fire in the room.

Watering

Keep the compost moist and make sure it is not allowed to dry out while the plant is growing and in flower. The watering can be reduced once the plant has flowered, but return to the normal amount after pruning or repotting in midsummer. Water from the top of the pot.

Feeding

Add liquid feed to the water during the active period for the plant. When the Poinsettia begins to die down naturally, stop feeding it until signs of growth are resumed.

Seasonal care

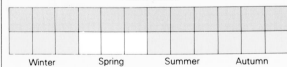

Winter   Spring   Summer   Autumn

When the plant begins to die down after flowering, cut back the main stems to a length of about 4in (10cm). Store the plant in a warm, dry place and wait until new growth is apparent. This will take about six weeks, and as soon as the plant resumes activity, it can be watered and repotted. Be careful not to overwater a Poinsettia as this can cause root rot and leaf discoloration.

Soil

Use a loam-based potting mixture for repotting in late spring. Remove the old soil and replant in the same container. Water the plant after potting but keep it only just moist until new growth has fully taken hold.

Unhealthy leaves Botrytis (**above**) often attacks Poinsettias. It is a grey mould that causes nasty wet blotches on the foliage, attacking the lower leaves first. It is unwise to buy a Poinsettia that has very few lower leaves, as they may have been removed because the plant is already suffering from this mould. To cure, remove badly affected leaves and treat with fungicide. Leaves regularly suffer discoloration (**top**) and this may simply be age, or alternatively, root rot. This develops if the soil is kept too wet, and air is unable to circulate round the roots of the plant. Eventually the leaves will drop off. There is no cure so excessive watering should be avoided.

PESTS AND DISEASES

White fly This is by far the most troublesome pest, and can easily be detected on the undersides of the leaves. It is notorious for increasing rapidly, and being fairly difficult to kill. There are numerous insecticides available – dichloran and malathion sprays are recommended – but they must be used intensively. Having killed off the parent flies, insecticide treatment must be repeated at four-day intervals to dispose of any larvae. A Poinsettia must be checked regularly for white fly throughout its life.

Botrytis This can occur (**see illustration above**) causing the plant to give off dust when it is moved or shaken. Household chemical sprays will cause spotting of a much smaller type than botrytis patches.

Root rot Another regular cause of discoloration in Poinsettias, (**see illustration above**), this causes a dramatic fading in the colour of leaves.

Fatsia and Fatshedera

The fatsia and the fatshedera are very closely related in as much as the fatsia is one of the parents of the fatshedera —the hedera obviously being the other. Both are hardy out-of-doors, and reasonably trouble-free plants in the home. While the fatsia has large, shallowly indented, fingered leaves, the fatshedera has similarly shaped leaves that are very much smaller. Both are green, but there are also variegated forms of each. The fatsia produces a compact bush while the fatshedera is much more upright, and will generally branch out if the growing tips are removed.

The best method of propagating the fatsia is by means of seed. To grow new fatshederas, tip or stem cuttings should be taken during spring and summer.

VARIETIES AND PURCHASING

These are both robust plants which are quite easy to grow. Check the leaves when buying the plant and choose one with glossy, bright green foliage. An overall browning of the plant may indicate the presence of red spider mites, so avoid a plant which does not look in the peak of condition.
Fatsia japonica This is often to be found under its other name of *Aralia sieboldii*. There is also a variegated form which is very decorative, but this is more difficult to manage and is seldom seen on sale.
Fatshedera lizei This fresh green plant has upright growth and is an ideal climbing plant, for instance, on an open staircase where the temperature may be too low for other plants.

Healthy plant The spreading leaves of *Fatsia japonica,* (**right**), form an attractive, almost tropical display. The mature plant may reach a height of 4ft (1.3m) but remains rounded and bushy, unlike the fatshedera which grows vertically. However, both plants are susceptible to aphids, which especially enjoy the young shoots (**below**) in the top growth of the plants. Mealy bugs and red spider mites may also attack both these plants.

AVOIDING PROBLEMS

Light and position

These plants are quite tolerant of bad conditions, but prefer good light, so long as it is not harsh sunlight. A room which is bright but not sunny, or an airy hallway, is ideal, but keep plants away from draughts coming through doors or windows.

Temperature range

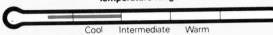

Cool   Intermediate   Warm

A temperature of below 60°F (15°C) is required but the plants are quite hardy and anywhere in the range 45°-60°F (7°-15°C) is suitable. Keep them well away from radiators, which exude dry heat which the plants cannot enjoy. The lower temperatures in the preferred range are adequate in winter.

Watering

Water the plants regularly but do not let them stand in water. They will require less moisture in winter, especially if the temperature is low. Be quite generous with the watering, but allow the soil to dry out slightly before repeating.

Feeding

Established plants will require frequent feeding. Add liquid feed to the water at regular intervals. As is usually the case, the plants may be fed less as watering is reduced, in this case during the inactive winter period.

Seasonal care

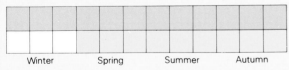

Winter   Spring   Summer   Autumn

Both plants will enjoy being placed out-of-doors in summer, if they are placed in a sheltered position, though not in full sun, and if their need for food and water is not neglected. Spray the leaves regularly when the plants are indoors. Cut back the stems if the plant becomes too leggy or the leaves have suffered from dry heat. The plants may be propagated from stem tip cuttings potted in the spring.

Soil

Plants in small pots will need potting on soon after they are bought. Once the plant has reached a pot of 5-7in (12.5-17cm) it can stay there quite happily for two or three years. Use loam-based mixture at all stages as peat is too thin.

PESTS AND DISEASES

Red spider mite Both plants are vulnerable to this pest, fatsia more than fatshedera. Browning of the leaves and hardening of soft new growth is the sign of spider mites. Thorough and repeated spraying with malathion is vital.

Aphids These greenfly are found on the younger leaves (**see illustration left below**) and are easy to see. Treat the plant by spraying with diazinon.

Mealy bug It is not difficult to detect this pest. At an early stage, wipe off the white bugs with cotton wool soaked in malathion.

Botrytis If the conditions in which the plant grows are cold, dank and shaded, it may develop mould. Remove badly affected leaves and spray the plant with dichloran.

Leaf problems Plants which are taken out-of-doors in summer are especially prone to damage from slugs and caterpillars which eat the leaves. Slug damage (**right**) is more serious than the less voracious attentions of the caterpillar (**above**). These creatures can find their way into the house even if the plant has not been outside. Cut away badly eaten leaves and remove all slugs from the plant.

107

Ferns

Fine foliage ferns

The finer foliaged ferns must rank among the oldest of houseplants, and they are as popular today as they were in the other heyday of indoor plants, the Victorian age, when they were well adapted to the relatively dark rooms of most homes. There are some varieties with silvery variegation to their foliage, but the vast majority are grown and enjoyed for their cool, soft greenery.

Coarse foliage ferns

It is probably more correct to say that these have large, rather than coarse, fronds as the Bird's Nest Fern, *Asplenium nidus avis*, has just about the smoothest and the most exquisite leaves of any green foliage plant. The Stagshorn Fern, *Platycerium alcicorne*, is coarser in appearance, on account of the waxy coating that completely covers the antler-shaped fronds. The asplenium has pale green fronds that in very mature specimen plants can be 3ft (1m) long arranged in the shape of a shuttlecock, and these can be a most impressive sight. As the name suggests, the Stagshorn Fern has decorative leaves that have a definite antler appearance to them. The fern also has anchor leaves which attach it to trees and other forms of aerial support, where the plant makes its natural home.

Healthy plants The Bird's Nest Fern, *Asplenium nidus avis,* (**above**) is one of the most popular varieties, its distinctive leaf pattern giving rise to its common name. Its fronds, which are undivided and glossy, spread themselves upwards to form a bowl shape, similar to that of a bird's nest. The fronds themselves are delicate during the first few weeks of growth and thus, since they can be easily damaged, should not be dusted. Mature fronds, however, benefit from an occasional dusting. The *Adiantum capillus-veneris,* or Venus Hair (**right**), is a beautiful, but delicate, plant, which must be looked after carefully, as it dislikes excessive heat, direct sunlight and a very dry atmosphere. It rarely grows higher than 12in (30cm).

AVOIDING PROBLEMS

Light and position

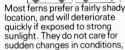

Most ferns prefer a fairly shady location, and will deteriorate quickly if exposed to strong sunlight. They do not care for sudden changes in conditions, abhor draughts and even those which like warm temperatures should not be placed near heating appliances.

Temperature range

Cool   Intermediate   Warm

There are a great number of different ferns and as a group they cover quite a wide range of preferred temperatures. In general, fine foliage ferns such as the nephrolepis and pteris need intermediate conditions of 55°-65°F (13°-18°C). The ferns with coarser foliage, such as the platyceriums, require more warmth, in a range of 60°-70°F (15°-21°C). Some ferns are quite hardy but are happiest in a humid atmosphere.

Watering

Ferns enjoy moisture on the foliage and can be sprayed quite generously. Watering should be frequent to help maintain humidity, but the plant container should not be allowed to become waterlogged. Avoid overwatering especially in lower temperatures.

Feeding

Feed the plants with weak liquid fertilizer at every watering while they are active and producing new foliage. Little or no food is needed in the winter.

Seasonal care

Winter   Spring   Summer   Autumn

The plants must be kept moist throughout the year and may prefer to be given rainwater. Although you must guard against overwatering, it is also important to take care that the roots are not allowed to dry out. Thorough cleaning in the centre of each plant during the autumn will reduce problems with rotting leaves which clog the plant and make it unsightly.

Soil

An open, peaty mixture is essential to the well-being of all types of ferns. The containers must be well-drained and a plant which is newly potted should be wetted mainly on the leaves and the soil kept only just moist.

VARIETIES AND PURCHASING

Though flowerless, ferns are extremely popular houseplants. The family consists of many different varieties, with common characteristics. Their method of reproduction is unusual; unlike most other plants, they reproduce by means of spores, rather than flowers or seeds. Ferns can be bought in many sizes, but, whatever their size, they will grow at a prodigious pace, given suitable conditions. Small plants, therefore, can be just as good a buy as large ones. Check any plant carefully before you buy it. The leaves should be fresh and green. Any plant with dry and shrivelled foliage should be passed over, although browning of leaf ends is only a sign that the plant was allowed to become too dry at some time and is not, in itself, a reason not to buy it. Watch out for signs of scale insects and mealy bugs, the chief pests. Their presence is normally easily detectable if you examine the leaves. Any asplenium should be checked for blemishes along the margins of its leaves, as these are very susceptible to damage. The anchor fronds of a platycerium should be green, fresh and not dried out; the latter is a sign of neglect. All ferns prefer shaded locations and quickly deteriorate if exposed to strong sunlight. Avoid draughts and do not position them near heating appliances. Grouping plants together is a good idea; they will invariably grow and look better.

Blechnum Many different varieties of fern are included in this genus, ranging from small creepers through to upright plants with small trunks. The most popular is *B.gibbum,* an attractive plant with a tidy rosette of fronds crowning its trunk. Other popular versions are *B.brasiliense,* whose pinnae are copper-coloured when young, turning green as the plant ages, and *B.occidentale.*

Pellaea rotundifolia The Button Fern is one of the two species of pellaea grown as houseplants. The other is *P. viridis* or Green Cliffbrake. The former's fronds arch downwards, carrying pairs of button-like pinnae. *P. viridis* has a bushy look.

Cyrtomium falcatum The Holly Fern is extremely decorative and long-lasting.

Phyllitis Only one species, the Hart's Tongue Fern, is commonly grown as a houseplant.

Polypodium The fronds of *P. aureum* rise from a long rhizome part-embedded in the potting mixture.

Davallia Two popular varieties are *D.canariensis* and *D.fejeensis.* The rhizomes are furry and will spread over the pot so that it is hidden.

Platycerium alcicorne The easiest of this family to grow indoors, it needs to be acclimatized gradually. It does best growing on bark or in a basket.

Pteris Three species do well as houseplants – *P. cretica, P. ensiformis* and *P. tremula.*

Blechnum

Cyrtomium

Phyllitis

Pellaea

Davallia fejeensis

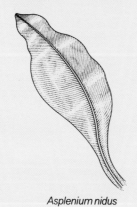
Asplenium nidus

Types of fern The possibilities of the fern family are almost endless. Many varieties are available in addition to the ones illustrated here; the commonest include the adiantum, asplenium, blechnum, cyrtomium, davallia, nephrolepis, pellaea, phyllitis, platycerium, polypodium, polystichum and pteris ferns. Because they invariably grow in places sheltered from direct sunlight in the wild, they thrive in places in the home where other houseplants are prone to languish. They like normal room temperatures, though high humidity is essential, as a surprising amount of water can be lost through the fronds of a fern in room conditions.

Polypodium

Davallia

Platycerium

Pteris

Three favourite ferns

Nephrolepis exaltata (**top**) is a splendid specimen, recognizable by its distinctive feathery appearance. It is seen at its best growing in a hanging basket or in a large pot, positioned on a pedestal. The best-known variety is the Boston Fern. The fronds can grow to a length of 6ft (2m). Another popular version is *N. cordofilia,* the Erect Swordfern. *Adiantum capillus-veneris* (**centre**), the Venus Hair, is one of the best-known of all the pot ferns. The triangular green fronds are comprised of fan-shaped, fragile pinnae. Though the Venus Hair likes a humid atmosphere, take care not to overwater it; it should be kept only slightly moist at the rootball. Other varieties of maidenhair ferns include *A. hispidulum, A. raddianum* and *A. tenerum. Microlepia speluncia* (**bottom**) is a new coarse fern raised in Holland. It should be treated in the same way as the nephrolepis ferns. They grow well in normal room temperatures, though the roots must never be allowed to become dry; the potting mixture should be kept moist. In common with nephrolepis ferns, cut out any unusual rogue fronds if they appear. This is a sign that the variety is reverting to the base species.

PESTS AND DISEASES

Coarse foliage ferns are relatively easy to care for, being less temperamental than some houseplants. Remember that an open, peaty potting mixture is essential and that pots and containers must be well drained, Some varieties, notably the platycerium, like to be rooted in bark. Do this by wrapping the roots in sphagnum moss soaked with liquid fertilizer. The roots can be attached easily to the bark and, eventually, will cling naturally by their anchor fronds. Such plants make very fine specimens indeed. They are watered by plunging the plant and anchorage into a bucket to soak them thoroughly. With all coarse foliage varieties, use rainwater for preference, plus a weak, liquid feed. When the plant is well soaked, allow it to dry out a little before repeating the process. At no time should the roots be allowed to become excessively dry. All fine foliage ferns prefer shaded locations and quickly deteriorate if exposed to strong sunlight. Keep the plants moist at all times; in dry conditions, it is a help if plant pots can be plunged up to their rims in moist peat. It is important to maintain humidity in the surrounding atmosphere, though the potting medium should never be allowed to become sodden for a long period. Feed weak liquid fertilizer at every watering while the plants are producing new foliage. A peaty, open mixture should be used at every stage of potting, following which, the soil and the foliage of plants should be well watered with a fine rose. Guard against too wet winter conditions when temperatures are low. A thorough cleaning out of the centres of plants each autumn will reduce the risk of leaves rotting and falling off.

Scale insect These present by far the most serious problem, as far as pests are concerned, since they can soon infest plants if left unchecked. To start with, they mostly trouble the reverse sides of the leaves. These should therefore be examined carefully as a matter of routine, so that remedial action can be taken at the earliest possible stage. Chemical treatment is best, but check carefully first to make sure the necessary insecticide, diazinon or malathion for example, will not damage the plant itself, as many of the ferns are sensitive to chemicals. Treat a specimen section of the plant to see if there is any reaction. The fronds of the asplenium can be wiped gently with a damp cloth to remove scales; this, however, is not recommended for the wax-covered fronds of the platycerium. When treating fine foliage ferns, wipe the insects carefully off the infected plant; brown scales may be scraped with a thumbnail. Again, check the insecticide is suitable before using it on the whole plant. Test a leaf, waiting about 10 days to see the result.

Mealy bug This is a less serious problem. The bugs can be eradicated by soaking a cotton wool bud in methylated spirits and dabbing directly onto the powdery white adult bugs. Take care also to treat the young bugs in their waxy white protective coverings. Mealy bugs are difficult to locate in older, fine foliage ferns. Part the foliage for close inspection and, if bugs are present, remove them as for the coarse ferns.

Unhealthy and healthy ferns

The asplenium (**left**) has been affected dramatically by a sudden change in its environment. Though most ferns are relatively easy to look after, careful observance of a few simple rules will ensure your plants remain healthy throughout their lives. Keep the room temperature constant, if possible, avoiding extremes of either hot or cold. If the temperature rises above 70°F (21°C), remember to increase the humidity. A simple way to achieve this is to spray the plants with water. If the temperature falls below about 60°F (15°C), reduce watering accordingly. With an asplenium, remember it is important to water plentifully during active growth, but that afterwards less is required. The fronds of a nephrolepis fern (**below**) illustrate a common cause of confusion. The top illustration shows scale, which should be treated with an insecticide; the bottom one shows brown areas, which are often thought to be scale insects, but, in fact, are spores.

Three common problems The adiantum (**far left**) is under-watered, while the plant (**left**) is overwatered. The trick with these ferns is to keep them only slightly moist at their roots; if the rootball is allowed to dry out and the plant is then overwatered to compensate for this, the results can be disastrous. When watering, try to control it, so that the plant is given sufficient water to moisten the potting mixture throughout its depth, but ensure that the top layer of the mixture dries out before watering is repeated. The asplenium (**right**) is suffering from slug damage. This is a common problem that can affect all plants, but is minor compared to the two other pests that can attack ferns — mealy bugs and scale insects. The marks are not only damaging, but also unsightly. Usually, the smooth pale green shuttlecock leaves of the *Asplenium nidus avis* place it among the cream of potted plants.

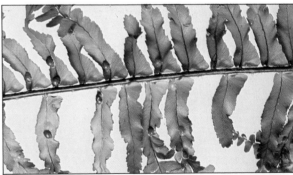

Ficus

Many houseplants are drawn from this diverse family of plants whether they are large, small or creeping. Most have green foliage, although there are some variegated forms which have a limited degree of popularity. All are propagated by means of cuttings of one kind or another, and need temperatures of around 70°F (21°C) to get them under way.

The leaves of the *F. benjamina* have a weeping habit and can be most attractive in many settings—especially placed over water by an indoor pool. The plant's small, oval-shaped, glossy green leaves are produced in abundance, and lost in abundance as well if the light levels are inadequate.

New plants are made by removing tip cuttings that are reasonably firm and about 4in (10cm) in length. In moist peat and a temperature of 70°F (21°C) rooting is not too difficult.

The well-known ubiquitous Rubber Plant is one of the most popular houseplants. *F. robusta* is the name of the modern version of an earlier plant, *F. elastica*, which has long been discontinued. The Rubber Plant today is a much tougher individual than its predecessor and is more able to withstand the vicissitudes of life in the home.

New plants are raised from cuttings prepared from individual leaves with a small section of stem attached, and, as a rule, are inserted in the autumn when plants are either dormant or at least less active. For rooting, a temperature of around 70°F (21°C) is needed.

VARIETIES AND PURCHASING

Because there are so many varieties of ficus, there is sure to be one to fit each personal requirement. When purchasing, look for clean, blemish-free leaves. The plants should have a little sparkle to them too. Those with dull and dowdy foliage will have less chance of surviving when introduced to the conditions of the average living room. Look also for missing leaves which are a sign of old age and poor culture. Besides *F. benjamina* and *F. robusta,* the most popular varieties, there are other members of the ficus family which make excellent houseplants.

F. 'Europa' This cream and green variegated form of the Rubber Plant is one of the most attractive of all the many ficus plants.

F. pumila This is also called the Creeping or Climbing Fig. It has little in common with the other plants being a small, creeping variety with thin, heart-shaped leaves which are usually pale green. *F. pumila* is generally used as a trailing plant, and it grows very well in moist, shady locations.

F. lyrata The Fiddle Leaf Fig has violin-shaped leaves attached to woody stems. The plant can reach tree proportions in time, and will require regular pruning to keep it under control. It grows quickly and tends to stay on a single stem. In poor conditions, rapid shedding of the leaves will occur.

F. benghalensis The Banyan Tree is valued for its branching habit and dark, oval leaves which can grow to 1ft (30cm) in length.

F. retusa This ficus, the Indian Laurel may occasionally bear small inedible fruit. The plant has dark green, elliptical leaves which grow to about 3in (8cm) on stems which branch profusely.

F. rubiginosa This plant is the Rusty Fig, a small tree with leathery, oval leaves which are rust-coloured underneath. *F.r. 'Variegata'* has leaves which are marbled with yellow markings.

F. sagittata This is a good trailing plant with leaves 2-3in (6-8cm) long.

AVOIDING PROBLEMS *(GENERAL)*

Light and position

There are many ficus varieties, each requiring slightly different lighting and positioning. All, with the exception of *F. pumila,* require good light and shade from direct sun. Healthy specimens will grow quite large and thus need ample space and positioning.

Temperature range

Cool   Intermediate   Warm

All except *F. diversifolia* require a minimum temperature of 60°-70°F (15°-21°C). *F. diversifolia* can withstand temperatures down to 45°F (7°C), provided watering is infrequent. The maximum temperature for all these plants is 75°F (23°C).

Watering

None of these plants like to be overwatered. A symptom of overwatering is yellowing and falling leaves. Water twice a week in summer and once a week in winter. Never let a plant stand in a dish of water.

Feeding

Liquid fertilizer can be added to the water every few days during the active growth period. Generally, ficus plants should be given larger and stronger doses than those recommended by the manufacturer or retailer.

Seasonal care

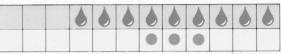

Winter   Spring   Summer   Autumn

All varieties need to be kept moist throughout the year, although less water is needed in winter than at other times. Water thoroughly and allow the soil to dry out before repeating. Repotting can be done annually in spring. Mature plants which do not need repotting can have the topsoil replenished. Prune the plant in spring and remember to dust the cuts with charcoal to prevent bleeding. As they age, some of these plants will develop aerial roots which should never be cut. Instead tie them back.

Soil

All large specimens need loam-based mixtures. The plants should be repotted when they have a solid rootball. Larger plants tend to push their roots through the pot bottom. Draw these back by carefully removing the rootball, pulling the roots with it.

AVOIDING PROBLEMS *(F. BENJAMINA)*

Light and position

F. benjamina is one species of the this family which requires plenty of light, but not direct

sunlight. If adequate light is not provided, the leaves will turn yellow and drop off.

Temperature range

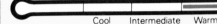

Cool   Intermediate   Warm

The Weeping Fig is happiest in temperatures between 65°-70°F (18°-21°C). The maximum temperature it will tolerate is 75°F

(23°C). This plant does not like draughts, so if near a window, make sure there are no cold breezes coming through.

Watering

As with all the ficus varieties, *F. benjamina* should not be overwatered or the leaves will inevitably go yellow and drop off.

Water no more than twice a week in summer and every 7 - 10 days in winter.

Feeding

Established plants will need copious feeding in whatever form you choose. Less feeding is required in winter, but plants that

continue to produce new growth will need a small amount even at this time.

Seasonal care

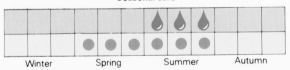

Winter   Spring   Summer   Autumn

Liquid fertilizer should be added to the water during the active growth period. A daily spraying of water will benefit this plant throughout the year. Repot once a year at most in the spring. Mature

plants need not be repotted but can have the topsoil replenished. Prune in spring but do not remove any aerial shoots. The plant can be propagated from stem cuttings taken in the spring.

Soil

Like many of the strong ficus plants, this will soon push its roots through the bottom of the pot. Withdraw the plant from its pot and carefully tease back the

roots through the drainage holes. When the rootball is a mass of roots, repot in a loam-based mixture.

AVOIDING PROBLEMS *(F. ROBUSTA)*

Light and position

Although the Rubber Plant will tolerate fairly shady conditions, it grows more quickly in good light. It will also benefit from direct sunlight for a few hours a day.

F. robusta prefers cool environments to dry and hot, otherwise it is a very adaptable plant.

Temperature range

Cool   Intermediate   Warm

Temperatures between 50°-60°F (10°-15°C) are best, but the Rubber Plant will tolerate a minimum of 40°F (4.5°C) in winter.

In very hot rooms, above 85°F (29°C), the leaves tend to lose their turgid appearance.

Watering

With most houseplants, the temptation is to overwater. This is one plant that should never be overwatered. In

winter the soil should be just moist, and in summer water twice a week at most.

Feeding

When plants are first purchased and brought indoors they should be fed immediately. Feeding should continue thereafter using a weak fertilizer with each

watering. Less is needed in winter. Plants which have just been repotted need no food for at least three months.

Seasonal care

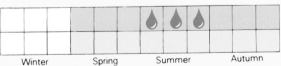

Winter   Spring   Summer   Autumn

Overgrown, larger plants can be pruned in autumn by cutting through the stem just above the leaf. Check the resultant flow of sap by covering the wound with moist peat. Clean the leaves

periodically with leaf cleaner, but avoid frequent use of chemicals; wiping with a damp sponge is usually sufficient. Less watering is required in winter when the plant is inactive.

Soil

A loam-based houseplant mixture is essential. Once in pots 7in (17cm) in diameter, sustain with regular feedings. The plant should be well rooted before repotting.

Water after potting and keep on the dry side for one month afterwards to allow the plant to root in the new soil.

Healthy plant Along with the ubiquitous Spider Plant, *F. robusta*, the Rubber Plant, (**left**) is the most popular houseplant today. The central stem usually grows straight, but branching can be induced by cutting off new growth. When purchasing, the leaves should be free from blemishes, dark green, shiny, and leathery in texture.

F. 'Europa' (**above**) has cream and green variegated leaves. The leaves of *F. robusta* (**below**) are thick and leathery with prominent midribs.

F. benjamina, the Weeping Fig (**below**), grows into a large, graceful tree. As it grows, its 'weeping' appearance becomes more pronounced. The plant does not have a definite rest period, but its leaves often turn yellow and drop off in winter. The leaves of *F. benjamina* (**left**) are 3-4in (6-10cm) long. They are light green when young, and they darken with age.

The common name of *F. lyrata,* the Fiddle Leaf Fig (**above**), is well expressed by its violin-shaped leaves (**left**). *F. pumila* (**below**) is a compact plant with branching leaves which tend to creep. It is also attractive if trained onto a pole.

PESTS AND DISEASES

All these plants can contract pests and diseases, but which type will depend on the individual plant.

Scale insect These can become a major problem if left unchecked to go about their destructive business. Black, crusty adult scale insects, or softer, flesh-coloured young insects attach themselves to leaves, branches, and almost every other part of the plant. *F. benjamina* is especially prone to these pests, so check the undersides of leaves frequently. For minor attacks, wipe the pests forcibly with malathion. More stubborn adults may need the encouragement of a thumb-nail to dislodge them. Control bad attacks with thorough and repeated saturation with malathion.

Mealy bug These usually appear on older plants and can be removed by spraying or wiping with malathion.

Root rot This is aggravated when roots are deprived of oxygen which in turn is caused by soil that is too wet and does not allow air to penetrate it. Because the plant is deprived of moisture and nutrition, the roots will turn brown and lifeless and the plant will shed its foliage. Let the soil dry out thoroughly so the plant may produce new roots. The obvious precaution is never to overwater the plant nor let the plant stay wet for long periods of time.

Mealy bug When found on a *F. lyrata* leaf (**above**) mealy bugs will lodge in the veins of the leaf. Saturate the leaf with a sponge soaked in malathion or methylated spirits.

Sooty mould Dark mould on a *F. benjamina* leaf (**left**) grows on the excreta of scale insects into which fungus mould then settles. To cure, wipe the leaves clean with soapy water. Scale insects (**above**) are either black and crusty as adults, or flesh-coloured when young. They will attach themselves anywhere on the plant. Sponge away with an insecticide. Root rot (**right**) tends to make the leaves yellow and eventually fall. Let the plant dry out thoroughly and do not overwater it in future.

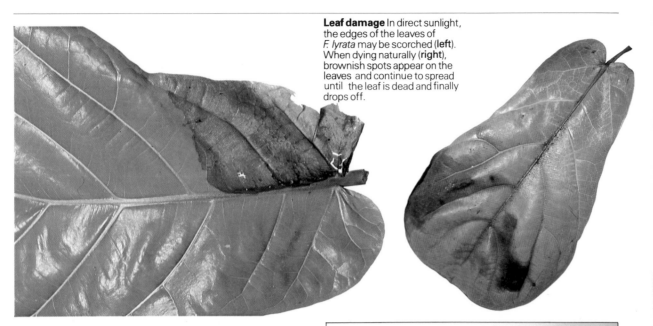

Leaf damage In direct sunlight, the edges of the leaves of *F. lyrata* may be scorched (**left**). When dying naturally (**right**), brownish spots appear on the leaves and continue to spread until the leaf is dead and finally drops off.

Underwatering To maintain healthy, lush growth, *F. pumila* (**above**) needs careful watering. Never allow the plant to become too dry or the paper-thin leaves will shrivel. Allow only the top ½in (12.5mm) of soil to become dry between waterings.

Overwatering This is a common mistake with *F. robusta* (**right**). A symptom of overwatering is drooping, lifeless leaves which will soon turn yellow and drop off. These plants need only moderate watering, even in active growth.

Fittonia

Both in appearance and habit fittonias are among the most delicate of all foliage plants. Originating from tropical South America, they produce insignificant dull yellow bracts, their main attraction being colourful, delicately veined foliage.

New plants are raised from cuttings taken during the warmer months of the year and placed in temperatures of around 70°F (21°C). The propagating mix is peat and sand, and moist, humid conditions should be the grower's aim.

Healthy plant Two species of fittonia are sold – *F. argyroneura* and *F. verschaffeltii.* The first has olive green leaves patterned with delicate silver veins; the second is veined in red or pink. A variety of the first, *F.a. 'Nana'* has silvery green leaves with strong white veining. Healthy plants are bushy. Avoid those with curling or dropping leaves.

Botrytis This fungus (right) is caused by cold damp conditions. Leaves that are badly affected develop a brown wet rot. Remove these leaves and treat the rest of the plant and those close to it with diazinon fungicide. Then check for warmth and good drainage.

PESTS AND DISEASES

Aphids These may attack the bracts and young shoots but can easily be cleared by spraying with pyrethrum or a systemic insecticide.
Red spider mite These pests may affect plants growing in very hot and dry conditions. Spray the plant with insecticide, especially the undersides of the leaves.

AVOIDING PROBLEMS

Light and position

This plant is that unusual specimen which actually enjoys a shady position. Although it will grow in reasonable light, it cannot abide direct sun or even too much indirect light. However, it is also damaged by exposure to draughts.

Temperature range

Cool   Intermediate   Warm

The fittonia must have warm temperatures, a minimum of 65°F (18°C) and preferably surroundings of 70°F (21°C). It will also tolerate higher summer temperatures, but it is then vital to keep up a high level of humidity. The plant appreciates an overhead spray with tepid water in any season.

Watering

The soil must be kept moist at all times, although the fittonia will require less water during the winter when it is inactive. To keep up humidity, stand the pot on a tray of damp pebbles, but make sure the base is not actually sitting in water.

Feeding

Feeding is not essential in this case, but a weak liquid feed with every watering will keep the plant in good condition. Stop feeding it altogether when it is dormant in winter.

Seasonal care

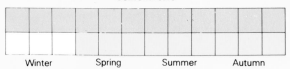

Winter   Spring   Summer   Autumn

If the conditions in which the plant is kept are naturally dry, especially in the summer, create humidity by placing the pot on a tray of damp pebbles and moisten the fittonia with an overhead spray. Otherwise it will simply wilt, but if it does so, it should revive without further harm when watered. Stem tip cuttings can be taken in spring and must be raised in a temperature of 75°F (23°C).

Soil

This plant prefers a small, shallow pot and potting on is seldom required more often than every other year. Use a potting mixture with a good proportion of peat and repot during the summer months.

Grevillea robusta

With the cost of larger plants ever on the increase, it is surprising that this plant is not much more popular than it is. Easily raised from seed it will develop into a plant of considerable height in only a few years, reaching tree proportions in eight to 10 years. By removing the top section of the plant, it can be reduced in height at almost any time. A further advantage is that it not only tolerates cooler conditions, but actually prefers them to warmer temperatures. The leaves are fern-like and have a silky sheen to them, hence the common name. *G. robusta* is indigenous to Australia and although there are other varieties, this one is the best and the most easily obtained.

Healthy plant *G. robusta,* the Silk Oak, is a fast-growing, evergreen plant. The foliage, which is dark green, tinged with brown when the leaves are young, has a downy upper surface, silky to the touch. These plants go well in a mixed pot with other plants when young while they still resemble ferns. In a few years, however, they can reach 6 ft (2m) and will need a sturdy pot of their own. Plants grown indoors will not produce flowers but will provide a pleasant feature for any cool room.

PESTS AND DISEASES

Red spider mite These can best be avoided by inspecting the undersides of the leaves at regular intervals with a magnifying glass. If the plant is affected, spray with insecticide or, if necessary, cut away the damaged leaves.

Sciarid fly This is a kind of fungus gnat which nests in the potting mixture and is not particularly harmful. The flies are black and can be cleared by watering the soil with malathion.

AVOIDING PROBLEMS

Light and position

Good light is essential to the grevillea, but it should be shielded from direct sun if in a window. It grows to quite a height and can be placed anywhere in a light, airy room, but in poor light it will shed some of the lower leaves.

Temperature range

Cool	Intermediate	Warm

Cool, but not draughty, conditions are required and extremes of temperature can kill the plant. Somewhere in the range 45°-55°F (7°-13°C) is suitable. At the other extreme, hot sun can scorch the leaves of the plant, leaving unpleasant brown marks, and in high summer the temperature in a sunny window may be far too high.

Watering

The grevillea dislikes extremes of any kind and it should be thoroughly but not excessively watered and allowed to dry out slightly before watering is repeated. However, at no time should the soil be allowed to dry out completely.

Feeding

Once established, the grevillea is a vigorous plant which requires regular feeding. The amount of fertilizer recommended by the manufacturer can be increased or administered more frequently, as the plant will respond well to a strong feed.

Seasonal care

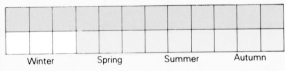

Winter	Spring	Summer	Autumn

The plant does not need any particular seasonal attention, but in common with many others, it is less active in winter and feeding can be decreased or stopped for a while until growth is stimulated once again. Overgrown plants can be trimmed back at any time, but should not be cut right down.

Soil

The soil should be a loam-based mixture with plenty of body to sustain the plant over a long period. Increase the pot sizes progressively and crock the bottom of a large container. The plant may remain in one pot for three years

● ● ●

Ivy

Hedera

These are among the most popular of plants sold for indoor decoration, although they are not particularly suited to rooms that are heated. Perhaps one of their most appealing qualities is that once they appear to have failed indoors, they can be planted out in the garden where they are likely to flourish.

There are many different varieties and almost all of them are propagated from easily rooted cuttings taken during the spring and summer months. Firm pieces of stem with two sound leaves attached are put into small pots filled with peaty compost and placed in a close atmosphere at a temperature in the region of 65°–70°F (18°–21°C). Several cuttings should be inserted in each pot to ensure that the eventual plant looks quite bushy.

Healthy plant When choosing hederas, avoid those that look dehydrated and have a number of dead leaves gathered at the base of the plant.
H. canariensis (**above**) is a tall species that can be grown quite easily. If you want the plant to become more bushy, pinch out the growing tips as they develop.

VARIETIES AND PURCHASING

Never buy an Ivy with long lengths of leafless stem at the top of each stalk, as this indicates the plant has already been attacked by pests. What is more, all the other plants in the shop are likely to be infested as well. There are only a few hedera species, but there are many varieties which have a wide range of leaves (**see illustration below**).

H. canariensis This is one of the tallest plants. It has large leaves 5in (12.5cm) long and 6in (15cm) wide which are the shape of a rounded triangle. The leaves are dark green with pale green veins. There is also a variegated form called *'Gloire de Marengo'* which has leaves bordered in cream and blotched with grey-green.

H. helix This is the English Ivy of which there are many varieties. Its familiarly shaped leaves have three or five lobes.

H.h. 'Chicago' This has medium-sized green leaves. There is a variegated form *H.h. 'Chicago Variegata'* which has creamy-bordered leaves.

It is a little more difficult to manage but worth growing as it is a very colourful plant.

H.h. 'Glacier' This is perhaps the hardiest of all the variegated Ivies. It has light and dark grey colouring.

H.h. 'Little Diamond' This also has grey coloured variegated foliage. Its leaves are a particularly pleasing diamond shape. The stems have a twisting appearance.

H.h. 'Sagittaefolia' As its name, derived from the Latin for 'arrow', suggests, the dark green leaves of this Ivy are arrow-shaped. There is also a variegated form, *H.h. 'Sagittaefolia Variegata'* which has green and pale yellow leaves. This makes an excellent trailing plant.

H. ivalace This hedera has glistening green leaves and reddish-brown stems. It is excellent for both indoor and outdoor use. It is seen to its best effect when grown as a hanging plant in the window of a cool room or out-of-doors on a sheltered patio where there are no cold winds.

PESTS AND DISEASES

Black spot Ivies are particularly susceptible to this. It will appear on plants that have been kept crowded together or in very damp conditions. It is a damaging fungus which should be treated immediately with a reliable fungicide.

Thrips These insects, which are also called thunderflies, are sometimes present in Ivies. They can be detected by grey streaking on the softer leaves. Remove any very badly damaged leaves, and spray thoroughly with an insecticide such as pyrethrum.

Scale insect These will lodge on the stem of the plant, or under its leaves. They should be wiped off with a wad of cotton wool soaked in methylated spirits, after which the whole plant should be treated with pesticide.

Aphids One of the most common houseplant pests, aphids may be detected on the leaves. Treat with a systemic insecticide. Aphids may also spread virus.

Unhealthy plant
If an Ivy is allowed to get too dry, it will become withered and unattractive (**left**). To cure this, mist the plant daily with water and move it to a cooler position. Light brown discoloration of the foliage and a dry appearance (**below**) suggests that red spider mites are present. The grey furry blotching (**below**) is caused by botrytis which should be treated with a fungicide.

AVOIDING PROBLEMS

Light and position

Ivies require light, cool environments. If poorly lit, variegated types will lose their colouring and should thus have 2-3 hours of sunlight each day. Keep other types out of direct sunlight and away from dry heat which can encourage red spider mites.

Temperature range

Cool   Intermediate   Warm

Ivies are generally sturdy enough to withstand a broad range of temperatures but they do not like wide fluctuations. Most respond well to temperatures between 50°-60°F (10°-15°C).

In temperatures higher than 65°F (18°C), provide a moist environment. In winter, let the plants rest in a cool temperature of 50°F (10°C).

Watering

Keep the compost moist in summer with regular waterings. In winter, water sparingly but do not let the compost dry out. Ivies like humidity, especially if the atmosphere is dry, as in summer. Mist frequently at these times, and also in winter if the room is dry and warm.

Feeding

Ivies are not fussy about feeding, and any fertilizer recommended by the manufacturer may be used. Feed actively growing plants with a standard liquid fertilizer every two weeks. Most Ivies grow prodigiously without assistance, so feeding may not be necessary.

Seasonal care

Winter	Spring	Summer	Autumn

In their growth period, Ivies can create dense foliage which should be cleaned out in autumn and spring by removing all dead or dying undergrowth. Water frequently in all seasons except winter when the soil should be kept fairly dry. Repot Ivies every two years in the spring in pots no larger than 5-6in (10-15cm) in diameter. Plants which are not repotted should have the top layer of compost replenished annually.

Soil

Peaty compost mixtures tend to produce soft growth, so use a mixture which contains enough loam to sustain the plant over a long period. This will also eliminate the need for frequent repotting. Tip cuttings should be potted in a mixture of moistened peat moss and coarse sand.

Heptapleurum

This little known plant came on the houseplant scene not much more than a decade ago and has made a considerable impression, as it is elegant, free-growing and reasonably easy to care for. There is a variegated form and also varieties with smaller leaves, but they all grow in a similar way. Naturally glossy green leaves, elliptic in shape, are arranged like fingers on slender stalks attached to a stout central stem. By removing the growing tip at an early age, plants may be encouraged to branch quite freely and take on a very bushy form. Alternatively, they can be left to grow on, in which case they simply extend to about 8–10ft (3m) as slender specimens.

Stem cuttings can be rooted in a temperature of around 70°F (21°C) if the conditions are close and moist. At potting time, three plants put into a 5in (12·5cm) pot will provide plants of considerable beauty as they mature.

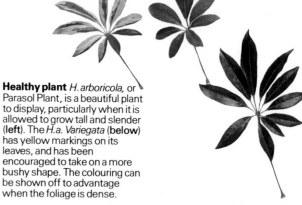

Healthy plant *H. arboricola*, or Parasol Plant, is a beautiful plant to display, particularly when it is allowed to grow tall and slender (**left**). The *H.a. Variegata* (**below**) has yellow markings on its leaves, and has been encouraged to take on a more bushy shape. The colouring can be shown off to advantage when the foliage is dense.

AVOIDING PROBLEMS

Light and position

All heptapleurums require good light. At least two to three hours a day are needed, but avoid direct sunlight. If lighting is poor, the leaves will grow abnormally long. Position the plant well away from radiators, draughts, and cold windows and doorways.

Temperature range

Cool   Intermediate   Warm

H. arboricola requires a minimum temperature of 60°F (15°C) all year long, and a maximum temperature of 70°F (21°C). In winter, keep the plant warm at not less than 60°F (15°C).

Heptapleurums also enjoy a moist, humid environment which can be created by standing the plants on trays of pebbles covered with water.

Watering

H. arboricola needs moderate watering. Allow the top inch (2.5cm) of soil to dry out between waterings. The soil should not dry out more than this, nor should it be watered so that it is thoroughly wetted. The plants also enjoy frequent misting.

Feeding

Do not overfeed. Feed only when the plants are well rooted in their pots. This can be determined by turning the plant out of its pot to check the amount of root growth. A standard fertilizer may be used every two weeks from spring until late autumn.

Seasonal care

Winter   Spring   Summer   Autumn

Heptapleurums should never be overwatered, but they should be watered more frequently during the active growth period between spring and summer. In spring the plants should be moved to pots 2in (5cm) larger. Continue to repot during the growth period as required. The plants can be propagated in spring from tip or stem cuttings.

Soil

Peat mixtures with a small amount of loam are best. Press the mixture down firmly in the pot, but not too tightly. Before repotting, make sure the plants have enough root growth to justify the move. When propagating, plant cuttings in a mixture of moistened peat moss and coarse sand.

Stem rot This can affect Parasol Plants causing them to become slimy, black and rotten near the base (**above**). The leaves will start to drop off as the condition becomes worse. Stem rot is usually brought on by overwatering, and there is no easy cure. If the rotten section is fairly high up the stem however, the top half of the plant can be cut off in the hope that the remaining healthy stem will sprout again. Heptapleurums will become droopy and discoloured if they are overwatered (**left**).

PESTS AND DISEASES

Aphids These occasionally attack young leaves and cause spotting. They can be controlled by using one of the many effective insecticides.
Mealy bug This is normally only found on larger plants with a tangled mass of growth in which it can go undetected. Spray thoroughly with insecticide or wipe bugs off the plant with a sponge that has been soaked in methylated spirits. Large yellow blotches often appear on the topmost leaves of heptapleurums. There is no simple explanation or cure, but fortunately most plants seem to grow out of this condition.
Red spider mite These may attack heptapleurums, particularly if the surroundings are unusually hot or dry. They are very small, and hard to detect with the naked eye as a result. Light brown leaf discoloration is a sign of their presence, which can be confirmed by thorough scrutiny of the undersides of the leaves with a magnifying glass. Treat with insecticide.

Hibiscus rosa sinensis

This is another much improved potted plant for indoor decoration, owing much of its undoubted success in recent years to the scientist rather than the grower of the plants. The discovery of growth-retarding chemicals has made it possible to grow these plants so that they can be in full flower when they are little more than 15in (38cm) high. This makes them ideal for the average room, ideal for handling and packing, and ideal in that they require less heated space on the benches in the greenhouse than many other houseplants. *H. rosa-sinensis* is woody, has glossy green leaves, and produces quite superb flowers in both single and double forms.

VARIETIES AND PURCHASING

H rosa-sinensis (see illustration below) This is the original Rose of China from which many hybrids have been produced. The flowers may be crimson, pink, yellow or white, and have long golden stamens.
H.r-s 'Cooperi' This is a variety of the Rose of China. Its leaves have olive green, pink and white markings and its flowers are red.
H. schizopetalus This is the Japanese hibiscus. Its delicate stems support orange-red flowers.
'Hawaiian hybrids' This group of hibiscus all have very large flowers. They include *'Surfrider,' 'Elegance'* and *'Firefly'*.

Healthy leaves Despite the differences in shape, these four leaves all came from the same plant.

Healthy plant A hibiscus (**below**) has glossy leaves and brilliant flowers. The leaves should grow right down to the top of the pot. When choosing one, check the buds and undersides of the leaves for aphids.

Dehydrated plant This hibiscus has not been given enough water with the result that the leaves are wilting.

Aphids These insects will attack both the buds and the open flowers, as well as the upper leaves. Remove aphids by running a finger and thumb along the plant, but if the attack is severe, immerse the plant in insecticide.

AVOIDING PROBLEMS

Light and position

In common with all flowering pot plants, the hibiscus needs very good light to retain its buds and go on to produce a satisfactory flowering. Keep the plant away from draughts and any place in the home which is likely to have sudden changes of temperature.

Temperature range

Cool   Intermediate   Warm

The plant prefers an even, moderate temperature of around 60°F (15°C) although the range in which it can exist without problems is 55°-65°F (13°-18°C). Any radical change in the temperature to either end of the scale may damage the plant and cause the buds to drop.

Watering

Water the plant well during dry weather and evenly all year round, allowing the top of the compost to dry before watering again. Do not make the plant waterlogged or the roots will rot. When the plant is in bud, it benefits from a daily overhead spray.

Feeding

Feed the hibiscus with weak liquid fertilizer, given at each watering, while the plant is in active growth. This can be discontinued in winter while the plant is resting.

Seasonal care

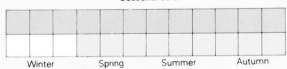

Winter   Spring   Summer   Autumn

When the plant is being well watered in the summer months, it is important that it should drain quickly through the soil when applied at the surface. In winter, even though the compost is kept at the right moisture content, some leaves will fall from the plant, but the new growth in spring refurbishes it. Pruning is only needed if growth is really out of hand and is best done when the plant has just finished flowering.

Soil

The hibiscus does not do well in peaty compost, but will enjoy a loam-based potting mixture. Pot the plant into a slightly larger pot each spring. It is not good practice to transfer a small, new plant into a large pot and wait for it to fill it.

127

Hydrangea macrophylla

Hydrangeas are available in the spring in white, pink and blue, the latter in fact being pink plants artificially treated with alum to persuade them to change colour. Blues will often vary, sometimes being nothing more than washed-out pink. This happens when the colouring chemical is used incorrectly. These plants will be out-of-doors most of the year, coming inside in the middle of winter to be forced into flower. If they are to do well for years after they have been bought, hydrangeas should be out-of-doors all summer, coming into a cool place in autumn, then to a warmer place in mid winter to encourage flowering for the spring.

VARIETIES AND PURCHASING

Plants are available from early until late spring. Look for fresh, green colouring and sturdy leaves. Avoid plants that are thin and weak with discoloured foliage. Multi-headed plants are usually the better buy. Try to obtain plants with both flowers and buds.

Hydrangeas are not usually offered by name but by colour and general appearance. *H. macrophylla* One of the best varieties for growing indoors, this has much larger flowers than other types. The flowers are either pink, red, blue, or deep blue.

Healthy plant Hydrangeas are attractive flowering plants but they need careful attention. The many different colours of the plant flowers are produced by the acidity of the soil in which they are grown. By changing the acid content, the owner can alter the colour of the flowers to blue (**see illustration above**), purple, pink, red, or deep blue. A group of hydrangeas in individual pots of differing soil can be placed in a large tub to produce a delightful rainbow of colours.

PESTS AND DISEASES

Aphids These are found on softer leaves and should be treated with an insecticide.
Red spider mite These appear on the undersides of leaves. In time, the mites produce tiny webs. Remove the worst leaves and treat with pest control.
Mildew This is seen as a white, powdery deposit on the top of leaves. Remove the worst leaves and treat with a fungicide.
Botrytis This fungus develops in large, wet patches on the leaves. Remove affected leaves and spray with a solution of dichloran.

Underwatering This is easily detected in the hydrangea because its leaves are normally thick and healthy. The first signs of underwatering will appear on the edges of leaves which will turn brown and curl under (below). In extreme cases, (bottom), the whole plant will wilt dramatically. To revive, immerse the pot in water and continue watering at regular intervals.

AVOIDING PROBLEMS

Light and position

Hydrangeas prefer to be positioned in a light, cool place. Leaf scorch may result if the plant is placed too close to a window, but this is usually minimal. If put out-of-doors, keep in light shade.

Temperature range

Cool   Intermediate   Warm

Keep in fairly cool conditions of 50°-60°F (10°-15°C). This will ensure that the plant will go on flowering much longer than if placed in a hot, dry location. Avoid direct sunlight and heat. When properly situated, hydrangeas will produce abundant, lush growth.

Watering

During active growth, the plants will need frequent watering. Allow the topsoil to dry out before watering, but avoid letting the plants wilt. Pots should have large drainage holes and a healthy layer of crocks and rotted leaves to help retain moisture.

Feeding

Hydrangeas usually have an abundance of strong foliage and will need weekly feeding to keep them strong and healthy. The acid in some soil can cause the flowers to go blue; adding alum will ensure that the flowers remain blue and do not revert to pink.

Seasonal care

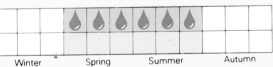

Winter   Spring   Summer   Autumn

Copious watering is required when the plants are in active growth, but none while the plants are in their dormant phase towards the end of the year. After flowering, shoots should be cut back to about half their length. Top sections of shoots that have not flowered can be treated in a heated propagator. The cuttings should have two leaves attached. Prune in early spring, removing any dead material, as well as dead flower heads.

Soil

Hydrangeas prefer heavier soil and a loam-based mixture is best. Pot in the spring when flowering is over. An all-purpose potting soil can be used. Make sure enough room is left at the top for heavy watering. The pots should also have good drainage.

Impatiens

This is another common plant that has undergone many changes in recent years. The plants today are generally more robust in habit, the flowers are more colourful and attractive, and the variegated foliage of many of the varieties is as colourful as the flowers. Cuttings about 4in (10cm) long, with the flowers removed, will root very readily either in water or in a peaty potting mixture. The cuttings should be provided with moist conditions, shade from the sun and a temperature in the region of 65°F (18°C). When the cuttings have rooted and started to grow, the tips should be removed to encourage branching.

Healthy plant Busy Lizzies are too often straggly, leggy plants with yellowing foliage and few flowers. A healthy plant (**below**) should be of compact shape, with glossy leaves and a profusion of bright flowers. When choosing one, make sure the leaves are clean and fresh, the flowers open, and lots of buds are visible. A well cared for Busy Lizzie will hardly ever stop flowering. Old plants tend to lose their beauty, so keep the stock fairly young, and be ruthless about pruning. The pathetic, straggling, limp Busy Lizzie is not a pleasant sight, but when in the peak of condition they are among the most attractive and cheering of houseplants.

VARIETIES AND PURCHASING

The Busy Lizzie is one of the most popular houseplants. Today there are many hybrids, which are compact plants with many flowers.

I. petersiana This one has burgundy-coloured foliage and rich red flowers. It grows to a height of 2-3ft (70cm-1m) and can attain a very attractive shape. It is rather prone to red spider mite and so the undersides of the leaves should be inspected carefully when buying.

I. wallerana It is from this species that many hybrids have been produced. It tends to grow too tall and droopy, unlike its descendents. The flowers of the hybrids can be all shades – white, pink, orange, or a combination of any two. Most of them do not have names but a few have been specially bred.

I. 'Red Magic' This is similar in appearance to *I. petersiana*. However, it is not as vulnerable to red spider. It usually grows to a height of 2ft (7cm) and has scarlet flowers. It is a hybrid of *I. wallerana*.

I. 'Arabesque' This is another hybrid of *I. wallerana*. Its leaves are veined with red and have yellow centres.

***I. 'New Guinea'* hybrids** These are the latest version of the Busy Lizzie. With their large flowers and vigorous growth, they are possibly the best buy, although they are slightly more expensive than the other varieties.

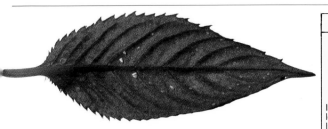

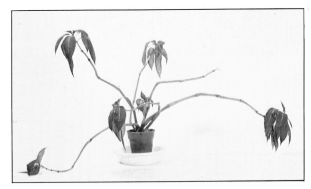

AVOIDING PROBLEMS

Light and position

If the Busy Lizzie is to produce a lot of flowers, it must have the lightest possible position although it is wise to protect it from very strong sunlight. It does not like draughts and will not do well in a shady position.

Temperature range

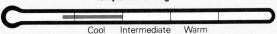

Cool   Intermediate   Warm

The Busy Lizzie will not flourish in temperatures below 55°F (13°C). Normal room temperatures are ideal. It may be possible to put the plant outside in summer, provided it is in a warm and sheltered spot. At very high temperatures over 75°F (23°C) the plant needs a humid atmosphere, so stand it on a tray of damp pebbles or moss.

Watering

The Busy Lizzie should be given moderate amounts of water at rest times, and plentiful supplies while it is growing. Never let the potting mixture dry out, and never let the plant stand in water for too long.

Feeding

This vigorous plant responds well to liberal feeding. During the spring and summer, which are periods of fast growth, it can be fed once a week with a standard fertilizer. Extend the interval to three weeks during the rest of the year.

Seasonal care

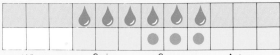

Winter   Spring   Summer   Autumn

Because the Busy Lizzie is so susceptible to pests it is important to keep a regular look-out for pests. Never neglect its water or feed if the plant is to remain at its best. In winter it should be kept a little warmer. In autumn, trim large plants back hard as otherwise they will be difficult to care for. Cuttings should be taken and rooted, to replace older plants when they are past their best.

Soil

For the vigorous growth of this plant, a peaty, loam-based mixture should be used. Young plants can be put into 5in (12.5cm) pots on purchase. In the first year, plants can be potted on twice.

PESTS AND DISEASES

Aphids Like all sucking insects, aphids love Busy Lizzies. They are usually found on the new growth and they should be treated with one of the many pesticides available.
Red spider mite Treat with insecticide, paying particular attention to the undersides of leaves. Smaller plants can be immersed in a bucket full of the insecticide.
White fly These are easy to spot as they fly away from the plant when it is moved. Treat with doses of insecticide.
Stem rot Wet and cold conditions may cause this – parts of the stem will be black. Remove the affected parts and treat with fungicide.
Sooty mould This is a fungus which develops on the honeydew of the aphids. Remove with a damp sponge.

Unhealthy plants White fly (**above top**) are a big problem with Busy Lizzies. They are difficult to eradicate – the insecticide should be used four times at four-day intervals. Red spiders (**above**) have a very detrimental effect on plants and Busy Lizzies are particularly vulnerable to them. Signs of their presence are poor growth and discoloured foliage. Wear rubber gloves if immersing plant in insecticide. The effects of dehydration and starvation are shown on this Busy Lizzie (**above centre**). Moderate feeding and watering are essential to these vigorous plants.

Kalanchoe beharensis

This is one of the most majestic of the many fine kalanchoes available, but it is also one of the most difficult to obtain as it is more of a botanical specimen than a commercial houseplant. The plant has triangular shaped leaves which are attached on their undersides to stout greyish green petioles, and these in turn are borne on stout stems that become very woody with age. Young leaves are also greyish green, maturing in time to an unusual dark brown colouring. The strong upright main stem will reach a height of around 10ft (3m) when roots are confined to pots 10in (25cm) in diameter, and it will not normally need to be staked.

The plant's leaves stand stiffly away from the central stem, and they have a natural tendency to die at a lower level as the plant increases in height. Many of the kalanchoes can be propagated from pieces of leaf and stem extremely easily, some of them not requiring any form of soil to encourage rooting. *K. beharensis* has the fascinating ability to develop perfectly shaped young plants along the fractures of broken sections of mature leaves. A leaf should be bent over until it fractures, with the broken piece left hanging, and new plants will then form along the fracture. When large enough to handle, these can be potted in sandy potting mixture.

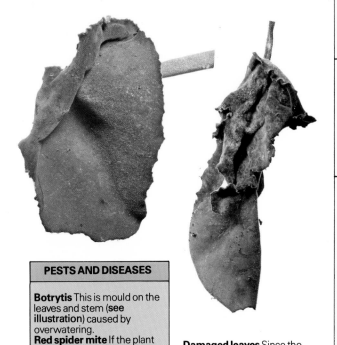

PESTS AND DISEASES

Botrytis This is mould on the leaves and stem (**see illustration**) caused by overwatering.
Red spider mite If the plant should be found to be inhabited by this pest, immediate action is vital. Spray the leaves with diazinon and repeat the treatments at intervals of a few days.

Damaged leaves Since the leaves stand out from the plant they are liable to damage from rough handling (**above left**). Botrytis (**above right**) occurs in damp conditions. Remove badly affected leaves and spray the plant with dichloran.

AVOIDING PROBLEMS

Light and position

Good light is essential to the Felt Plant and it will even tolerate quite bright sun without coming to undue harm. Sunlight tends to enhance the appearance of the leaves. It cannot thrive in poor light or in a draughty position.

Temperature range

Cool   Intermediate   Warm

The kalanchoe survives happily in a broad temperature range, as high as 75°F (23°C) or down to 55°F (13°C). In fact, it can exist in even cooler conditions, but this is inadvisable, and the temperature should never be lower than 50°F (10°C), especially in a damp atmosphere.

Watering

Water the plant sparingly, but enough to keep the soil moist throughout the year, which means that it will requre little watering in winter. Overwatering is particularly damaging in cooler temperatures and when growth is less active.

Feeding

If the potting mixture is sufficiently nutritional, little feeding is needed and it is certainly not essential. A little feeding in spring and summer when the plant is developing new growth is beneficial.

Seasonal care

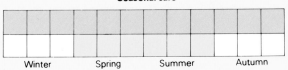

Winter   Spring   Summer   Autumn

The kalanchoe does not need special care, but it is not entirely easy to grow and the watering and conditions of light and temperature which it requires should be strictly adhered to. Although the fleshy leaves can survive temporary neglect, remember to check the soil carefully and moisten it whenever necessary.

Soil

Use a loam-based potting mixture and repot the plant in spring if this is necessary. Propagate from stem tip cuttings, which should root easily, or pot out baby plants which will form along a fractured leaf.

Healthy plant The open arrangement of spreading, triangular leaves in the *k. beharensis* makes it an attractive and unusual plant. In the wild it would grow to quite a size, but indoor cultivation is unlikely to produce a plant of more than 2-3ft (1m). The dense covering of fine hairs on the leaves gives the plant its common names of the Felt or Velvet Plant. As the plant develops, the lower leaves die away naturally. If the shape becomes leggy and unbalanced it may need a little support, but this should not happen at the size normally reached indoors.

Marantaceae

There are numerous marantas but only a few of them are suitable for room culture. Most are much too difficult to grow as they need the warm and humid conditions of a proper greenhouse. *M. leuconeura Kerchoveana* has two common names. Rabbit Tracks came about because of the similarity between the plant's leaf blotches and the paw prints of a rabbit, although this rather stretches the imagination! Prayer Plant is a much better common name. It relates to the way in which the leaves fold together like hands in prayer with the approach of darkness. In a moist atmosphere, at a temperature of 70°F (21°C), cuttings with a pair of leaves will root fairly easily.

Healthy plant Plants of the marantaceae family are striking and exotic, with their bold leaf patterning and lush colours. The marantas which are most commonly grown as houseplants are *M. leuconeura Kerchoveana* (**below left**) and *M. leuconeura Erythrophylla* (**below right**). Unusually for plants carrying bright colour, the marantas prefer a rather shady location and may become papery and lifeless if exposed to the sun. They require warm, moist conditions and if properly cared for, the leaves will remain attractive and healthy. The origin of the common name Rabbit Tracks, given to *M. leuconeura Kerchoveana,* is clearly apparent from the heavy black markings on the rich, green leaf (**top right**). The pattern of vivid red veins on dark green leaves patched with lighter green (**right**) of the *Erythrophylla* makes it particularly appealing.

Calathea and stromanthe

Anyone seeking a challenge with houseplant growing could well meet their match here, as these plants can present very testing problems. Almost all of them have highly coloured leaves with delicately interwoven patterns. They grow in clumps that can be separated and potted individually to provide fresh plants. To succeed with this, it is important that the divided clumps should not be too small as they are then difficult to re-establish in their own right. When dividing, the inevitable collection of dead leaves around the base of the parent plant should be trimmed off and the divided pieces should not be crammed into very small pots. The smaller plants will now require a pure peat mixture and a warm, humid atmosphere to help them become established.

Healthy plant Calatheas and stromanthes also belong to the marantaceae, but they are rather more delicate and subtly coloured than the marantas. *Calathea makoyana* (**below**), commonly called the Peacock Plant, has thin, almost transparent leaves (**right**), predominantly green on the top with light markings and a rich reddish brown on the undersides. *Stromanthe amibilis* (**below right**) is a rather sturdier plant with broad, spatulate leaves (**top right**). Calatheas are temperamental plants and will quickly react to too much sun or too low a temperature by shrivelling up completely. In common with other marantaceae, these plants require stable, warm conditions, but the calatheas will prove the most difficult members of the family.

VARIETIES AND PURCHASING

Exercise careful choice when buying plants of the marantaceae family, especially with the delicate calatheas. If the retailer has allowed the plants to be exposed to cold temperatures for any length of time, the plant will be damaged and may soon die. Avoid plants with brown leaf tips, or leaves which have any sign of ill health. These are not plants which will recover happily once given the correct care.
Maranta leuconeura Kerchoveana has green colouring with dark blotches on the leaves. It is a plant of compact habit, seldom growing very high at all.
M. leuconeura Erythrophylla This may alternatively be labelled *M. leuconeura Tricolor,* a name suggested by the bright markings and rich red vein pattern on the dark green leaves. It is one of the easier plants to care for in

this species.
Calathea makoyana The paper thin leaves of this plant, commonly called the Peacock Plant, are carried on slender petioles and are reddish brown on the undersides. The veins of the leaves form a delicate pattern and the plant itself is extremely sensitive and cannot be revived after a period of neglect or ill treatment.
C. zebrina This is sometimes known as the Zebra Plant, although this common name is more generally used for another houseplant. *C. zebrina* has stripey leaves of dark and light green, slightly velvety in texture and the undersides are a rich reddish purple.
Stromanthe amabilis Another typical member of the marantaceae, and not the most difficult to care for, the stromanthe has a fresh, open arrangement of leaves.

The leaves of a maranta will curl and wither if the plant becomes too dry and cold. Raise the temperature and humidity gradually.

This leaf shows the drastic results to a plant which is cold and overwatered. The limp leaf is brown and patchy, curling at the edges.

PESTS AND DISEASES

Most of these plants will be marked because of rough handling or bad culture. They may also develop spotting if exposed to household aerosols such as spray polish or air freshener. Marantaceae are as vulnerable to even momentary carelessness as they are to pests.
Red spider mite Marantas may be slightly more liable to this pest than calatheas. It is extremely difficult to detect but hardening of leaves and a general lack of vigour in the plant may be signs of infestation. Inspect the undersides of leaves with a magnifying glass as soon as you suspect spider mites, because once they have taken hold they are difficult, if not impossible, to eradicate. If the trouble is still at an early stage, spray the plant with malathion, with particular attention to the undersides of leaves. Alternatively, insert a systemic insecticide such as disulfoton in the soil. Test the solution on a single leaf of a plant and allow a day or two for it to take effect before

spraying the whole plant. Repeated treatments will be necessary, but may be to no avail if the mites have really taken hold.
Symphalids These small white insects which dance in the soil may affect a calathea. They are quite harmless to the plant but may be an unsightly nuisance. If you wish to get rid of them, water the soil with malathion.
Sciarid fly Plants which stand in the same pot over a long period may be visited by these small black fungus gnats. Again, they live in the soil and are not especially harmful. Overwatering, causing dank conditions around the plant and in the pot, encourages both sciarid flies and symphalids. Watering with malathion removes both pests.

A plant which suddenly acquires torn and ragged edges may be suffering from the unwanted attentions of a curious cat or dog.

Dehydration This is extremely damaging to marantaceae, as shown by this *Maranta leuconeura Erythrophylla* (**below**) which has been neglected to a catastrophic degree. Whole leaves are limp and discoloured and the stems are spindly and weak. If the plant can be retrieved, be careful not to shock it further by swamping it with food and water. Gradually moisten it with tepid water and keep it warm.

AVOIDING PROBLEMS

Light and position

These plants must have a shady position as sunlight will damage the foliage. The colouring is actually improved by poor light.

As they require warmth, a location in a window or near a door is unsuitable, being too cold and draughty.

Temperature range

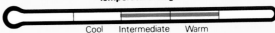

Cool   Intermediate   Warm

The temperature must be no lower than 65°F (18°C) and preferably higher. A stable temperature of 70°F (21°C) is ideal for all types and the calathea can be warmer still, at 75°F (23°C).

Moisture in the atmosphere is essential and to encourage this, a group of small plants can be placed together in a shallow container filled with moist peat.

Watering

Regular watering is necessary but wait until the soil feels fairly dry as overwatering is as bad for the plant as lack of moisture. Put in

the water at the top of the pot and let it drain through the soil, but do not leave the plant standing in the excess.

Feeding

Occasional doses of a heavy feed will not be beneficial. Give the plants weak liquid fertilizer when they are watered, except during

the winter, when they will require feed once a month at most, and then only if they are active.

Seasonal care

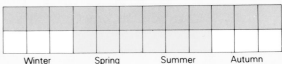

Winter   Spring   Summer   Autumn

In common with the majority of plants, marantaceae need more attention in the summer and during the growing period than in the winter. Plants can be cleaned and freshened occasionally by

sponging the leaves gently. Never use plant cleaning chemicals and take care not to damage the leaves which are quite tender and vulnerable. Tepid water is better appreciated than cold.

Soil

A peat-based mixture is the best choice, but it should contain some loam to provide nourishment to the plants.

Frequent potting is not necessary and a plant should never be put in a pot that is too large. A 7in (17cm) pot should be the maximum size.

Monstera deliciosa

Blessed with numerous common names, the monstera has immense appeal. Indigenous to Mexico, it now grows naturally in most tropical regions, and in almost every collection of tropical and indoor plants. Easily raised from seed, the monstera is therefore an ideal plant for the commercial grower who can produce uniform quality plants with little difficulty, so long as the reasonably undemanding cultural requirements are provided. Indoors, the naturally glossy green leaves, interesting habit of growth and ease of culture ensure that the monstera will always be among the top 10 foliage houseplants.

Endless questions are asked about this attractive plant, chief among them being what should be done about the natural aerial roots that protrude from the main stem of the plant. Where there is an excessive amount of these roots, it will do no harm to remove some of them, but it is really much better to tie the roots neatly to the main stem of the plant so that they may grow naturally into the soil in the pot when they are long enough. The important thing to remember is that these roots will draw up food and moisture to nourish the plant, so any drastic removal of the roots would weaken it.

Healthy plant The *Monstera deliciosa* (**left**) is a hardy plant with tough, glossy leaves. Mature plants can reach a height of 20ft (6m) and look attractive displayed on their own. The leaves are neat and rounded (**below**), deeply serrated and perforated in older plants. The leaves benefit from occasional cleaning with a damp cloth, but do not attempt to clean new, soft leaves, as these are easily damaged.

Underwatered plant This plant (**right**) is suffering from underwatering, causing the leaves to wilt and eventually die. Signs of underwatering will only show if the soil is extremely dry and the atmosphere is dry as well. The remedy is to water the plant regularly and provide a moister atmosphere. Monsteras should be watered and sprayed liberally in the spring and summer; in the winter it is sufficient just to keep the soil moist.

PURCHASING

Select a firm, compact plant, with glossy, green, unblemished leaves. Check that the soft, new leaves at the top of the plant are undamaged. Other common names for the monstera include Splitleaf Plant and Window Plant.

Damaged leaf A dark brown colour around the outside of a leaf (**below**) is a sign that the soil is much too wet and that the temperature is also too low. Increasing the temperature and reducing the watering is the cure, but steps may also have to be taken to dry out the soil. Leaves damaged in this way will not recover and should be removed.

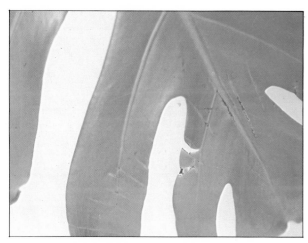

AVOIDING PROBLEMS

Light and position

Ideal conditions will produce a large, healthy plant. Avoid strong sunlight and dark corners. Sun will scorch the leaves, while poor light will restrict growth and result in smaller, less serrated leaves. Monsteras are happiest in locations with ample space.

Temperature range

Cool   Intermediate   Warm

A temperature range of 60°-70°F (15°-21°C) is ideal. Excessive heat should be avoided or the lush leaves will begin to curl and droop. Avoid wet conditions around the roots if lower temperatures are likely to prevail which may cause the roots to rot.

Watering

Monsteras should be kept moist, especially if in dry surroundings. The roots which grow from the main stem can be put into containers of water, reducing the plant's need for frequent watering. Sponge the leaves with water to keep them clean.

Feeding

This plant produces masses of roots in its active period, so it must be given regular feeding at this time. During less active periods, feed only if new leaves are being produced. Large plants which have been in their pots a long time need frequent feeding.

Seasonal care

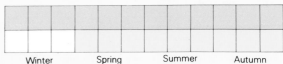

Winter   Spring   Summer   Autumn

When in the active growth period, feed and water monsteras generously. Give less of both at other times. Clean the leaves occasionally, but never wipe soft new leaves at the top of the stem because these are easily damaged. If the plant is healthy, potting can be done at any time of year but should be avoided during the colder months.

Soil

The potting mixture for monsteras should be primarily composed of peat, sand, and an appropriate fertilizer. Older plants will benefit from a mixture containing a good amount of sterilized loam.

●●

Musa

The musa, or Banana Plant, is a relative newcomer to the world of houseplants. Its change to the household environment came when a leading seedsman offered banana seed, at a surprisingly high price, in his catalogue. Experimentally minded houseplant growers put the three precious seeds very optimistically into the soil in their propagators, only to find that in many instances they all germinated. It soon became obvious that the Banana Plant can grow very successfully indoors if the temperature is adequate. New plants can also be started by removing the suckers that form around the base of older stems and potting them up individually.

Healthy plant The leaves grow in a sheaf curving out from a central stem. The lower leaves are shed naturally as they yellow and curl.

AVOIDING PROBLEMS

Light and position

Providing a window area is neither too hot and exposed to fierce sun, nor cold and draughty, the plant will enjoy being kept in

maximum light. Do not leave it pressed against a windowpane in high summer.

Temperature range

Cool Intermediate Warm

A minimum temperature of 60°F (15°C) is vital to the Banana Plant and it will do better in a range of 65°-70°F (18°-21°C). The plant was once considered an unlikely candidate for indoor cultivation,

but if cared for well in the correct temperatures it will flourish. Keep the atmosphere quite humid but do not leave the plant wet from spraying if it is in the sun.

Watering

The Banana Plant needs plenty of water, but should not be left to stand in a full saucer. Water from the top and drain off the excess.

Give less water in winter but be careful not to let the roots of the plant dry.

Feeding

This is a large, fairly quick-growing plant and it needs plenty of nourishment. Feed it

every time it is watered, except in winter when it becomes inactive.

Seasonal care

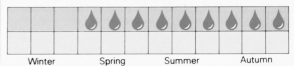

Winter Spring Summer Autumn

Keep the plant clean and remove the lower leaves when they yellow and begin to die. This happens quite naturally and is not a sign of ill-health. Give moisture whenever needed throughout the year and check that the soil is

always draining well. The plant is propagated in spring by splitting off new suckers from the mother plant and potting them out separately. These new plants require high temperature and humidity.

Soil

Pot on a plant in loam-based mixture at any time during spring or summer if it seems necessary. The mature plant will probably live

happily in a 10in (25cm) pot if it is well fed. Pot it firmly and put crocks in the base of the pot to ensure good drainage.

VARIETIES

The plants can be grown from seed in a propagating case which can be heated to about 70°F (21°C). Young plants may be found in a good plant shop, but be sure they have not been damaged by careless handling. Insist that the plant is carefully wrapped before taking it home.
M. cavendishii If the roots of this plant are confined, it may grow to as much as 6ft (2m) and even, in time, produce fruit, but this cannot be expected.
M. ensete Rubra This is known as the Dwarf Banana and is the best for room conditions. It will grow from seed into a sizeable plant with rich, red leaves.

PESTS AND DISEASES

Red spider mite This is the worst pest that will afflict this plant and is extremely difficult to detect on the foliage. Check the undersides of leaves with a magnifying glass to locate the insects and their tiny webs. Wipe or spray the leaves very gently with diazinon. Spider mites may need quite persistent treatment over a period of time, and if they have fully taken hold before they are noticed, may be impossible to remove.
Mealy bug The characteristic white, waxy balls of the mealy bug may be partly hidden between the leaves and stem of the plant. Saturate the foliage with malathion to remove them.

Pachystachys lutea

Although it belongs to the same family as the aphelandra and has similar yellow bracts, the pachystachys has very inferior foliage. While the aphelandra has attractive silver and green bars of colour across each leaf, this plant is a very dull, pale green in comparison. One compensation is that there are many more bracts and, if anything, the pachystachys is a little bit easier to care for. One drawback with this plant is that it does not travel very well, so, unless handling has been especially careful, plants are often not in particularly good condition when they reach the retailer.

Healthy plant A well-cared for plant which is pruned slightly in spring retains a neat, bushy shape, showing the bracts to advantage.

The healthy leaf (**top**) is a rather dull green but looks fresh and clean. Tiny holes (**above**) may be due to pests or a visiting caterpillar.

PURCHASING

Select a plant with a fresh and open appearance to the foliage. Plants which have been tightly packed for long before going on sale look sad and cramped. The Lollipop Plant may be bought with lots of buds developing among the top leaves, but avoid one which already has a mass of white flowers, as this is a sign of ageing. The bracts are continually developing as old ones are removed. The lower leaves will sometimes drop, so choose a plant with leaves all down the stem.
P. lutea This is the only variety which is truly suitable for indoor culture and is therefore the only one usually found on sale.

PESTS AND DISEASES

Aphids Check young growth regularly for the presence of these small green pests. They weaken the plant and cause distortion of the foliage. Spray the foliage generously with malathion.
Mealy bug These powdery white bugs attack only older plants and will be found amongst the bracts. Remove old bracts and burn them. Spray the plant thoroughly with diazinon to treat the remaining bugs and repeat after seven days to ensure their young are eliminated.
Botrytis Plants which are too moist and cramped may develop brown patches on their lower leaves. Remove affected leaves and spray the plant with dichloran.

AVOIDING PROBLEMS

Light and position

The plant requires the lightest position possible without being in danger from direct, hot sun which scorches the leaves. Weak winter sunlight or morning and evening sun will not harm it. The Lollipop Plant is quite delicate and must not be in a draught.

Temperature range

| Cool | Intermediate | Warm |

Warmth is an important requirement and the best temperatures are 65°-70°F (18°-21°C), although the plant is adequately warm at 60°F (15°C) or more, particularly in winter. In cooler conditions the leaves will drop. The plant will also appreciate a reasonable humidity, which can be achieved by standing the pot on wet pebbles, but the plant dislikes being sprayed when in flower.

Watering

Water from the top of the soil to keep it moist, but be sure the water drains through and do not leave the base of the pot standing in excess water. Make sure it is not waterlogged, but at the same time never let the compost dry out completely in winter. Reduce watering in winter.

Feeding

Add liquid food to the water so the plant is well-nourished in the growing period. The food should be gradually reduced, along with the watering, when the plant rests in winter.

Seasonal care

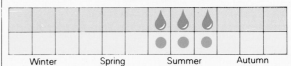

| Winter | Spring | Summer | Autumn |

When the plant has flowered, the remaining yellow bracts should be removed. If they are left on the plant to rot it may develop botrytis. At the same time the stems can be cut back to half their size. The plant is kept to a neat shape if it is carefully pruned in the spring, and a leggy plant can be cut right down to about 2in (5cm) to start fresh growth. Keep soil moist at all times but water less in the winter.

Soil

Pot the Lollipop Plant in a loam-based mixture. A plant can be potted into a slightly larger container in the spring following the year when it is purchased, in time to encourage the new season's growth. Do not hurry it into a pot which is too big.

Palms

There are many types of palm, almost all of them fairly tough, but the majority are rather too vigorous for today's average living accommodation. The best known is the Parlour Palm, *Neanthe bella* (*Chamaedorea elegans*). This is a neat, slow-growing plant that many people have in their homes and which is very easily produced from seed by the commercial grower. Although there are many palm varieties most of them require similar treatment and temperatures, and they all attract the same sort of pests.

There are two kentias which are available—the Kentia Palm, (*K. forsteriana*), by far the most popular, and the Sentry Palm (*K. belmoreana*). The first has broader and fewer leaflets to each individual hand of leaves, but they both attract the same culture and pests.

Kentias have been popular for indoor decoration since Victorian times and, in spite of the amount they cost, there seems to be little change in their popularity today.

Healthy plants *Neanthe bella* (**above**) does best in moist conditions. If the plant is allowed to become too dry, its leaf tips are liable to turn brown. Insufficient humidity may also lead to infestation by red spider mites. The plant takes several years to mature. It produces small yellow flowers, but its chief attraction is its mass of green leaves. *Kentia fosteriana* (**left**) is easy to look after and extremely elegant. Growth is very slow, so it is often best to grow several plants in a single pot. Kentias are often classified today as *Howea* palms.

AVOIDING PROBLEMS

Light and position

Most palms grow naturally in places where there is intense heat and sunlight. So, to encourage them to grow well indoors, place new plants where they will enjoy 2-3 hours of direct sun a day.

Temperature range

Cool   Intermediate   Warm

During the active growth period, a warm environment of 60°-70°F (15°-21°C) is best. During winter, hardier varieties, such as chamaerops, livistona and washingtonia, can tolerate temperatures down to 45°F (7°C). Other types should not be subjected to temperatures below 55°F (13°C).

Watering

The amount of water needed will depend on the individual palm. In general, water thoroughly during the active growth period. In winter, the cooler the room, the less water required. All palms like to be sprayed occasionally with tepid water.

Feeding

Smaller plants will do well with a weak feed every watering, but phoenix palms must have heavy feedings at weekly intervals during summer, and fortnightly in winter. For all palms, in winter use a weak feed or else stop feeding altogether.

Seasonal care

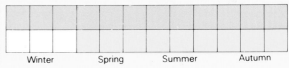

Winter   Spring   Summer   Autumn

All palms should be watered and fed thoroughly during the active period. Stop feeding and water only moderately during the rest period. Do not clean leaves with chemical mixtures; use a sponge and water instead. Most palms are very difficult to propagate and the seed can take up to two years to germinate. Palms are sensitive to changes in environment so if moving the plant out-of-doors in summer, acclimatize it gradually. Be sure to bring the plant back indoors before the temperature drops too low.

Soil

Smaller plants can be potted every two years using a loam-based mixture with leaf mould added. Good drainage is essential for all palms. Repot only when the roots have filled the pot and have begun to protrude through the drainage holes.

Dry conditions This leaf (left) is suffering from a lack of humidity, which has turned the tips of its fronds brown. To overcome this problem, stand the pot on a bed of peat moss, or a tray of moist pebbles. Mist-spray the plant regularly.

Two problems The *Neanthe bella* (above) has been underwatered. It also carries the symptoms of red spider mite — light brown patches on the edges and eventually over the whole of some leaves. Daily mist spraying acts as a preventative, since it keeps up the humidity.

Chemical danger All palms, like the *Kentia forsteriana* (above) are extremely sensitive to chemicals. Leaves should always be cleaned with a damp sponge, never a chemical cleaner. Similarly, always consult a retailer before using an insecticide.

Root growth The *Chamaerops humilis* (left) needs careful attention when grown indoors. They should be repotted every 2-3 years, the signal for this being the spread of brittle roots on the surface of the potting mixture. Repot the plant carefully, making sure tha palm is planted firmly, but taking care not to damage its roots.

PESTS AND DISEASES

Red spider mite This is the chief enemy of all palms. As a preventative, keep the plant in fairly humid conditions and mist-spray regularly. If infestation is suspected, remove a sample and examine it under a magnifying glass as, in its initial stages, this tiny pest is easy to miss. Treat by thoroughly spraying the foliage with a recommended insecticide.

Scale insect These infest the stem and underside of the leaves. Like red spider mites, they are difficult to spot. Treat with insecticide.

Earthworms These can block drainage holes in the pot so that the soil becomes too wet, with the result that roots rot and die, shortly followed by the leaves.

VARIETIES AND PURCHASING

Palms fall into two main divisions – those with pinnate (feathery) fronds and those with palmate (fan-like) ones. Always choose plants that are free from blemishes and have a bright, fresh look to them. Check carefully for the presence of pests, such as the red spider mite and scale insect.

Caryota There are two common varieties, *C. mitis,* the Burmese Fishtail Palm, and *C. urens,* the Wine Palm. They like warmth, should be watered plentifully and fed once a month during the active growth period.

Kentia The slender build of *K. belmoreana* and *K. forsteriana* belies their stamina. They are able to thrive even in difficult conditions, though they do not like temperatures below 55°F (13°C).

Phoenix *P. canariensis* is hardier than *P. dactylifera* or *P. roebelenii.* The last needs frequent repotting, as it grows quickly. Suckers can be used for propagation.

Chamaedorea As well as *C. elegans, C. erumpens* and *C. seifrizii* are also popular. They all need plenty of water in the active growth period. In winter, however, water only just enough to moisten the potting mixture.

Microcoelum *M. weddellianum* must not be potted in a pot that is too big for it and must be kept at a minimum temperature of 60°F (15°C).

Trachycarpus *T. fortunei,* the Windmill Palm, is a slender-stemmed plant, bearing attractive, fan-shaped leaves. These must be removed when age makes them unsightly.

Chrysalidocarpus *C. lutescens,* the Yellow Palm, produces clusters of reed-like stems. The small suckers that grow at its base can again be used for propagation.

Rhapis *R. excelsa,* the Little Lady Palm, and *R. humilis,* the Slender Lady Palm, are slow-growing, producing fan-shaped dark green leaves. They will both do well in pots that seem a little small for them.

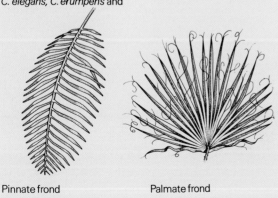

Pinnate frond

Palmate frond

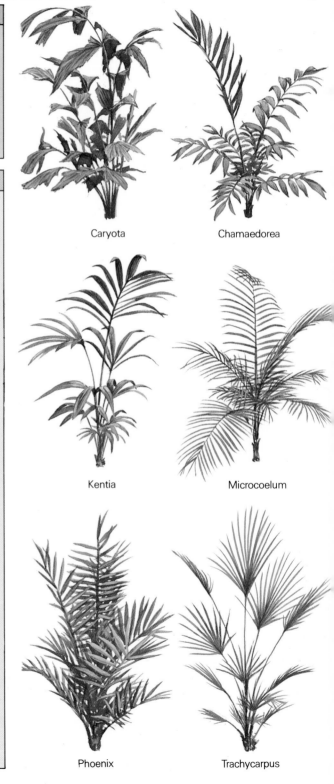

Caryota

Chamaedorea

Kentia

Microcoelum

Phoenix

Trachycarpus

Chrysalidocarpus

Rhapis

Propagation The *Neanthe bella,* which is also known as *Collinia elegans* and *Chamaedorea elegans,* (**right**) is difficult, but not impossible to propagate. Seeds can be gathered in the spring and placed in a heated propagator. A high temperature — at least 80°F (26°C) — is necessary, plus intense humidity. It is easier to propagate from the varieties that produce offsets. Allow these to develop leaves and roots, then cut them carefully from their parent. Plant them in moistened potting mixture, covering the pot with a plastic bag for a few weeks until they have taken root.

Passiflora

Indigenous to tropical South America, this plant grows at an extraordinary rate if the conditions are favourable. The intricately formed flower, which is predominantly blue, received its common name after Christian missionaries compared it to various elements of the Crucifixion. For example, they saw the crown of thorns in the purple rays of the corola. Whether or not it is a good houseplant is another matter, as there is not much to be admired in the foliage once the flowers have passed, and it is quite possible that after it has been bought the plant will not flower at all. In mild climates it will survive out-of-doors if it is given a sheltered position.

Healthy plant It is usual to buy the plant already trained around a hoop, which makes it look decorative. It is quite an easy plant to keep although the attractive flowers (**above**) may take a long time to open fully.

AVOIDING PROBLEMS

Light and position

The best possible light is needed and the plant should be placed in a window, although it is necessary to watch for scorching in direct sun. The plant can be placed outdoors in summer, but be sure to remember it and attend to its needs.

Temperature range

| | Cool | Intermediate | Warm | |

The passiflora likes a moderate temperature range, 55°-65°F (13°-18°C). It will not be harmed by warmer temperatures, but heat encourages red spider mite. In cooler conditions the plant maintains less active growth and will keep an attractive shape. In any temperature within the preferred range, keep the environment well ventilated.

Watering

Give the plant plenty of water, especially in summer when it may need watering three times a week. Reduce watering in winter, but do not let the soil dry out completely.

Feeding

The plant will flower more freely if the roots are confined, and if it is kept pot-bound regular feeding is essential. Give liquid feed with a high potash content, once a week in summer and about fortnightly in the autumn and cooler months.

Seasonal care

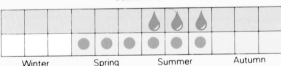

| Winter | Spring | Summer | Autumn |

Keep the soil moist at all times but be careful not to overwater in the winter. Growth can be extremely active so keep the plant in conditions which restrict it slightly and prune out unwanted stems in the autumn, after the plant has flowered. The passiflora is best grown on its own as it will tend to outgrow and swamp any companions.

Soil

Frequent potting on of this plant is not recommended, and when it is done, must be embarked upon carefully. Crock the bottom of the pot and use a loam-based mixture. Peaty soil will be of no use at all. Repot in early summer and press the soil well down around the roots.

VARIETIES

Plants may be bought at any time of year, but look their best in summer when the flowers are emerging. Look for a plant with fresh, green leaves, as yellowing may be a sign that red spider mites are already in evidence. Check the buds on a plant carefully, and ensure that some of the flowers have already developed.
P. caerulea This is the best variety for indoor growing, and few others are likely to be seen for sale. The flowers are almost always a blue-purple colour but occasionally you may see pink or red. The plant has a natural climbing habit, having clasping tendrils that cling to anything within their range.

PESTS AND DISEASES

Aphids The young, growing tips of the plant are vulnerable to this pest. Spray the plant with diazinon or malathion and repeat the treatment as necessary to clear them altogether.
Red spider mite These will be found on the undersides of leaves which may look yellow and lacking in vigour. Thorough and repeated spraying with malathion is vital at the earliest possible stage.
White fly This is an infrequent visitor but may prove difficult to kill. Spray the plant with diazinon at four-day intervals and repeat the treatment at least four times to kill the flies and eradicate all their young.

Pelargonium

Most pelargoniums, which commonly tend to be called Geraniums, will do well indoors, but they must have the lightest possible position if their flowers are to open satisfactorily, and they are to continue to flower well. There are many types, but the Regal pelargonium is most associated with indoor culture. Cuttings can be taken at almost any time during the summer, but it is best to leave them until late summer so that young plants are overwintered and ready for potting on and getting under way in the spring. Cuttings 3–4in (7·5–10cm) long root very easily and need no special treatment. Older plants that have flowered should be pruned back in the autumn and kept on the dry side until the following spring.

VARIETIES AND PURCHASING

There are so many varieties of pelargonium that it is impossible to give a full list. Flowers in colours ranging from white, through pink and red to deep plum are available, some as delicate sprays and others in rich, heavy flower heads. In addition, some varieties have leaf markings in dark red or cream. When selecting a plant, look for a full, bushy specimen and check the undersides of leaves to make sure there are no pests already at work. In all respects, pelargoniums are handsome, decorative plants which are quite easy to keep in the home.

P. domesticum Otherwise known as the Regal pelargonium, this is the most popular of domestic varieties and when well kept is a pleasing and impressive sight.

P. zonale This has red-brown markings on the leaves and bears its flower heads for several months.

Healthy plant Part of the great pleasure of these plants is the fresh and vigorous effect of the contrast between the clear, bright colours of the flowers and the rich green leaves, enhanced if several plants are kept together.

AVOIDING PROBLEMS

Light and position

Full light is essential for pelargoniums and they prefer an airy atmosphere, although they do not care for draughts. There are many varieties and they all enjoy sunshine, especially when flowering, but guard against scorched leaves in really hot weather.

Temperature range

Cool   Intermediate   Warm

Pelargoniums appreciate a cool or moderate range of temperature. They will exist happily in 50°F (10°C) but prefer a slightly higher temperature, nearer to 60°F (15°C). In summer they can tolerate rather warmer conditions for a while and a dry, rather than humid, atmosphere is best.

Watering

Introduce water at the top of the pot and let it sink down through the soil. After 15 minutes, empty the excess water from the saucer.

The plants do not care for overhead spraying and this may start rotting in the leaves.

Feeding

Excessive feeding will encourage a leafy plant, but at the expense of the flowers. Give no more than an average amount of liquid feed in summer as the plants are watered. They will not require winter feeding.

Seasonal care

Winter   Spring   Summer   Autumn

Water the plants quite generously in summer, moistening the soil often, but keep them fairly dry during the winter and in the lower temperature of 50°F (10°C). The top growth of the plant can be severely cut back during the winter rest. This reduces the likelihood of disease in congested foliage and also allows for more attractive growth in spring. Cuttings taken in late summer provide plants for the following year.

Soil

Use a loam-based or peat-based compost. Repotting should not be done too frequently as the plant can benefit from being slightly pot-bound. Young cuttings should be potted on, but do not repot fully grown plants.

PESTS AND DISEASES

Aphids These little greenfly can be a nuisance on young plants. They suck the sap from soft growth and deposit sticky honeydew on the foliage. (**see illustration right below**).

White fly This is a more prevalent problem and also more difficult to treat. The small white insects sit on the undersides of leaves (**see illustration below**) and dance about when the plant is disturbed. They may occur in great numbers and will spread quickly from one plant to another. Like the aphids, they weaken the plant by sucking the sap and again leave a sticky deposit. Spray the leaves with diazinon and repeat the treatment every four days until the plant is clean. Repeated spraying also kills the young flies which are hatching out.

Black leg This is a fungal disease which attacks the stems of pelargoniums. It occurs in conditions which are too wet and airless. There is no useful treatment and the plants must be destroyed, so make sure the same conditions will not prevail for plants which replace those affected.

Vine weevils Adult beetles can be damaging to the leaves, but it is the grubs which live in the compost and attack the roots of the plant which are most dangerous. As soon as you notice this condition, soak the soil thoroughly with rotenone. Spraying the plant with this insecticide is a useful precaution which may prevent the outbreak.

Rust A disease which is not common in houseplants, this may appear on pelargoniums in dank, airless conditions. You will notice brown spores on the undersides of the leaves. Remove the diseased leaves and treat the plant with a suitable insecticide.

Virus There is no single, easily described symptom of virus infection. If certain areas of the plant are distorted or stunted, or the leaves develop pale green or yellow patches, it may have a virus. This may have been present when you bought the plant or insects may have carried in the infection. Either way, there is nothing to be done, so make sure there can be no other cause and then dispose of the plant.

Mealy bug These white bugs, the adults large and waxy and the young wrapped in cottony fluff, are easily seen on the plant (**see illustration right below**). A severe infestation is difficult to control and leads to the leaves of the plant yellowing and dropping. At this stage, spray the leaves generously with malathion, but if there are only a few pests, wipe them off carefully with cotton wool soaked in malathion.

Botrytis This is a grey mould caused by cold, wet conditions (**see illustration above right**). Cut away affected leaves and spray with dichloran.

White fly These can be clearly seen against the leaf colouring. They must be quickly treated before they do any more damage.

Pests White fly is a tricky pest to eradicate and causes great harm to the plant. The problem is compounded if the plant is at the same time suffering from botrytis (**left**). Any attempt to cure it would require a chemical assault which would probably do more harm than good to a plant so weakened and it is doubtful that treatment could be effective. Remove and destroy a badly affected plant before the trouble spreads. A simultaneous infestation of mealy bug and white fly (**below left**) is not quite such a disaster, as thorough and repeated spraying with malathion should kill both pests. Make sure the undersides of leaves are well soaked. Aphids alone (**below**) are destructive enough. Spray the plant as soon as you notice the problem and repeat the treatment as necessary.

149

Peperomia

These plants seldom reach a height of more than 10in (25cm). The Desert Privet has attractive cream and green variegation on rounded leaves that are attached to succulent stems. The Little Fantasy plant is very dark green with crinkled leaves that are small and rounded, sprouting not from stems but from soil level. This is a dwarf variety that rarely grows above 6in (15cm) in height.

Little Fantasy is propagated from individual leaves, while the Desert Privet is propagated from leaves with a piece of stem attached. They should be inserted in a peat and sand mixture in small pots and the temperature should be in the region of 70°F (21°C).

Healthy plant *Peperomia magnoliifolia*, the Desert Privet, is a small plant which generally grows to a height of 6in (15cm).

It has attractive rounded leaves which are variegated in cream and green. The leaves grow from thick, fleshy stems.

AVOIDING PROBLEMS

Light and position

Because of their neat size and shape, peperomias are essentially windowsill plants. The window should provide good light, but not direct midday sun.

These are excellent plants for mixing with other types. They are not, however, suitable for bottle-gardens.

Temperature range

Cool   Intermediate   Warm

A modest temperature of 55°-65° F (13°-18°C) is best although this can drop to 50°F (10°C) in winter if

watering is also reduced. The maximum summer temperature should be 75°C (23°C).

Watering

Peperomias should be watered only sparingly, every 10 days in summer and every two weeks in winter. Use lime-free water. The

plants store water in their leaves, and if overwatered, these will quickly rot.

Feeding

Peperomias will usually be growing in a soil-less mixture which lacks essential nutrients, so feed with a weak fertilizer with each

watering. In summer, feed every two weeks using half the recommended dosage.

Seasonal care

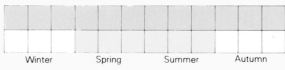

Winter   Spring   Summer   Autumn

These can be difficult plants to keep growing from year to year, but it is well worth the effort. Peperomias should be watered very moderately throughout the year. Generally, these plants do

not develop extensive root systems and will not require repotting. If necessary, repot only in the spring. Propagate from cuttings.

Soil

These plants do much better in loam-based soil-less mixtures than in conventional soils. Repotting should be done every

second year at most. When repotting, use shallow containers rather than deep pots. Never repot in winter.

VARIETIES AND PURCHASING

When purchasing peperomias, select sturdy, compact plants with distinct markings. Look for damaged leaves and any discoloration. Carefully inspect the soil area for rot which could quickly lead to irreversible problems. There are some 400 members of this family.

P. magnoliifolia 'Variegata' This is also known as Desert Privet. It has green leaves with cream markings.

P. hederifolia has pale grey leaves which are indented.

P. scandens 'Variegata' has small green and cream leaves.

PESTS AND DISEASES

It is fairly easy to tell when something is wrong with most peperomias. If the leaves of the plant turn dull and pale, it is receiving too much sun. If the leaves begin to drop off, the plant could be sitting in a cold draught. Leaves that develop what look like blisters are suffering from overwatering. Besides regulating the water supply, check to make sure the plant is not standing in water and that proper drainage is provided. Let the plant dry out thoroughly and water only moderately thereafter. There are many pests and diseases common to these plants.

Red spider mite These can be an occasional problem. On variegated types, red spider can be difficult to see and a magnifying glass might be necessary to locate them. This should be carried out regularly anyway, even if their presence is not suspected because once the pests appear, they usually maintain a firm foothold. In advanced stages, the plant will have a thick, dry appearance. Close inspection at this point will probably reveal fine webs on the undersides of leaves and the stems of the plant. If the plant has not been badly infected, an insecticide may clear up the problem. If the plant is overrun with the pests, it could prove pointless to attempt total recovery. Drastic as it might seem, the best action is to burn the plant to prevent the pests from spreading onto other plants which might be nearby.

Other varieties *P. lanceolata* (**above**) sends out shoots in an ivy-like fashion. The leaves of *P. lanceolata* (**below left**) have broad, pale green stripes with tiny veins. In good health, *P. obtusifolia* (**left**) has strong leathery leaves which are a deep purplish green colour. The stems of the plant are purple. The leaves of *P. orba 'Princess Astrid'* (**below**) are round and fleshy with fine veins.

Botrytis Due to incorrect watering, the disease starts at the rotting base of the plant. When the fungus begins to flourish, there is little hope. Treat with fungicide as soon as it is noticed, and cut out any rotting leaves which may infect other parts of the plant.

Philodendron

Philodendrons are certainly some of the most important foliage houseplants. Although there are a few variegated forms, they are mostly green to reddish brown in colour. Some are majestic and upright, others are radiating and equally majestic, while some are plants that are content to creep along the ground.

All philodendrons produce aerial roots of some kind from their stems, or trunks, which are used in their natural jungle habitat for entwining around tree trunks, so enabling them to climb into the upper air. Besides their climbing facility these roots can also spread out over the floor of the jungle and provide the parent with nourishment and moisture. Bearing this in mind, it is important not to remove too many of these roots from plants that are growing indoors. It is much better to tie them neatly to the main stem of the plant or its support and allow the tip of the root to enter the soil when it is long enough. With the low growing, radiating types, any very long roots can be wound around the base of the plant on top of the soil, while smaller roots can be encouraged to enter the soil by making a hole with a pencil and carefully inserting the root into it.

New plants can be raised by a variety of methods. The most productive is from seed that is reasonably easy to germinate in a temperature of around 70°F (21°C). The seed should be sown in shallow boxes or pans filled with peat and sand that is not allowed to dry out. Most seed will be large enough to sow at approximately $\frac{1}{2}$in (1·25cm) intervals before being covered with a very thin layer of the propagating mixture. Seedlings can be left in the propagating mixture until they have made several small leaves when they can be transferred to small pots filled with a peaty potting mixture.

Almost all the philodendrons, other than the stockier radiating kinds, can be propagated from pieces of stem with one or two leaves attached. A peat and sand mixture can be used and a temperature of around 70°F (21°C) is necessary if the plants are to do well.

Healthy varieties P. 'Red Emerald' (**top**) is a hybrid, noted for its burgundy-red leaves. It is a slower climber than other philodendrons, but makes up for this by an increased spread. The plant (**far right**) was produced by hydroculture.
P. hastatum (**above**) is distinguished by its broad, arrow-shaped leaves (**left**). These are bright green in colour and attached to long stalks. They must be staked if the plant is to remain erect. It can reach a height of 20ft (6m) in optimum conditions.
P. scandens (**right**) is known as the Sweetheart Plant on account of its distinctive heart-shaped leaves. These can be allowed to climb or trail, depending on requirements. The plant does particularly well in hanging baskets, where the trailing effect of its growth is most attractive.

VARIETIES AND PURCHASING

Philodendrons are available throughout the year and are easy plants to handle and care for, as they do not require much in the way of special attention. One area in which they may need assistance is help in climbing. Here, wrapping a piece of dampened sphagnum moss around a stake so that the plant's aerial roots can cling to it is not only more attractive than training and tying, it is also better for the plant. Keep the moss moist and remember to apply enough to allow for the eventual growth of the plant. Your new plant should have no damaged or missing leaves. Remember, too, that the leaves of young plants can be entirely different in both size and shape when they reach maturity, so it is well worth a little research before you buy.

P. bipennifolium Commonly known as the Panda Plant, this is one of the many varieties whose leaves change as the plant becomes older. At first, they are heart-shaped; as the plant matures, they shape themselves like a violin. The plant can grow to a height of 6ft (2m) and needs to be supported securely.

P. bipinnatifidum This is a radiating type, with fingered green leaves spreading from a central trunk. It can reach a height of 10ft (3m), but this is seldom attained indoors. Its aerial roots are very strong. These should be directed into the soil when they are long enough. This will help support the trunk as well as providing added moisture and nourishment.

P. hastatum This is an attractive plant, with broad arrow-shaped leaves, ideal for display. The stems of the plant must be supported with a stake.

P. 'Red Emerald' This hybrid has red stalks and stems. Its new leaves are totally red at first but, after a few weeks, the tops turn green.

P. scandens This is one of the easiest philodendrons to cultivate. Pinch out some of the growing tips regularly to stop the plant straggling.

P. wendlandii A non-climbing species, this has leaves arranged in the shape of a shuttlecock.

P. imbe A fast climber, this can reach a height of 8ft (2.5m) in a couple of years if it is supported securely. Its heart-shaped leaves are thin, but firm, in texture. They are carried on long stalks, which lead off vertically from the plant's stems, so the plant looks layered.

P. pedatum This is a slow climber, with shiny green leaves divided into five lobes.

AVOIDING PROBLEMS

Light and position

All philodendrons must be given locations that will provide them with protection from direct sunlight and draughts. Choose a suitable position for each type.

Radiating plants will need ample space around them. Place climbing and trailing species where they have enough height to grow.

Temperature range

Cool   Intermediate   Warm

Philodendrons will thrive best in temperatures between 60°-70°F (15°-21°C) but above all should not suffer a drop in temperature below 55°F (13°C). The maximum

summer temperature at which they are comfortable is 75°F (21°C) and at all times they will appreciate occasional mist-spraying.

Watering

Water these plants in the growing period enough to moisten the potting mixture and then allow the top layer of the soil to dry out before watering again. In the

short mid-winter rest period give them just enough water to prevent the soil from drying out completely.

Feeding

The larger the plant and the longer it has been in the same pot, the stronger or more frequent feeds it will require. For smaller plants,

best results are obtained by including weak fertilizer in the water each time the soil is moistened.

Seasonal care

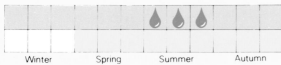

Winter   Spring   Summer   Autumn

These are plants for all seasons but they should be kept out of colder areas at all times. They have a short mid-winter rest period during which time they should have just enough water to

prevent the soil from drying out. Water in moderation for the rest of the year while the plants are in active growth and new shoots are being formed.

Soil

Use a peat-based mixture with some loam and pot on only when the roots completely fill the pot. Many of the larger plants (in pots over 10in (25cm) in diameter) are

best left where they are. Extremely large plants or those that will climb readily if tied to a stake should be started in tubs.

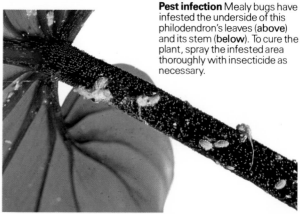

Pest infection Mealy bugs have infested the underside of this philodendron's leaves (**above**) and its stem (**below**). To cure the plant, spray the infested area thoroughly with insecticide as necessary.

PESTS AND DISEASES

Once in their final pots, most philodendrons need little more than regular feeding and watering. The larger the plant, the more food it will require, though only moderate amounts of water are needed. All philodendrons should be protected from direct sunlight, while they are happiest at around 65°F (18°C).
Mealy bug These can be troublesome on some plants as they get older, but, fortunately, the open growth of most philodendrons makes it easy to deal with the pests. Spray insecticide heavily and directly onto them.

Black leg This attacks cuttings during the propagation stage in unhygienic conditions. There is no cure so the cuttings must be burned.
Root failure Due to wet and cold conditions, this can cause the plant's collapse. The same can happen in too dry conditions, but this can be avoided with care.
Slugs These can be troublesome on plants with soft, tender leaves. Use a recommended slug repellant around the base of the plant to eradicate them.

Leaf damage Slugs have found the leaves of this *P. scandens* tender to eat (**below** and **right**). There is also leaf spot (**right**), which may be the result of either scorch or lack of water. If other similar marks are on the plant, the chances are that they are natural. Deal with the slugs by putting poison around the base of the plant.

Too dry The brown marks on the leaf (**above**) are natural, but the leaf is drooping because the plant is too dry. Soak the plant in a bucket of water and allow it to drain. Also check you are feeding it enough.

Sooty mould The black marks (**right**) are an indication of sooty mould. This grows on sticky honeydew deposited by aphids and other pests. To cure, wipe the leaves with a damp cloth.

155

Pilea

Many of these plants are compact, easy to propagate from cuttings, and not too difficult to manage. Cuttings can be taken at any time if suitable conditions are available. Sound pieces about 3in (7·5cm) in length should be taken from the ends of plant stems, and inserted in a peaty mixture at a temperature of 65°–70°F (18°–21°C). As an alternative to pure peat, the cutting can be inserted straight into 3in (7·5cm) pots filled with a good houseplant soil—at least five pieces should go into each pot.

Healthy plant Pileas come in creeping as well as upright growing varieties. They are popular for mixed displays because the different varieties encompass a wide range of size, colour and leaf texture. They look attractive when displayed with other small plants and they are suitable for bottlegardens. The *P. cadierei* or Aluminium Plant (**above**) is perhaps the best-known and it is relatively easy to care for. It can be distinguished by the silver patches on each leaf (**left**).

AVOIDING PROBLEMS

Light and position

Pileas flourish in shady surroundings and should never be placed near a bright light or in direct sunlight. They grow best in the summer, positioned at a short distance from a window.

Temperature range

Cool	Intermediate	Warm

These plants must be protected from cold draughts and they thrive in an atmosphere that is both hot and humid. It is not advisable to keep them in temperatures of less than 55°F (13°C) as they are unlikely to survive. Temperatures between 60°-70°F (15°-21°C) are much more suitable.

Watering

All varieties of pilea should be watered cautiously so that the potting mixture is damp throughout, without ever being sodden. The top half of the mixture or soil can be allowed to dry out before another watering is necessary. Pileas should never be completely immersed in water.

Feeding

Once they are well established, pileas should be fed each time they are watered. Although small, they are greedy plants, and they may need a stronger dosage than the fertilizer manufacturers usually recommend.

Seasonal care

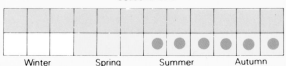

Winter	Spring	Summer	Autumn

Trimming and pruning should be done in the spring. However, the dead leaves should be removed regularly and the growing tips should be pinched out occasionally to ensure a bushy growth. Pileas may require slightly more water during the summer as this is the period of most growth. After three or four years these plants may become straggly and messy. When they start to deteriorate, cuttings should be taken and new plants propagated.

Soil

Potting mixtures without soil are suitable for pileas, and repotting should be done in the spring or summer. As small plants, they are displayed to their best advantage in half pots rather than full-size ones.

P. spruceana Two of the varieties in this strain are extremely popular as houseplants. The Silver Tree (**above**) is a short plant with upright growth, the common name deriving from the broad silver stripe of the leaf marking (**left**). Markings on *P.s. 'Norfolk'* react quickly to the light, taking a warm tone in bright light and bluish when shaded.

PESTS AND DISEASES

Pileas are not among those houseplants which are constantly prone to problems of this kind, but there are a few things which may trouble them from time to time. Although they are not particularly temperamental plants, strong, direct sun or cold draughts will inhibit them and cause damage. Leaves pressed against a windowpane during a cold winter are especially at risk and may turn black when chilled.

Mealy bug These are quite a common pest in pileas, mainly found among the lower stems of the plant. Left to their work, they will cause so much damage that in time the plant may lose its leaves completely. Mealy bugs are easy to see on the stems or under the leaves, being white against the green and brownish colouring of the foliage. Young bugs wrapped in their woolly protection are particularly visible. To treat the whole plant effectively, immerse it in a bucket filled with malathion solution. If the infestation is very light, spray under the plant's leaves.

Red spider mite This is not usually troublesome but may occasionally be present and, when it is, must be dealt with immediately. Check regularly for spider mites by examining the undersides of leaves. Use a magnifying glass as the insects are tiny and easily missed. Because the foliage of a pilea is quite dense, immersion in a bucket of insecticide is the most effective treatment for this pest, as well as for the mealy bugs.

Botrytis This greyish-brown mould (**see illustration below**) attacks the leaves of the plant, causing them to rot. The whole plant may also become dusty-looking. This fungal disease is encouraged by damp cold conditions and exacerbated if dead leaves become trapped in the living foliage and start to rot. Treat botrytis by spraying the whole plant with dichloran, but first thoroughly clean away badly affected leaves and dead or rotten matter.

VARIETIES AND PURCHASING

Fresh young plants should be selected in preference to larger ones. The latter may have used up all the goodness from the soil in which they are growing, and are more difficult to establish indoors.

P. cadierei Also known as the Aluminium Plant or Watermelon Plant, this is the most popular variety of pilea. It grows to approximately 1ft (30cm) in height, whereas the very similar dwarf variety, *P.c. Minima* only ever reaches 6in (15cm).

P. involucrata This plant is more frequently called the Friendship Plant and is thought by some to be identical to another pilea, *P. spruceana*. In the summer it should produce minute pink flowers, and it adapts to different conditions more easily than most of the other varieties.

P. mollis The leaves on this pilea have bronze markings, and are a brighter green than the leaves of *P. cadierei*. The rough surface of the leaves gave rise to the plant's common name, Moon Valley.

P. muscosa This pilea resembles a fern. It never grows higher than 10in (25cm) and usually blooms throughout the summer.

Botrytis This unpleasant fungus (**above**) has attacked a *P. cadierei nana,* causing the whole plant to droop and have a generally dull appearance.

Already the bottom leaves are grey-brown and rotting. Immediate spraying with dichloran is vital and rotted leaves must be removed.

Pittosporum

P. tenuifolium is native to New Zealand and is usually grown as a semi-hardy shrub, its foliage being used in the commercial flower trade as a useful material for including with flower arrangements. However, it is also an excellent potted plant, and there are numerous other improved varieties becoming available that should make these very fine foliage shrubs most popular. The pittosporum has woody stems and small leaves which are a glistening, glossy green, some with grey colouring in them, while others are overset with yellow, and many are attractively variegated.

VARIETIES

P. tenuifolium This has greyish green foliage. It develops into an erect, flourishing plant of about 5ft (1.5m).
P. garnetti This makes a neat ball of silver and grey variegated foliage. It is quite hardy outdoors.
P. eugenioides This may grow to 10-12ft (3-4m), but the grey leaves with white margins can be pruned back at any time.

PESTS AND DISEASES

Aphids These are not usually troublesome to this plant but they may affect new leaves. Spraying with malathion quickly controls them.
Red spider mite These are hard to spot underneath leaves but must be treated quickly with diazinon spray. Sooty mould can also cause problems (**See illustration below**).

Unhealthy leaves Dehydration and exposure to bright sun through the glass of a window cause leaves to brown and curl at the edges (**left**). Water the plant and change its position if necessary. Sooty mould (**below**) is the result of secretions from scale insects. Wipe the leaves of the plant gently with malathion, or spray it on, and at the same time take steps to remove all the pests and their young.

AVOIDING PROBLEMS

Light and position

Good light, even quite bright sun, is necessary if the plants are to retain their leaves and keep their colour. Some protection may be needed if they are growing by the glass in a window, to prevent the leaves being scorched.

Temperature range

Cool   Intermediate   Warm

Avoid keeping a pittosporum in a warm atmosphere, it really prefers cool, airy conditions with a low temperature range of 50°-60°F (10°-15°C). Combining this with its need for bright light can be a problem in a hot summer, so if the plant usually lives in a window, remember to move it further into the room on very sunny days.

Watering

Water the plants thoroughly and regularly as they will suffer if allowed to become too dry. However, let the soil dry slightly before giving more water each time. A plant which is too dry will quickly revive again when it is watered.

Feeding

The plant can be given liquid fertilizer once a week in spring, summer and autumn, but reduce the feed in winter, giving it not more than once every three weeks.

Seasonal care

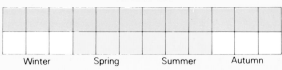

Winter   Spring   Summer   Autumn

Pittosporums are not the most demanding of plants and providing they get simple, regular attention throughout the growing season there is no reason why they should not do well. In summer, the plants can be placed outdoors in a sheltered place, but be sure to care for them as much as if they were indoors. Less attention is needed in winter, so reduce the frequency of feeding and watering.

Soil

Pot the plant firmly in loam-based mixture, but crock the bottom of the pot before putting in the soil. The pots should not be too large, to keep the growth in check, and by the time the plant has reached a 7in (17cm) pot it can remain there for three years.

Healthy plant Pittosporums are very attractive foliage plants, being bushy and strong when healthy. The glossy green leaves of *P. tenuifolium* are often cut for use in florists' arrangements. They can be bought at any time of year, and a better choice may be had from a retailer of outdoor shrubs, rather than a small houseplant shop. However, if the plant is at any time subject to a considerable change in conditions, try to break it in gradually or it may be unsettled. If the plant is kept in a light, airy place it will flourish. Some fairly new varieties of pittosporum have natural spots in their leaves, but the emergence of spotting during the life of a plant may indicate that it is being harmed by household sprays.

Primula

The wide variety of primulas have flowers which place them among the most delicate and beautiful of all the plants used for indoor decoration. Most are grown from seed, and will continue to flower for many months. *P. obconica* seems quite content to produce flowers throughout the whole year. However, it is sometimes known as the Poison Primula, because it can be a major problem for anyone with sensitive skin. It is possible for someone to become irritated by being in the same room as the plant, without actually touching it.

Healthy plant The best season for primulas is spring, and with their fresh colours and vibrant green leaves, they are appropriate symbols of the season. A group of plants with different coloured flowers makes a delightful display. To ensure that they are at their best, choose plants that are clean and fresh green in appearance with a few flowers showing and plenty of buds.

VARIETIES AND PURCHASING

There are many varieties of these most delicate and beautiful plants.

P. acaulis The flowers of this variety appear during the winter. They have no stalks and, nestling among the leaves, look very like primroses.

P. malacoides This is sometimes known as the Fairy Primrose. Slender stems above clusters of pale green leaves support the star-shaped flowers which may be red, pink or white. The plants may grow up to 18in (45cm) tall.

P. obconica This is often called the Poison Primula because of its effect on people with sensitive skins who may come out in a rash after contact with the plant. However, for those who are immune, it is a very good houseplant, being quite strong and producing flowers almost continuously throughout the year. It is less delicate in appearance than other varieties.

PESTS AND DISEASES

Aphids The soft foliage of the primula is vulnerable to all sucking insects, but aphids are the most troublesome. They may be detected by the white 'skeletons' that they shed when moulting. If they are not dealt with rapidly, the flowers and leaves may become distorted and sticky. Any reliable insecticide will control them.

Red spider mite It is essential to inspect the undersides of the leaves regularly, as if red spiders go unnoticed for too long, they can do great damage. They are encouraged by hot, dry conditions, so if primulas are kept in a moist, cool environment, which in any case suits them better, they are less likely to attract these pests. If red spiders do infest the plant, it must be treated with a recommended insecticide immediately, with particular attention being paid to the undersides of the leaves.

Vine weevils These are sometimes seen on the foliage but it is the maggots in the soil that do most of the damage. If they do occur, the soil should be drenched with an insecticide solution.

Botrytis (see illustrations below) Plants may contract this disease if they are in poor cultural conditions, particularly when there is poor air circulation. It causes wet patches on the leaves, or, if the plant is potted too deeply, its entire centre may be affected.

Botrytis This fungal disease may attack both the flower buds (**above**) and the leaves (**below**) of a primula. The whole plant should be treated with a fungicide as soon as signs of rot have appeared.

AVOIDING PROBLEMS

Light and position

Primulas need plenty of light but should be kept out of direct sunlight. As the plants should be kept moist, it is a good idea to plunge their pots to the rim in larger containers filled with moisture-retaining moss or peat.

Temperature range

Cool   Intermediate   Warm

Primulas like a fairly cool environment, between 50°-60°F (10°-15°C), especially when they are in flower. If the room temperature exceeds 60°F (15°C), the flowers are liable to fall more quickly. If the plants must be temporarily kept in a warmer environment, it is important to provide them with added humidity by standing them on trays of moistened pebbles and spraying their leaves.

Watering

Primulas thrive on plentiful supplies of water. Water copiously, ensuring that the potting mixture is thoroughly moist. However, care must be taken to ensure that the plant is not actually standing in water.

Feeding

From the time when the first flower stalks start to appear the plants should be fed every two weeks with a weak solution of standard fertilizer. This will extend the flowering period as long as possible.

Seasonal care

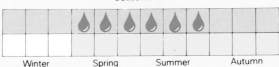

Winter   Spring   Summer   Autumn

Although sodden soil is harmful, plants should be kept moist at all times. It is possible to prolong the flowering period by picking the dead flowers as soon as they fade. *P. malacoides* is an annual but *P. obconica* can be potted on to flower more freely the following year. After *P. acaulis* has flowered it can be planted in the garden.

Soil

If on purchase the plants appear to be pot-bound, they should be repotted into larger pots immediately to give them room for development. Use a loam-based mixture and do not ram the soil into the pots too firmly.

Rhoicissus

The rhoicissus is among the toughest of all the dark green foliage plants, and when all else fails it could well be the best plant to try to establish indoors. It is a climbing plant with tri-lobed, glossy green leaves. Although it does not produce any flowers, it is invaluable for covering wall areas in difficult corners.

New plants are raised from 3–4in (7·5–10cm) cuttings and inserted in peat in a temperature of around (70°F (21°C).

Mealy bug The fluffy white young of the mealy bug are usually easy to see, looking like tiny lumps of cotton wool stuck on the stems or leaves of the plant (**below**). The adults have a powdery texture and resemble pale woodlice. If the infestation is not too advanced, treat the bugs with a sponge soaked in malathion, wearing rubber gloves to protect your hands. If there are many bugs, spray the plant thoroughly instead.

Healthy plant The rhoicissus is an elegant plant and really quite easy to care for; if it is allowed to climb or trail it will attractively fill an awkward corner where other plants have failed. The growth can be trained to a framework set in the pot, but as the plant can grow to 10ft (3m), it is very effective in a stairwell or supported against a wall. It is a resilient plant, and should it have suffered from poor culture or neglect, should recover quickly when given the right conditions.

PESTS AND DISEASES

Mealy bug These powdery white bugs and their young may infest congested growth in older plants (**see illustration above**). Spray the plant with malathion or soak a sponge with solution and wipe the bugs away.
Root mealy bug Similar to the leaf bugs, these attack the roots of a plant which has stayed in one pot for a long time. Water malathion solution into the soil.

Healthy leaves The two rhoicissus varieties have quite similar leaves (**above**).

Scorched leaf Browning at the tip is a sign of scorching or overwatering.

AVOIDING PROBLEMS

Light and position

These plants will enjoy a bright or lightly shaded position, but cannot tolerate exposure to direct, strong sun. Provided it is not subjected to this or to cold draughts, it will do well almost anywhere.

Temperature range

Cool   Intermediate   Warm

The rhoicissus copes with lower temperatures but really prefers a range of 60°-70°F (15°-21°C). It will benefit from light spraying in summer, when warmer conditions are prevalent, but is extremely adaptable and in winter will even put up with fumes from oil or gas heating appliances.

Watering

Water the plant well in summer and during the period of active growth, but check the condition of the soil carefully as overwatering may damage the plant, causing the leaves to droop and even rot completely. Reduce watering in winter when the temperature is cool.

Feeding

Once established, the plants require frequent feeding. Give liquid food in the water at least once a week while in active growth. Reduce or discontinue the feeding when the plant is dormant in winter.

Seasonal care

Winter   Spring   Summer   Autumn

The plants require no more than the usual care, with the soil kept moist but not sodden under any conditions. Untidy growth may be trimmed back in the autumn and if young shoots at the top of the stems are pinched out regularly, a healthy, bushy growth will result. Take cuttings in spring or early summer, using growing tips furnished with a couple of full leaves.

Soil

Annual potting is necessary, transferring the plant to a slightly larger container each time until the plant is in a 10in (25cm) pot. Then sustain the plant with regular feeding and change just the topsoil occasionally, using a loam-based mixture.

Saintpaulia

Although these plants are generally difficult to manage, this does not seem to be a deterrent, as worldwide they are among the most popular of all the potted flowering house-plants. The leaves are mostly rounded, hairy and attached to short stalks that sprout from soil level, forming a neat rosette that is a background for the flowers when they appear. Flowers of many colours are now available in single and double forms, and a collection of plants growing in ideal conditions will provide a display of flowers throughout the year. Plants can be propagated from individual leaves with stalk attached. These are put into clean peat in a propagating case in a temperature of not less than 70°F (21°C).

VARIETIES AND PURCHASING

The wide variety of African Violets available today vary in colour and in flower shape and formation. However, a few points should be borne in mind when buying. Select a plant with firm, non-drooping leaves, and, if possible, avoid purchasing from cold premises. Plants with blemishes on the foliage and sign of root or stem rot should always be passed over. Try to choose a plant which is in bud, as this will afford more lasting pleasure than one in full flower.

S. ionantha This is the only variety of African Violet in cultivation. All the many examples commercially available are hybrids of *S. ionantha*.

Healthy plant The African Violet (**above**) is one of the most popular flowering houseplants. It is available in a wide variety of colours and flower shapes. This example of *S. ionantha Rococo* has pink flowers and double blooms.

AVOIDING PROBLEMS

Light and position

The African Violet requires good light and will tolerate direct sunlight so long as this is not magnified by the glass of a greenhouse or windowpane. It is important that this plant should be protected from all draughts.

Temperature range

Cool   Intermediate   Warm

A good nursery will not sell African Violets until the milder weather has arrived. They are plants which do not like being chilled and flourish in a temperature of 65°-70°F (18°-21°C). The warmth and humidity of bathrooms and kitchens provide ideal conditions for growth.

Watering

During the summer, spray plants occasionally with a fine mist of rainwater. Hard water causes white spots and patches on the foliage. In cold weather, water sparingly; if kept slightly dry plants will often survive in low temperatures.

Feeding

It is important that the leaves of this plant should be kept as dry as possible when feeding. Add a liquid fertilizer to the soil when watering, taking care to use a weak solution regularly rather than giving an occasional large feed.

Seasonal care

Winter   Spring   Summer   Autumn

The main difference in the care of the saintpaulia from season to season is in the amount of water required. Throughout the year, the plant should never be overwatered, but in cold weather it is even more important not to allow the soil to become too wet. Use tepid rather than cold water at all times. Remove dead flowers and leaves as soon as you notice them.

Soil

In general, small pots are more suitable than large ones. African Violets flourish in peat-based potting composts. A soil-less mixture is also suitable but if used it must be kept sufficiently moist.

Fungal diseases Overwatering can lead to problems with African Violets, such as mildew (**above**) and botrytis (**below**). Never overwater. Treat outbreaks with fungicide.

PESTS AND DISEASES

The recent varieties of African Violet tend to be tougher than their predecessors, but care still needs to be taken when caring for the plants. Overwatering and wetting the leaves can cause problems.
Root rot Most types of root rot are aggravated by wet soil conditions which prevent oxygen reaching the roots of the plant. Affected roots are brown and lifeless. In the early stages, treat by allowing the plant to dry out and to stay dry for several days. In an advanced state, the whole plant collapses and the leaves go limp. At this stage the plant must be destroyed.

Mildew This should be treated with a suitable fungicide such as dichloran.
Botrytis This fungus disease should also be treated with fungicide. If the attack is severe, destroy the plant.
Aphids These insects may attack the plant's soft, tender leaves. Treat with a systemic insecticide, and avoid wetting the leaves if possible. If the leaves are wet, do not place the plant in the sun.
Cyclamen mite Although generally uncommon, this pest can be fatal as there is no known cure. The plant should be burned so that the pest cannot spread.

Sansevieria

The common name of Mother-in-Law's Tongue is given to the best known of these plants, *S. trifasciata'Laurentii'*, which has upright fleshy leaves that are mottled green in the centre and margined with a broad band of yellow. Occasionally plants will be seen without the yellow band, which indicates that they have been grown from a leaf section cutting, rather than from divided plants that will retain the yellow leaf margin.

Young plants will retain their leaf colouring if they are propagated by removing well developed plantlets from around the parent stem with as much root attached as possible.

Healthy plant *S. trifasciata 'Laurentii',* or Mother-in-Law's Tongue, is a tall-growing variety with striped, beautifully marbled leaves up to 3ft (1m) high. The leaves have spiny tips which should not be damaged as this will prevent the leaf growing. The healthy plant will grow slowly but will last for years. It must be well rooted to save it from toppling over.The

Mother-in-Law's Tongue will tolerate a wide range of conditions, enjoying high temperatures and direct sunlight. It should not be overwatered or overfed. Sansevierias are loved both because they are easy to care for and also because they create a simple and dramatic sculptural effect.

VARIETIES AND PURCHASING

Sansevierias are one of the most popular houseplants. They are long-lived, inexpensive and easy to care for, being well suited to thrive in rooms with central heating. They are also one of the simplest plants to use to dramatic effect – either by themselves or with a group of other plants. These plants, members of the lily family, originate in West Africa and are named after an eighteenth-century Italian prince, Raimondo di Sangro of San Severo. About 50 species are found in the wild but only five or six are grown as indoor plants, although new types have recently been created. The genus has two basic types – tall-growing and low-growing – all with stiff, pointed leaves, marbled or striped in green, golden yellow or white. The tall-growing types easily become top heavy, and it is important to choose one that is well rooted, and potted in a heavy clay pot. All of these plants should have unblemished leaves with clean, sharp edges and the spiny tips of the leaves must be intact or they will not grow.
S. trifasciata Varieties of this plant are the best-known of this genus.

St.t. 'Laurentii' This is the most popular variety. The tall, sword-shaped leaves edged with yellow and marbled with hues of green can reach 3ft (1m)
S.t. 'Moonshine' This is a quite new variety, which has apparently iridescent tall, pale green leaves edged with a very dark fine line.
S.t. 'Hahnii' One of the low-growing varieties, this has a rosette of stiff, sharply pointed leaves about 6in (25cm) in height.
S.t. 'Golden Hahnii' Also low-growing, this is more spectacular, with bright golden margins to its leaves, giving a false sense of swirling movement.
S.t. 'Silver Hahnii' This has silver-green leaves lightly speckled with dark green. Three other species can be grown easily indoors.
S. cylindrica This has narrow cylindrical leaves up to 3ft (1m) long spread in a starkly beautiful fan.
S. liberica This has broad, stiff leaves with lengthwise bands of dazzling white.
S. zeylanica Another tall species, this has leaves 2-3ft (60-100cm) long, grey-green and banded with dark green.

AVOIDING PROBLEMS

Light and position

Sansevierias thrive in good light and will do well on a sunny windowsill in a bright room. They will also tolerate partial shade but will stop growing in complete shade. Plants that have been left in the shade for a long time should be moved into full sunlight by gradual stages.

Temperature range

Cool   Intermediate   Warm

These plants, natives of the tropics, thrive in summer temperatures of 65°-80°F (18°-27°C). They will also survive at temperatures of 55°F (13°C) but will not continue to grow below 60°F (15°C). Between 55°-60°F (13°-15°C) make sure that the soil is almost dry and, above all, protect these plants from extremes of cold.

Watering

In the growing period water Sansevierias in such a way as to moisten the whole pot but allow the top layers of the mixture to dry out in between waterings. In the rest period wait until the top half of the mixture has dried out before watering again. Do not overwater.

Feeding

Use a liquid fertilizer once every three or four weeks in the growing period but at only half the normal strength. Do not allow the feed to spot the leaves and take care not to overfeed.

Seasonal care

Winter   Spring   Summer   Autumn

These very easy plants can be left alone in a warm room with a good light for the whole year with some water and very little feeding in the growing period. They will thrive at 65°-80°F (18°-27°C) all the year round without damage but should be protected from temperatures below 55°F (13°C) at all times. New plants can be grown in two ways. Either break away one of the offshoots with its section of rhizome and pot it or take a leaf, strip it into 2in (5cm) pieces, and plant them upright several to a pot.

Soil

Use a loam-based mixture and ideally use a heavier than usual pot as these plants will easily become top heavy. Place plenty of crocks, broken pieces of pot, in the base to ensure good drainage. Sansevierias like to be root-bound and will need repotting only when the pot breaks.

Dry leaf It is a great pity to spoil the elegant lines of this fine plant by simple errors in its care. The dried leaf (**left**) is quite rare because these plants usually thrive in high temperatures. Like all plants from tropical zones, however, they can suffer when too much direct heat is concentrated on a leaf. One way this can happen is if the plant is put where frosted glass focuses the sun's rays or immediately in front of a radiator. It may also be caused by the habit of these plants to become top-heavy and then topple over, touching the windowpane. Always give the plant a pot with a good solid base and keep to a regular, if sparse, watering plan. Overwatering is, however, by far the most common source of problems with sansevierias.

PESTS AND DISEASES

Pest rarely attack these plants and most problems are caused by poor culture.
Basal stem rot The most common problem, this is caused by overwatering. The main stem of the plant becomes wet and mushy and if it is left untreated the plant will fall over and die. Reduce watering and keep the centre of the plant free from moisture.
Brown patches on leaves These are also usually caused by overwatering. Water less often but do not let the plant dry out completely.
Damaged leaf edges These suggest that the plant is not firmly fixed in its pot. Place the pot inside a larger container and if the leaves are scorched move the plant away from the window.
Loss of colour This indicates a lack of light. Move the plant nearer to the window.
Mealy bug Sometimes these pests attack this plant. Wipe off the white woolly patches with a piece of cotton wool dipped in methylated spirits or spray with a systemic insecticide or malathion.
Vine weevils If these start to eat away the eges of the leaves spray immediately with lindane insecticide.

Saxifraga sarmentosa

These are natural trailing plants that produce perfectly shaped plantlets on slender strands that hang down and give the plant its common name. 'Thousands' is a little exaggerated, but young plants are produced in large quantities nonetheless.

New plants are the easiest things in the world to propagate. Any plantlets should be allowed to develop into a reasonable size and then removed and put individually in small pots.

Healthy plant The Mother of Thousands is a popular and attractive hanging plant. It has rounded shaped leaves of different sizes and trailing reddish shoots.

AVOIDING PROBLEMS

Light and position

Ideally, these plants should be suspended in hanging pots or small baskets in a window area where they will get plenty of light. They must be protected from strong direct sunlight however, as this can burn the foliage. Larger plants also look very effective on slender pedestals with the plantlets trailing down.

Temperature range

Cool Intermediate Warm

The Mother of Thousands grows well in cool conditions, but will survive in any temperature between 55°-75°F (13°-23°C). If the plant is being kept in fairly warm surroundings, a high level of humidity is advisable.

Saxifrages must be protected from draughts and will not tolerate continual shade. If they are never exposed to any sunlight the leaves will become discoloured.

Watering

These plants should be watered regularly, so that the potting mixture stays moist without ever being too wet. Less water is required during the winter period, as there is more danger of root rot at this time.

Feeding

Saxifrages benefit from a weak concentration of food whenever the plant is watered. Fertilizer in tablet form is the ideal nutrient for hanging plants. It can be pressed into the soil and will last for several weeks as long as the soil is watered regularly.

Seasonal care

Winter Spring Summer Autumn

It is a good idea to remove any dead and dying leaves during the autumn period. The Mother of Thousands plant tends to become rather straggly by the end of the summer period, particularly if the weather has been very warm. In the spring months, these plants can be moved into larger pots as necessary. It is not worth preserving these plants for more than about three years as they become messy looking, and are very easy to propagate.

Soil

Soil-less mixtures are fine provided you do not forget to water the plants. Once they have dried out however, they are difficult to moisten thoroughly again, and for this reason a loam-based mixture is recommended for these hanging plants. This mixture should feel light and spongy.

VARIETIES AND PURCHASING

It is important to select plants that are free of blemishes. The underside of the foliage should be checked thoroughly for any signs of pest infestation. If the saxifrages are wanted for hanging pots, it is advisable to purchase several small plants and pot them together. Larger hanging pots are more pleasing as well as being easier to keep moist. *S. sarmentosa,* or *S. stolonifera,* is easily the most popular type of saxifrage available today.

PESTS AND DISEASES

Red spider mite The dark red colouring of the underside of this plant's leaf is perfect camouflage for this pest. Leaves should be inspected with a magnifying glass if this mite is to be detected. It is difficult to spray the undersides of the smaller overlapping leaves, so a more efficient method is immersing the affected plant in a bucket of insecticide for several minutes. Rubber gloves should be worn.

Mealy bug These pests are powdery white in colour and they wrap their young in a waxy covering resembling cotton wool. To ensure that the young of both spider mite and mealy bug are eliminated, it is advisable to repeat the immersing exercise at 10-day intervals until the plant is clean. Saxifrage plants may also suffer from botrytis or aphids.

Healthy leaf This leaf (**above**) is dark green with silver veining on top, a deep red underside and irregular edges. The leaf and the stalk, which can be quite long, are covered with light hair.

Unhealthy plant The saxifrage plant is often a victim of botrytis (**left**). This grey mould attacks the leaves at the base of the plant; the plant then becomes brown, shrivelled and eventually dies. Once botrytis has got a firm hold, it is extremely difficult to save the plant. Aphids tend to attack the younger leaves (**above**), but are easy to see and can be eradicated with a variety of insecticides. They suck the plant's sap causing the leaves to become yellow and distorted.

Schefflera

Belonging to the same family as the heptapleurum, the schefflera grows in a similar way, but is a very much more robust houseplant. In some parts of the world it is known as *Brassaia actinophylla* while in Britain it is known as *S. actinophylla*. In tropical regions the schefflera grows to become a substantial tree, given the name Umbrella Tree because its foliage radiates like the spokes of an umbrella. These plants are strong growing and they may, in time, achieve a height of around 15ft (5m).

New plants are almost invariably raised from seed which is started into growth in temperatures of around 70°F (21°C).

Healthy plant The schefflera is an excellent plant for people who are unwilling or unable to provide constant care and attention. Able to withstand most environmental conditions, in an ideal situation it will grow to a strapping height of 8ft (2.5m). When young, *S. actinophylla* can be quite unattractive, with spindly stems and over-sized leaves. When full grown, however, the plant becomes a handsome specimen with rich, glossy leaves exploding outward from the top of each stem.

AVOIDING PROBLEMS

Light and position

The Umbrella Tree is an accommodating plant that will tolerate many locations but prefers light shade or indirect sunlight. Young plants can be mixed in with other houseplants, but full-grown plants are best viewed when they are standing alone as a special feature.

Temperature range

	Cool	Intermediate	Warm	

To keep the Umbrella Tree happy, reasonable warmth of around 60°-70°F (15°-21°C) is needed, 65°F (18°C) being about right. These plants also like humidity, so avoid dry heat. If the room in which they are situated is dry, place the plants in pots in shallow trays filled with pebbles and water.

Watering

The larger the plant, the more water it will require, except in winter when it becomes inactive. Keep the soil moist at all times. Good drainage is essential. A pointed stick can be used to loosen the top of the soil to assist drainage.

Feeding

At all stages of development, a proprietary liquid fertilizer can be used with every watering. As the plant develops, two different fertilizers can be used to satisfy the plant's various needs.

Seasonal care

Winter	Spring	Summer	Autumn

The soil of the Umbrella Tree should be kept moist at all times of the year, but only minimum watering is required during the winter months. The plants can be propagated in late winter from either seed or stem cuttings. Pot at any time except in winter when the plant is vulnerable to damage and radical changes in environment.

VARIETIES

Each type of schefflera is slightly different in size and appearance and should be purchased according to where it is to be situated. If, for example, the plant is to be the focal point of a room, then a full-sized plant is best because scheffleras can take a while to reach their full adult height. For all types, the health of the plant can be determined by the condition of its leaves. Purchase plants whose leaves are free of blemishes, firm and supple and not drooping. The surface of the leaves should be rich and glossy with a polished appearance.
S. actinophylla This is the most common and largest variety available. Look for one that has well-shaped and proportioned leaves. Scheffleras today are often sold under the name *Brassaia*.

PESTS AND DISEASES

While scheffleras are prone to the pests and diseases common to all houseplants, they are also less likely to contract them. Most of these problems can be avoided by carefully spraying and wiping the leaves of the plant every two months.
Aphids These are often a problem on young leaves but are easily treated if caught in time. A commercial insecticide will clear up the problem quite easily.
Red spider mite This pest tends to be found on plants growing in hot, dry environments. Light brown leaf discoloration is a sign of their presence. To cure, use a recommended insecticide which should be sprayed on the undersides of the leaves at weekly intervals.
Mealy bug This is mostly seen on older plants, but even then is not often found on the tough foliage of the schefflera. Because the bugs are easily seen, they can easily be treated with a commerical insecticide.

Soil

In four years' time, the robust Umbrella Tree may well need a pot 10in (25cm) in diameter. Once in a large pot, the potting mixture should sustain the plant for a number of years. A good mixture contains a fair amount of loam, but should not be too heavy.

Scindapsus

The scindapsus is one of the most remarkable foliage plants of them all. From being tender and difficult to care for a decade or so ago, they are now among the most rewarding of indoor plants. Obviously a tougher selected strain has been developed to make the radical change possible and today the scindapsus is a decorative plant with mustard and green variegation that is tolerant of a wide range of conditions in the home. Even when placed at the furthest point from the light source, the variegation is rarely affected—a quality that is unusual in most plants with variegated foliage.

Propagation is done vegetatively by inserting pieces of firm stem with two good leaves attached. A temperature of about 70°F (21°C) and a peat and sand mixture that is kept moist, but not waterlogged, are required.

Healthy plant There are about 20 species of scindapsus, each with a characteristic tendency to wrap itself around the nearest object. All the varieties can be grown either upright on a pole, or in a hanging basket.

VARIETIES

Scindapsus plants come in many shapes and sizes and most shops will have a selection. Some will be displayed as climbing, others trailing. Choose plants with firm leaves that stand out cleanly from the stem. Ignore any with curled, drooping leaves.
S. aureus (above). This is a green and mustard variegated plant, and probably the best buy. It may also be sold as Pothos.
S.a. 'Marble Queen' This plant (**above right**) has marbled white and green foliage. It is more difficult to care for than other types.

PESTS AND DISEASES

Some problems scindapsus is prone to include:
Botrytis (see illustration below). This causes wet, brown patches on the leaves. Remove any leaves which are infected.
Aphids These are found on the leaves of young plants. Wipe with insecticide.
Mealy bug Treat the bugs with methylated spirits.

AVOIDING PROBLEMS

Light and position

All scindapsus plants abhor strong, direct light. They also do not like shade, except for *S. aureus* which will maintain its distinctive yellow streaks if kept in low light. Bright, indirect light is ideal for most types. The plants can be grown in either a trailing or an upright fashion.

Temperature range

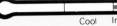

Cool   Intermediate   Warm

In their active period, these plants prosper in normal room temperatures between 60°-70°F (15°-21°C), 65°F (18°C) being ideal. In winter, a temperature of 60°F (15°C) will give the plant a chance to rest, and they can tolerate a temperature of 50°F (10°C). If the room is dry as well as warm, stand the plants in their pots on trays of pebbles and water.

Watering

The scindapsus does not like to be overwatered and should be allowed to dry out between waterings. During active growth water moderately. In winter, when the plant is dormant, water only enough to keep the potting mixture slightly moist.

Feeding

Being fairly sturdy, the scindapsus does not need large amounts of fertilizer. Small, established plants should have a weak feed with each watering. Larger plants will welcome a stronger dosage. During active growth, apply a liquid fertilizer every two weeks.

Seasonal care

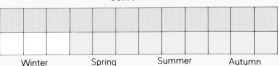

Winter   Spring   Summer   Autumn

Keep the potting mixture moist throughout the year by watering every four or five days in summer and every seven to eight days in winter. Prune in early spring. If a bushier plant is desired, prune the main growth well back.

Stem cuttings can be rooted in spring in either water or soil. The plants can be moved to a pot one size larger each spring. When the maximum size has been reached, replenish the topsoil rather than repotting.

Soil

Avoid putting plants in pots too large for their size. When repotting, the new pots should be only 1-2in (2.5-5cm) larger. Use a soil-based potting mixture with a small amount of loam added. When propagating, plant cuttings in a moistened mixture of peat moss and coarse sand.

Sinningia

This plant should really be referred to by its proper name, *Sinningia speciosa*, but its common name rolls off the tongue much more easily. Commercially, Gloxinias are raised annually from seed sown early in the year. As the year progresses the seedlings develop a corm and in time the plants find their way to a retailer. Following flowering indoors, the plant will die down naturally in the autumn and, if kept dry at a winter temperature of around 55°F (13°C), the corm can be retained until the following spring. Then it can be planted to produce a bigger and better plant. The corm should have all the dry soil removed from around it and be potted almost to its full depth in a houseplant potting mixture, with the rounded side of the corm going into the soil. This should be kept fairly dry until new growth is under way, when water can gradually be given more generously.

VARIETIES

S. speciosa This comes in many different forms. When the plants are fully grown they should have one or two of their spectacular, trumpet-shaped flowers open, but the chief thing to look for is an ample supply of buds that will flower during the coming weeks. To produce the maximum number of flowers, use a high potash fertilizer with each watering, rather than a nitrogen based product.

Botrytis This is a fungus disease that often attacks plants which have been planted too closely together in dank conditions. The signs are wet blotches on leaves (**below**). If left untreated, the whole plant will rot and eventually disintegrate. Remove any infected leaves immediately and treat the plant with a recommended fungicide.

Three problems The sooty mould (**above**) is a sign of an aphid attack, while the leaf marks (**above right**) are the result of red spider. Combat both with insecticide. Overwatering (**below**) leads to rot and botrytis.

AVOIDING PROBLEMS

Light and position

Find the lightest possible location for these plants, but avoid direct sunlight which can scorch the softer new leaves. Poor light will lead to thin leaves and the flowers will be weak and sparse. Protect from midday sun during the summer months.

Temperature range

Cool   Intermediate   Warm

A room temperature of around 60°F (15°C) during summer is best. In winter keep the corms dry and frost free at around 50°F (10°C). The maximum summer temperature should be 75°F (23°C).

Watering

In summer water generously two to three times a week. Water the plant at the soil level and avoid wetting the leaves or flowers. Gradually reduce watering in the autumn when the plant begins its dormant period. When growth has stopped, allow to dry out completely.

Feeding

No feeding is necessary as plants are becoming established. Those purchased in full growth should be fed with every watering. A weak feed is best, but for many flowers use a high potash fertilizer. Nitrogenous types will produce more leaves than flowers.

Seasonal care

Winter   Spring   Summer   Autumn

Keep the soil moist while the plant is in flower, then gradually give it less water and keep it dry over the winter months. Pruning is generally not needed except to remove dead or damaged leaves and flowers. Young plants grown from seed or cuttings should be potted two or three times during the active growth period. Old tubers should be potted once in early spring. New plants can also be grown from seed at this time. Leaf cuttings can be taken when the leaves are mature in summer.

Soil

Any good household potting mixture will suit the Gloxinia. Repot in the first year only if the pot is smaller than 5in (10cm) in diameter. Do this on purchasing. Do not feed for six weeks after potting.

PESTS AND DISEASES

Given the right temperature and, above all, an adequate amount of humidity, *S. speciosa* will do well. Most pests are relatively easy to combat.
Aphids These are the most troublesome pest, but they are easy to identify. Treat with an insecticide.
Botrytis This is frequently the result of overwatering. Remove infected leaves – the signs are wet blotches – as soon as they develop. Treat the healthy part of the plant with fungicide to prevent any further outbreaks.
Red spider mite These appear on the underside of leaves, if plants are growing in too hot or dry conditions.

173

Solanum capsicastrum

This plant gives its name to a very large family that includes the tomato and the potato. However, its chief use is as a decorative potted plant that bears attractively coloured berries at the latter end of the year. Plants are started from seed in the spring and, when established in their pots, they are placed out-of-doors until there is risk of frost. They are then taken into frames or greenhouses that offer cool conditions, to be grown on and flowered hopefully for Christmas trading. The plants have dull green leaves on twiggy stems and are nothing without their coloured berries.

Healthy plant The Christmas Cherry was originally brought from Brazil in the seventeenth century. It is a charming plant, whether placed indoors or in window boxes.

AVOIDING PROBLEMS

Light and position

The Christmas Cherry should never be placed in dark corners. If it is, it will shed its berries at an alarming rate, and its leaves will turn yellow and fall. Find the lightest location for these plants. Because they can tolerate cool conditions, windowsills are ideal.

Temperature range

Cool   Intermediate   Warm

A temperature range of 50°-60° F (10°-15° C) suits the plant best and will encourage it to produce more berries. A light and airy windowsill is ideal. In summer, the plants should be placed out-of-doors if possible.

Watering

During active growth, water profusely every other day. Do not let the soil dry out, even in winter. If keeping for a second season, make sure the soil is dry while the plant is dormant. After pruning, water every two weeks.

Feeding

Purchased plants will have been in their pots for some time, so regular weekly feeding with a fairly potent liquid fertilizer is necessary from the time they arrive indoors. No feeding is required after potting or pruning for about six weeks.

Seasonal care

Winter   Spring   Summer   Autumn

Plants should be kept moist at all times, but on the dry side at the end of the active growth period. If kept for a second year, repot when the plant is pruned in spring. Cut the plants back to half their size in early spring and stand out-of-doors until the middle of summer. Restrict growth in autumn by pinching the non-flowering tips. Plants will easily germinate from seed in early spring.

Soil

A loam-based mixture should be used and plants should be repotted quite firmly. Large plants in small pots will suffer, so repot to 5in (12·5cm) pots at the outset. Seed-raised plants should be potted gradually from one size to the next. Never move a plant to a pot that is too large for it.

VARIETIES

Plants may be purchased in a variety of pot sizes, but whatever the size, select plants that have green foliage down to the soil level. Yellow leaves are an indication of root disorder. The plants may have green, orange, and red berries all at the same time. The berries are poisonous and should be kept away from children and pets.
S. capsicastrum The common variety with fruit about the size of a marble.
S. pseudocapsicum Commonly known as the Jerusalem Cherry, this has larger berries than *S. capsicastrum*.

PESTS AND DISEASES

The Christmas Cherry is prone to the usual problems of most houseplants.
Aphids These are usually found on young growth in summer. They are a nuisance and should be dealt with immediately with an insecticide.
White fly This problem is controlled only with persistent spraying with insecticide. Treat four times a day at four-day intervals for 16 days.
Botrytis This is not common but can be found in wet, airless conditions. Remove the affected leaves and treat with fungicide.
Red spider mite These cause discoloration.

Sparmannia africana

This plant's common name of African Windflower is derived from the unusual way in which its exposed stamens fold outwards when blown by a breeze of wind. The name Zimmerlinden is the lovely sounding German name for what in English speaking parts of the world is the Indoor Lime. Surprisingly, these plants are not as popular as they ought to be, for they are easy to manage, grow at a prodigious rate and are not prone to many troubles in the way of pests. Its stems are erect and woody, and its lime green leaves are large, with flowers appearing on the mature plant. Propagating new plants presents few problems as cuttings can be grown in temperatures of 70°F (21°C) at any time of the year as long as adequate conditions are provided.

Healthy plant A member of the lime family, the sparmannia is similar in appearance to the lime but it has softer leaves. When a fair size it bears white flowers with purple stamens which are sensitive to wind and touch.

VARIETIES

The African Windflower can sometimes be difficult to purchase. There is no particular season for the African Windflower, so if they are available they may be purchased at any time of year. If you buy a leggy and neglected plant, it will quickly respond to regular feeding and potting into fresh soil.
S. africana This is generally the only variety grown commercially.

PESTS AND DISEASES

Sparmannia is more prone to pests than diseases.
Red spider mite These will appear only when the plant is growing in hot and dry conditions. When first noticed, treat immediately with a recommended insecticide.
Symphalids These white pests can be eradicated by watering with a malathion solution. When watered the flies seem to jump around on top of the soil.
Sciarid fly These can cause a little damage to the root tissue of the plant. Treat by watering with a malathion solution.

AVOIDING PROBLEMS

Light and position

The African Windflower will benefit from good light, but guard against strong sunlight. Draughty windows can lead to an alarming loss of leaves. Because mature plants will have lost many of their lower leaves, they are best viewed when placed on the floor.

Temperature range

Cool | Intermediate | Warm

These plants enjoy fairly cool and consistent temperatures of 60°-65°F (15°-18°C). In winter, the plants can withstand temperatures as low as 45°F (7°C). If the temperature drops this low, keep the plant on the dry side and water only every 10 days or so.

Watering

S. africana should be watered profusely in the summer — once a day or at least every other day. Water in winter according to the room temperature. In normal conditions, once a week should be sufficient.

Feeding

This plant grows many roots, so regular weekly feeding with a fairly potent fertilizer is essential. Feed in winter only if the plant is producing new leaves. Regular growth requires regular feeding; no growth only needs minimal feeding.

Seasonal care

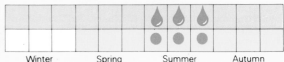

Winter | Spring | Summer | Autumn

Throughout the year, the plant should be watered sufficiently so that the soil does not dry out. During the first year of growth, the plant will probably need to be repotted two or three times. After this, annual repotting in the spring is enough. If the plant is left in its original pot, it will flower sooner. Prune in the spring. If the plant becomes very leggy, it can be cut back completely after flowering. Stem tip cuttings can be rooted in peat and sand in spring.

Soil

A new plant should have its roots inspected. If there is a mass of roots filling the pot, it will need new soil. Use a loam-based mixture and keep in a minimum temperature of 65°F (18°C). Water thoroughly after potting, then keep on the dry side until new growth begins.

Spathiphyllum

There can be few more simple or more effective contrasts than creamy white flowers set off against dark green foliage, and this is what the exotic spathiphyllums have to offer. The common name clearly derives from the manner in which spathe flowers are held erect on stiff stalks not unlike a sail. Although they belong to the same family as the anthuriums, the flowers of the spathiphyllum do not have the same lasting qualities when used as cut flowers. However, this is a small drawback as they will continue for many weeks if left on the plant.

Plants are propagated by the age old method of division. This simply means that the plant is removed from its pot and the clump of congested small plants is reduced to individual pieces or to smaller clumps which are potted up individually. The pieces should be removed with as much root attached as possible and they ought to be potted into 5in (12·5cm) pots using a standard houseplant potting mixture.

Healthy plant S. 'Mauna Loa' (**right**) is a pleasing, elegant plant When choosing a plant, look for clean foliage and flowers that are in bud rather than full out. Drooping or discoloured plants are unhealthy. The spathe eventually turns green. It is still attractive for a few weeks, but after that time it is a good idea to remove it.

VARIETIES AND PURCHASING

These plants are normally only found in specialist retail shops as they need considerable care after they have been acquired.

S. wallisii The maximum height this variety achieves is 1ft (30cm). The leaves, which grow in thick clusters, are about 6in (16cm) long and 4in (10cm) wide. The flowers, on long stalks, appear in spring and sometimes again in late summer. This variety, however, is not often found in retailers' stock. The cream or yellow coloured spadix of each flower is enclosed by the white spathe which gives rise to its common name, White Sails or Peace Lily.

S. 'Mauna Loa' This is a hybrid, and far more popular than the other variety. It has large green leaves and majestic flowers which usually appear in spring. However, the plant does sometimes bloom at other times of the year. The flower stalks may be 15-20in long (38-50cm) and they give the flowers a very graceful appearance. The flowers have a fragrant smell, and altogether, the spathiphyllum is one of the most attractive of houseplants.

PESTS AND DISEASES

Aphids These pests tend to attack the young, maturing leaves in the centre of the plant. As soon as they are noticed, steps should be taken to treat the plant, as they can cause considerable damage. Use an insecticide to get rid of them.

Red spider mite If the atmosphere is too hot and dry, the spathiphyllum may be attacked by red spider mite. It is wise to spray the leaves regularly, concentrating on the undersides. If the plant does become infested, use a reliable insecticide and improve the growing conditions.

Mealy bug This pest is not a frequent visitor to the spathiphyllum, but the leaves should be checked for it occasionally as it tends to be hidden between the congested leaves. If there are only a few, they can be wiped away with a pad soaked in methylated spirits. Larger numbers can be removed by soaking with an insecticide such as malathion.

Unhealthy leaf (above). If the spathiphyllum is not given enough food regularly, its leaves will go patchy and the edges will become yellow and ragged.

This spathiphyllum has produced an exotic white flower which is set off well against its foliage when both the flower and leaves are healthy (**above**).

AVOIDING PROBLEMS

Light and position

Spathiphyllums like a sunny position but direct sunlight should be avoided. They are beautifully shaped plants and so are at their best advantage when they can be viewed from all sides.

Temperature range

Cool   Intermediate   Warm

Spathiphyllums should be kept at temperatures between 60°-70°F (15°-21°C). If they are kept at about 65°F (18°C) they should grow for most of the year. They do not like draughts and they need a humid atmosphere, so keep them on trays of moist pebbles or moss.

Watering

The spathiphyllum should be watered with moderate amounts – the potting mixture should never dry out completely. Avoid overwatering, as this could result in wilting.

Feeding

Use a standard liquid fertilizer and administer every two weeks while the plant is growing. Older and more established plants may benefit from a slightly stronger solution than the manufacturer recommends.

Seasonal care

Winter   Spring   Summer   Autumn

The plant grows fastest in summer and should receive greater quantities of water then. Avoid water-logging – worms in the soil may block up the drainage holes with their casts so check for these. Decrease the amount of food in winter. Avoid accidental spraying with household aerosols as this may cause spotting of the leaves.

Soil

The plants should be repotted every spring in a loam-based mixture. Ensure that they are properly drained by putting a few pieces of broken clay pots in the bottom of the new containers.

Stephanotis floribunda

These are natural climbing plants, with tough, leathery, evergreen foliage, whose main attraction is the almost over-powering fragrance of the waxy white flowers that are borne in clusters of five to nine. The individual flowers are trumpet shaped with short stalks, and are much favoured by florists for bridal bouquets. New plants can be raised from cuttings of older growth taken in the spring and placed in a peaty mixture at a temperature of around 70°F (21°C). Plants may also be raised from seed that is produced from large, fruit-like seed pods which ripen in the autumn to expose small seeds attached to the most beautiful, silky white 'parachutes'.

Healthy plant The main attraction of these climbing plants is their mass of scented white flowers.

VARIETIES

Buy in summer, looking for healthy young plants that are fresh and green, with some flowers open and lots of buds on show. Avoid ones with yellowing foliage, or ones that have had such foliage removed. This is a sign of poor culture and root failure.
S. floribunda This is generally the only variety available.

AVOIDING PROBLEMS

Light and position

Always place the plant in the lightest possible place. Full sun may scorch some of the leaves, but this is not unduly harmful. The plant's natural climbing habit makes it essential that some sort of framework be provided for the plant to cling to.

Temperature range

Cool   Intermediate   Warm

A modest temperature of around 60°F (15°C) throughout the year is fine for these plants. In winter keep them cooler at 55°F (13°C). In summer, do not let the temperature rise above 75°F (23°C).

Watering

In summer, water two or three times a week and in winter, once a week. Use lime-free, tepid water whenever possible. Spray the plants once a week in summer but avoid wetting the flowers.

Feeding

Avoid giving excess food, but ensure that the plants have a weak feed with every watering while in active growth. In winter, when the plant is not flowering, feeding is not necessary.

Seasonal care

Winter	Spring	Summer	Autumn

Water stephanotis plants well during spring and summer but avoid too wet conditions by allowing the soil to dry out between applications. The plant can be trimmed to shape after flowering in autumn, or the growing frame can be extended to cope with new growth. Stem tip cuttings should be made in spring.

Soil

Pot in the spring when the plants are getting under way for the new season. Never move plants into containers much larger than the existing pot. Use conventional houseplant potting soil; peaty mixtures are not satisfactory.

PESTS AND DISEASES

The main enemies of *S. floribunda* are bugs and insects, but be careful not to water excessively or let the leaves become sun-scorched.
Scale insects These can only be eradicated by thorough application of malathion. Spray three times over 10 days
Sooty mould This is a harmless black fungus caused by scale insects. Wipe off with a sponge dipped in insecticide or soapy water.
Root mealy bug Eradicate with an insecticide.

Streptocarpus

Indigenous to South Africa, the original Cape Primrose, *S. 'Constant Nymph'*, with its profusion of delicate blue flowers, was for many years the only streptocarpus available. Now there are many fine hybrids offering a wealth of colour, and having the considerable added benefit that their leaves are smaller and very much less brittle. This makes it possible for the grower to pack them and get them to customers in a much better condition than was possible with the original variety. Its stemless leaves are coarse and they grow upwards with the plant's pretty flowers pushing up from among them.

New plants can be raised from seed, or particular varieties can be reproduced from leaf cuttings. These can be made by dividing the leaf up into sections about 3in (7·5cm) long, or by slitting firm leaves down the centre vein and placing them on their sides partially buried in peaty compost. The temperatures should be kept around 70°F (21°C).

Propagation This brightly-coloured streptocarpus (**below**) has reached the stage where new plants can be propagated from leaf cuttings (**right**).

AVOIDING PROBLEMS

Light and position

For the plant to continue to bloom throughout the spring and summer, it will need the lightest possible position, but not exposed to bright midday sun. During the winter months when not in flower, less light is tolerated.

Temperature range

Cool   Intermediate   Warm

Streptocarpus plants do not like heat, so an average temperature of 55°-60°F (13°-18°C) is best, with a constant of 60°F (15°C) being ideal. Should the temperature drop lower, keep the soil dry because the plant will become nearly dormant. In summer, a maximum of 75°F (23°C) is preferred.

Watering

Never let the plant stand in water or it will rot. In summer, water two or three times a week. In winter, water once a week or less. If possible, use soft, tepid water.

Feeding

Never feed the plant if it has just been potted, and feed sparingly during the winter. While in flower and well established, a greater number of flowers can be encouraged by using a fertilizer with a high proportion of potash.

Seasonal care

Winter   Spring   Summer   Autumn

Water thoroughly when in active growth and less in winter. At all times the soil should be allowed to dry out between waterings. Never clean leaves with chemicals. When not in flower, foliage can be cleaned by holding a hand over the soil in the pot and inverting the pot into a bucket of tepid, soapy water. Keep the plant out of the sun while it is drying.

Soil

While in small pots, a peaty mixture is best but when the pot reaches 5in (12.5cm) in diameter use a mixture that contains some loam. Good drainage is essential. Avoid putting plants in pots that are too large.

PESTS AND DISEASES

Streptocarpus is prone to three main pests and diseases, though not severely.
Aphids Either spray the flower stalks with insecticide, or simply remove by carefully running a thumb and finger along the stem.
Red spider mite This is not common, but can affect plants that are too dry and hot. Saturate the underside of leaves with insecticide.
Botrytis This is a result of dank, airless conditions, causing wet, brown patches of rot on foliage. Treat with a fungicide.

VARIETIES

Purchase in late spring to take advantage of the long flowering season. Select plants that are sturdy and fresh, with some flowers open and plenty of buds. Avoid any with damp leaves hanging over the side of the pot.
S. 'Constant Nymph' This long-established plant has attractive blue flowers, but brittle leaves that can be damaged easily.
S. 'Concorde Hybrid' This is a smaller plant, which comes in a wide range of colours and is less fragile.

Tolmiea menziesii

These houseplants develop into neat mounds of pale green foliage, and produce perfectly shaped little plants in the area where the leaf is attached to the petiole. The plantlets can be removed and potted separately and they give the plant its amusing common name.

Healthy plant The Piggy-back Plant is compact and fresh looking (**above**). New plantlets grow out of leaf edges (**below**).

VARIETIES

Select plants that seem young and green. Those with a dry yellow appearance may well be suffering from red spider mites. Larger plants may appear good value, but the smaller ones adapt better to indoor conditions, and usually prove more satisfactory. It is a robust indoor plant, but is equally hardy outdoors. The *Tolmiea menziesii*, Piggy-back Plant, Youth on Age or Mother of Thousands, is the only known variety of this species.

PESTS AND DISEASES

Red spider mite These get onto the underside of the plant's pale green leaves, and are difficult to detect with the naked eye. Spraying the plant with insecticide is inefficient as the leaves overlap, making the operation difficult. It is advisable to immerse the plant for about five minutes in a bucket of insecticide. Rubber gloves should be worn.

Aphids These can be a problem on young leaves in the spring and summer months, but can usually be controlled by an insecticide.
Mealy bug These pests may occur among the congested foliage of older plants. As they tend to lodge in the more inaccessible places, plants again should be immersed in insecticide, rather than being sprayed.

AVOIDING PROBLEMS

Light and position

T. menziesii is not a fussy plant, and it can adapt to most locations apart from very sunny positions near the window. It should always be positioned in plenty of space so that the extra little plants can grow comfortably.

Temperature range

Cool Intermediate Warm

This plant abhors very hot conditions, which will also encourage red spider mites. It will grow well in temperatures between 45°-60°F (7°-15°C) although the leaves will become paler, the lower the light level. Piggy-back Plants must be protected from draughts, and do not thrive in continual shade.

Watering

Regular moderate waterings are required by these plants during the summer period. In the winter however, tolmeias should only be watered occasionally when the potting mixture has become dry.

Feeding

Weak liquid fertilizer should be applied with each watering, much less being required during the winter period. Alternatively, fertilizer in pellet form can be pushed into the potting mixture.

Seasonal care

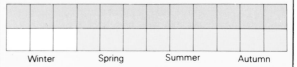

Winter   Spring   Summer   Autumn

Excesses of very wet and rock hard soil should always be avoided. Piggy-back Plants should regularly have all their dead leaves removed. New baby plants can be removed by hand at any time in the spring or summer period and potted again separately. They will grow very rapidly reaching a respectable size after only a few months. Tolmieas require considerably less food and water during the winter months.

Soil

Shallow pots are the most suitable for Piggy-back Plants, and they rarely need to be larger than 5in (12.5cm) in diameter. If the plants outgrow these, it is advisable to divide the plant or to start again with easily rooted plantlets. Loam-based mixtures are the most suitable for tolmieas.

Tradescantia

The numerous varieties of tradescantia are among the easiest to grow and the least expensive of all the indoor plants. They can also be very attractive if given a little bit extra care and attention.

During the summer months, cuttings about 3–4in (7·5–10cm) in length taken from the ends of sturdy growths will root easily in any good houseplant soil mixture. Up to seven cuttings should be inserted in each small pot, and both pot and cuttings should be placed in a sealed plastic bag to reduce transpiration, so encouraging rooting.

Tradescantia relations

Among the tradescantia, there is a small selection of slightly more difficult plants that are only occasionally offered for sale. Almost all of them are grown for their decorative foliage rather than their flowers.

Most plants are propagated from cuttings, but are a little more difficult to rear than the common types, needing slightly higher temperatures in the region of 65°F (18°C). Also, if black leg rot is to be avoided on cutting stems where they enter the soil, particular attention must be paid to watering which should be minimal until rooting has taken place. The siderasis is propagated very easily by dividing clumps into smaller sections, and the rhoeos can be propagated either from cuttings, or they may be allowed to set seed which is not difficult to germinate in a temperature of around 65°F (18°C).

Healthy plant The tradescantia, also called Wandering Jew or Inch Plant, can be displayed in a hanging basket (**left**) or in a wall pot. The trailing stems can grow as long as 1ft (30cm). If a tradescantia is properly cared for, its leaves should be a striking combination of cream and green stripes.

AVOIDING PROBLEMS

Light and position

For tradescantias to retain the variegated colours of their leaves, it is essential that they are placed in plenty of light but protected from very strong sun. They are often positioned so that they can trail over shady windowsills.

Temperature range

Cool   Intermediate   Warm

Cool conditions are ideal for this plant, 50°-60°F (10°-15°C), but it cannot tolerate draughts, very cold areas or continual shade. It is also advisable to keep tradescantias well away from all heating appliances. They will survive in dry surroundings, but grow better in a more humid atmosphere. Chilly temperatures may cause leaf discoloration.

Watering

Tradescantias should be watered regularly, but the colours of the leaves will become dimmer if the soil or potting mixture is allowed to become too wet. Less water will be required during the winter period when the plants are not so active.

Feeding

These plants will respond well to feeds of weak liquid fertilizer at every watering. Obviously this will be less frequent during the winter months, but it is important that feeding does not stop completely during this time.

Seasonal care

Winter   Spring   Summer   Autumn

The green shoots that occasionally appear on tradescantias should be carefully removed, as they are very vigorous and will quickly lose their variegated colouring, so marring their appearance. If the leaves become at all dry and shrivelled, they should be taken off the bases of the longer stems. Less water is needed in winter when the plants are less active, especially as during this period they are more prone to root rot from over-watering.

Soil

There is a belief that these plants thrive on little nourishment but this is not the case. Young tradescantias must be potted with great care if they are to do well. A good houseplant mixture should be used, and ideally it should be loam-based.

PESTS AND DISEASES

Aphids These do not often attack this plant, but they may occasionally get onto soft new leaves and cause discoloration. There are a variety of insecticides that should control them.
Red spider mite These may be troublesome. To cure, spray with malathion. Red spider will cause discoloration. Another possible cause of this is root rot from overwatering (**see illustration above right**).

VARIETIES

It is advisable to buy tradescantias during the spring.
T. fluminensis This has striped leaves with purple undersides.
T.f. 'Quicksilver' This variety is tougher and grows faster than *T. fluminensis.*
T. albiflora 'Albovittata' This form has a silvery foliage.
T.a. 'Tricolor' The leaves of this plant are striped white and purple.

Yucca elephantipes

In tropical South America, one or other of the almost indestructible yuccas is often used to mark out boundaries— hence its common name. Only recently have they become popular as indoor plants, being elegant individual plants for important locations. Stout stems of the yucca are imported, cut down and shipped almost as if they were miniature tree trunks. On arrival at their nursery destination, the various sized stem sections are propagated in beds of peat at a temperature of around 75°F (23°C). Amazingly for such large and solid sections, almost all of them produce roots and leaves, which is a testimony to the tough character of these splendid plants.

Healthy plant Yuccas are easily identified by their sword-shaped leaves and very thick stems.

AVOIDING PROBLEMS

Light and position

Yuccas must be given the lightest possible surroundings and will tolerate full sun. If the leaves are too close to the glass however, there is a danger of discoloration through scorching.

Temperature range

Cool　　Intermediate　　Warm

These plants are both versatile and resilient. Any temperature between 50°-70°F (10°-21°C) will suit them, providing the soil is not too wet when low temperatures are anticipated. If the surroundings are not well lit, yuccas should be kept as cool as possible. They are tolerant of a very dry atmosphere.

Watering

Yuccas need plenty of water but should never be overwatered or left to stand in water or botytris may set in. They should be kept fairly dry during the winter period

Feeding

Once they are well established in their pots, these plants should be fed with liquid fertilizer at each watering. Fertilizer in tablet form can be pushed into the soil at intervals recommended by the manufacturer.

Seasonal care

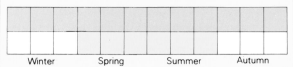

Winter　　Spring　　Summer　　Autumn

During the summer months, the yucca plant may remain out-of-doors in a sheltered position, with watering and feeding going on as normal. Leaf tips may occasionally become brown as a result of excessive watering. The plant must be positioned carefully so that it gets sufficient sunlight each day. Older plants may produce cream coloured flowers in the summer.

PESTS AND DISEASES

Scale insect These may attack the Yucca plant clinging to the foliage, and occasionally the stem, like miniature limpets. They suck the sap which weakens the plant.

Sooty mould This is a messy though harmless fungus that settles on the excreta of the scale insects leaving an unsightly black deposit. Scale insects and sooty mould can both be wiped off with a sponge soaked in soapy water.

Stem rot This may set in if the yucca is over-watered. As the base rots, the plant will start to keel over.

VARIETIES

All plants should have bright green foliage that is firm to the touch. The cost will vary according to the height of the plant and the number of stems that there are in the pot.
Y. elephantipes The Spineless Yucca, has much softer leaves than other varieties.
Y. aloifolia Spanish Bayonet has extremely sharp leaves, hence its name, so it should be touched and moved with caution. There are several varieties of the *Y. aloifolia* such as *Y.a. 'Variegata'* and *Y.a. 'Marginata'* that have white and yellow markings

Soil

Peaty mixtures are quite useless as this is a robust plant. It will overbalance very easily if it is not provided with the anchorage that a loam-based mixture offers. Clay pots are more suitable than light plastic ones.

Zebrina pendula

Similar in habit to the tradescantias, this is one of the most attractive of the common indoor plants. Its foliage has an overall silvery sheen when the plants are well grown, and the undersides of the leaves are a rich shade of burgundy. They are perfect hanging basket plants that are best prepared by potting five or six small plants in the basket in spring. The earlier growing tips should be pinched out to encourage branching and fuller, more attractive growth. In fact, the ends of each stem can be removed at a length of some 4in (10cm) and inserted in potting soil as cuttings that will root readily in spring and summer.

Healthy plant Another type of Wandering Jew, Wandering Sailor or Inch Plant, zebrinas are admired for their variegated leaves and general lustre. They grow very quickly, but must be fed and watered regularly and kept in suitable surroundings. If these plants are neglected (**right**) they will thin out becoming brown and withered.

AVOIDING PROBLEMS

Light and position

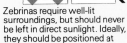

Zebrinas require well-lit surroundings, but should never be left in direct sunlight. Ideally, they should be positioned at head height in hanging baskets or suspended pots, so that they can be cultivated with ease.

Temperature range

Cool   Intermediate   Warm

Extremes of temperature should be avoided, but anywhere between 55°-65°F (13°-18°C) is suitable. These plants must be kept out of draughts and away from all kinds of heating appliances. At lower temperatures they will grow more slowly, and chilling may cause the leaves to drop.

Watering

Regular watering is essential, and most hanging plants tend to get neglected in this respect. The potting mixture should be moist throughout but never too wet.

Feeding

It is not advisable to starve Inch Plants in an attempt to improve the leaf colour. Zebrinas thrive on weak liquid fertilizer applied each time the plant is watered.

Seasonal care

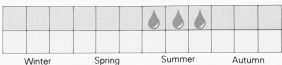

Winter   Spring   Summer   Autumn

To prevent plants from becoming straggly and unattractive as they age, it is wise to trim back untidy growth periodically. The growing tips of any shoots that appear to be outpacing their neighbours shoud be pinched out. When large plants start to deteriorate new cuttings should be taken. It is not necessary to feed plants that have been newly potted.

Soil

Use a loam-based mixture, potting plants in larger containers as soon as the existing ones are filled with roots. Unless zebrinas are going into hanging baskets, they will rarely need pots larger than 5in (12.5cm) in diameter.

PESTS AND DISEASES

Aphids These are sometimes a problem if there are a lot about, and they may cause spotting. They can be eradicated with an insecticide spray, or if there are only a few, simply remove between finger and thumb.
Red spider mite These may attack zebrinas, but they are very hard to see with the naked eye. Leaves that are affected will start to take on a very dry and lifeless appearance, but insecticide spray containing dicofol or malathion should cure the plant. On the whole, zebrinas tend to stay free of pests and diseases if they are kept clean.

VARIETIES

Avoid buying tired old plants with long straggling strands of growth. They may seem good value, but the younger ones are more likely to be free of blemishes and leaf damage.
Z. pendula This is the best-known plant with its purple flowers and silver striped leaves.
Z.p. Quadricolor This is similar, much less common, and has reddish brown, green, silver and pink striped foliage.
Z.p. 'Discolor' This has leaves with a brown tinge that are narrower than those of the other varieties.
Z.p. purpusii This plant has purple leaves.

Glossary

A

Aerial root A root which grows up above the level of the soil, often seen in philodendrons and the *Monstera deliciosa,* which can extract moisture from the air.
Alternate An arrangement of leaves on a stem in which they grow singly on opposite sides and at different levels.
Annual A plant which completes its whole life-cycle within one year of being grown from seed.
Aquatic This term is given to a plant which lives wholly or partially in water.
Axil The angle between a leaf or leaf stalk and the stem on which it is carried. A growth from the axil is called an axillary bud.

B

Biennial A plant which flowers and seeds in the year following its own growth from seed, thus completing its life within two years.
Bloom This term is often used to mean a flower but, more specifically, refers to a waxy or powdery coating on the leaves or fruits of certain plants. This coating is usually white or has a pale blue tinge.
Bract A modified leaf, shaped like a leaf or flower petal. Bracts are often highly coloured, as in the Poinsettia, and may support a less showy flower.
Bromeliad A member of the Bromeliaceae, or pineapple family. Bromeliads are epiphytic plants and can be grown supported on tree bark rather than in soil.
Bulb A fleshy bud growing underground which stores food and protects new growth within its overlapping layers.

C

Capillary action The upward movement of liquid in areas of confinement. This principle is used in watering plants from below, as the water rises through spaces in the soil.
Chlorosis A condition when the leaves of a plant become pale or yellowed due to lack of chlorophyll. This may be caused by insufficient nutrients in the soil.

Compost In the context of houseplant growing, this term means a mixture of soil and other ingredients in which the plant is potted, otherwise called a potting mixture.
Conservatory A room with specially controlled heat and humidity, in which houseplants are grown.
Corm The swollen base of a stem formed underground which protects new growth and stores food, and is used for propagation.
Creeper A plant with trailing growth which puts down roots at intervals along the growth.
Crocks Broken pieces of a ceramic pot, or stones and ceramic material, placed in the base of a pot to allow free drainage through the soil.
Crown The part of a plant from which the roots and stems grow, forming the base of the plant.
Cultivar A term for a plant, which has been bred in cultivation, rather than originating in the wild.
Cutting A piece of a plant which is used to raise a new plant, such as a leaf or stem tip which may be potted to develop roots.

D

Deciduous A term describing plants which shed their leaves when inactive, usually during the winter.
Division A method of growing new plants by splitting the root-ball of a mature plant and potting the sections separately.
Dormant period A temporary period in which a plant ceases to grow at all. This often occurs during the winter months.

E

Epiphyte A plant which can derive moisture and nutrients from the air or decaying plant matter and therefore does not need to grow in soil, but can support itself when growing in bark or shallow moss.
Evergreen A plant which keeps a mass of foliage throughout the year, shedding a few leaves at a time.
Exotic This term strictly refers to plants foreign to the country in which they are being grown, but is also commonly used for

brightly coloured, succulent or unusual plants.

F

Floret A single, small flower which is one of many making up a large compound flower head as in a daisy or cineraria.
Foliage plant A plant which is grown indoors to display the beauty of its leaves. Although some bear flowers, these are usually insignificant.
Foliar feed Fertilizer which is sprayed on to the leaves of the plant and can be rapidly absorbed.
Frond An alternative term for the leaf of a fern or palm.
Fungicide A chemical used to control disease and destroy fungus growths on a plant.
Fungus A parasitic form of plant life including microscopic organisms which cause such houseplant diseases as mildew and botrytis.

G

Genus A term which refers to a group of plants with similar characteristics which can be sub-divided into separate species. Several genera of fundamentally similar plants make up a family.
Germination The earliest stage in the growth of a plant, when a seed begins to sprout.
Grafting A means of joining a stem or shoot of one plant to another plant which is still rooted.
Growing shoot A shoot which extends the growth of the plant from a stem tip.

H

Habit The normal growth pattern of a plant, whether trailing, creeping, bushy or climbing, for instance.
Half-hardy A term for a plant which can adjust to cool conditions but cannot survive in extremely cold temperatures or wintering out-of-doors.
Hardy A term describing a plant which can withstand prolonged exposure to cold temperatures and even frost.
Honeydew The sticky secretion left on plants by

insects such as aphids and whitefly.
Humidifier A piece of equipment which will maintain or increase the level of humidity in a room.
Humus A substance consisting of decayed organic matter which can be used to make a rich topsoil.
Hybrid A plant which is bred by cross-fertilizing two plants of the same family, although not necessarily of the same genus or variety.
Hydroculture A method of growing plants without putting them in soil. Instead, the pots are filled with pebbles and the plants are fed nutrients when they are watered.

I

Inflorescence A term commonly applied to a cluster of flowers, a head or spike growing on one main stem, but also a general term for the flowering of a plant.
Inorganic A word descriptive of a fertilizer or chemical which is not derived from living matter.
Insecticide A chemical or organic substance used to control any insects.

L

Lateral shoot A shoot growing sideways from a main stem at any point below the tip.
Leaf cutting Part of a leaf or a whole leaf used to propagate a new plant.
Leaflet A small, single leaf which is one of a number growing from a stem to form a compound leaf.
Leaf mould A component of some potting mixtures which consists exclusively of rotted down leaves.
Leggy A term describing tall growth of a plant when the stems become spindly and bear fewer leaves, especially at the lower ends.
Loam A high quality soil used in potting mixtures, which contains a good balance of clay, sand and decayed matter.

M

Margin The edge of one section of a plant, most usually applied to the edge of the leaf.
Midrib The main rib of a leaf which divides the length centrally. The midrib usually stands out from the surface of the underside of a leaf.
Mouth The open end of a tubular or bell-shaped flower.

N

Node A joint or swelling on the stem, of a plant from which leaves, buds or lateral shoots appear.

O

Offset A small, new plant which develops naturally from its parent and can be detached and propagated separately.
Opposite An arrangement of leaves on a stem where they grow in pairs, one on either side of the stem.
Organic A word describing matter such as fertilizer or compost which is derived from living tissue.

P

Palmate A term for a leaf consisting of three or more leaflets radiating from a single stalk in an arrangement resembling an open hand.
Peat Also known as peat moss, this is a substance used in potting composed of partially decayed organic matter. It is particularly valued for its air and moisture retaining characteristics.
Perennial A term applied to a plant which lives indefinitely. In houseplants, this means surviving through at least three seasons of growth, and often much more.
Petiole A stem or stalk which carries a leaf.
pH balance A means of measuring the acidity or alkaline content of the soil.
Photosynthesis The process in a plant by which the leaves are nourished. For effective photosynthesis plants require water, air and adequate exposure to light.
Pinching out This refers to the procedure in which new growing tips are removed by pinching them between the fingertips to encourage branching and bushiness elsewhere on the plant.
Pinnate The term for a compound leaf in which the leaflets are carried in pairs on opposite sides of the stem. In plants where there is a further division of each part of the compound leaf, the arrangement is called bipinnate.
Plantlet A small plant produced on the runners or stems of a parent plant.
Pot-bound The condition in which the roots of a plant are crowded inside the pot. This usually prevents healthy growth although some plants do well if slightly pot-bound.
Potting on Transferring a plant to a larger container to allow continued growth of the roots.
Propagation Techniques of forming a new plant by means of cuttings or divisions of a mature plant.
Pruning Cutting back the growth of a plant selectively to encourage bushiness, a compact shape and better flowering.

R

Repotting Transferring a plant to a new container or renewing the soil in the pot to revitalize the growth.
Resting period A season in which there is little or no new growth in the plant. This period is not necessarily accompanied by decline or falling leaves.
Rhizome A thick, horizontal stem, usually growing underground, from which buds and roots are grown.
Rootball The dense mass of matted roots and the compost trapped in them which are visible when a plant is removed from its pot.
Rosette The name given to an arrangement of clustered leaves radiating from a central area, either carried on a single stem or on separate stems.
Runner A trailing stem which runs horizontally along the soil and roots at intervals to form new plants.

S

Sharp sand A coarse sand, free of lime, sometimes used in potting mixtures.
Shrub A plant with branching, woody stems which remains relatively small and compact in growth, unlike a tree.
Spadix A fleshy spike which carries small flowers embedded in its surface.
Spathe A large bract, often brightly coloured, which acts as a protective sheath for a spadix.
Species A sub-division of a genus of plants forming a distinct grouping of plants which can fertilize each other and grow from seed without being specially cultivated.
Sphagnum moss A spongy bog moss, useful in cultivating houseplants because of its high capacity to hold water.
Spore The reproductive cell of a fern or moss, acting in the same way as a seed from a flowering plant. Ferns usually carry spores in raised cases on the undersides of the fronds.
Sport A plant variety which arises as a natural mutation from the parent plant.
Strike The term used to describe the rooting of a stem or leaf cutting.
Succulent A plant which can withstand a period of very dry conditions, having fleshy stems and leaves which are able to store moisture.
Systemic A term describing an insecticide or fungicide which is absorbed into the tissues of the plant through the soil or leaves and poisons the organism or insect living on the plant.

T

Tendril A fine, twining thread arising from the leaf or stem of a plant which clings to a frame or surface, enabling the plant to climb.
Terrestrial A plant which grows in soil in its natural habitat, as opposed to an epiphytic or an aquatic plant.
Top-dressing Freshening the soil in which a plant is growing by replacing the top layer, rather than repotting or potting on the whole plant.
Transpiration The natural process in which water evaporates through the pores in leaves.
Tuber A swollen stem, usually underground, which stores food and produces new growth.

V

Variegated A term which refers to plants with patterned, spotted or blotchy leaves. Most common variegations are green broken by cream, white or silver, but some plants have brighter colours on the leaves.
Variety A member of a plant species which differs from the others by a natural alteration such as in the colour of the leaves or flowers. The term is often applied to plants bred in cultivation, which strictly should be called cultivars.
Vein A strand of tissue in a leaf which conducts moisture and nutrients. Large veins may be known as ribs.

W

Whorl A radiating arrangement of three or more leaves around a node on a plant's stem.

Index

A

Acalypha hispida 44-45
  diseased plant 44-45
  feeding 45
  healthy leaf 44
  healthy plant 44
  light and position 45
  potting 44
  propagation 44
  red spider mite 45
  seasonal care 45
  soil 45
  temperature range 45
  watering 45
Acanthaceae:
  Aphelandra 52-53
  Beloperone guttata 66-67
  Fittonia 120
  Pachystachys lutea 141
Adiantum capillus-veneris 108-109, 111
Aechmea 46-47
  A. fulgens discolor 46
  A. rhodocyanea (A. fasciata) 46
  browning leaf 47
  discoloured bract 47
  feeding 46
  healthy leaf 47
  healthy plant 47
  leaf texture 47
  light and position 46
  pests and diseases 47
  propagation 46
  seasonal care 46
  soil 46
  temperature range 46
  varieties and purchasing 46
  watering 46
Aerial root 184
African Violet (Saintpaulia) 34, 164-165
African Windflower/ Hemp (Sparmannia africana) 175
Agavaceae:
  Dracaena 102-103
  Yucca elephantipes 182
Aglaonema 48-49
  A. crispum 'Silver Queen' 48
  A. modestum 49
  A. pseudobracteatum 48
  A. trewbii 48
  botrytis 49
  damaged leaf 49
  feeding 49
  healthy leaf 48
  healthy plant 48
  leaf spot 49
  light and position 49
  pests and diseases 48
  potting 48
  propagation 48
  seasonal care 49
  soil 49
  temperature range 49
  watering 49
Alternate leaves 184
Aluminium Plant (Pilea cadierei) 156-157

Amarillidaceae:
  Clivia miniata 88-89
Ananas:
  A. bractatus variegatus 72
  A. comosus 72
Annual 184
Anthurium 50-51
  A. andraeanum 51
  A. guatemala 51
  A. scherzerianum 51
  brown patches 51
  feeding 50
  flower wilting 51
  healthy plant 50
  leaves turning yellow 51
  light and position 50
  natural and unnatural deaths 51
  seasonal care 50
  soil 50
  temperature range 50
  varieties and purchasing 51
  watering 50
Aphelandra 52-53
  A. chamissoniana 53
  A. squarrosa Brockfeld 53
  A. s. Dania 53
  A. s. Louisae 53
  feeding 52
  healthy plant 52
  light and position 52
  pests and diseases 53, 53
  propagation 52
  seasonal care 52
  soil 52
  temperature range 52
  varieties and purchasing 53
  watering 52
Aphids 21, 24
Aquatic 184
Araceae:
  Aglaonema 48-49
  Anthurium 50-51
  Dieffenbachia 98-101
  Monstera deliciosa 138-139
  Philodendron 152-155
  Scindapsus 171
  Spathiphyllum 176-177
Aralia elegantissima 54-55
  feeding 54
  healthy plant 55
  light and position 54
  pests and diseases 54, 55
  propagation 54
  seasonal care 54
  soil 54
  temperature range 54
  watering 54
Aralia sieboldii see Fatsia japonica
Araliaceae:
  Aralia elegantissima 54-55
  Fatsia and Fatshedera 106-107
  Hedera 122-123
  Heptapleurum 124-125
  Schefflera 170
Araucaria 56-57
  feeding 57
  healthy plant 56
  light and position 57
  pests and diseases 56
  seasonal care 57

soil 57
temperature range 57
unhealthy plant 57
varieties and purchasing 57
watering 57
Araucariaceae:
  Araucaria 56-57
Asclepiadaceae:
  Stephanotis floribunda 178
Aspidistra lurida (A. eliator) 59-59
  A. l. 'Variegata' 58
  damaged leaves 59
  feeding 59
  healthy plant 58
  light and position 59
  pests and diseases 59
  propagation 58
  seasonal care 59
  soil 59
  temperature range 59
  varieties and purchasing 58
  watering 59
Asplenium nidus avis 108, 108
Astrophytum 76, 77
Australian Laurel (Pittosporum) 158-159
Australian Pine (Araucaria) 56-57
Axil 184
Azalea indica 60-61
  A. obtusum 60
  dehydration 61
  feeding 61
  healthy plant 60
  light and position 61
  pests and diseases 61, 61
  seasonal care 61
  soil 61
  temperature range 61
  varieties and purchasing 60
  watering 16, 16, 61

B

Balsaminaceae:
  Impatiens 130-131
Banana Plant (Musa) 140
Banyan Tree (Ficus benghalensis) 114
Begonia 62-65
  B. glaucophylla 63
  B. haageana 63
  B. 'President Carnot' 63
  creepers and climbers 64
  feeding 65
  foliage 62, 62-63
  healthy flowering cane type 64
  light and position 65
  Reiger or Schwabenland strain 65
  seasonal care 65
  soil 65
  starved B. solonanthea 64
  temperature range 65
  tuberous 64
  varieties and purchasing 63
  watering 65
  B. hiemalis Reiger 63
    botrytis 65
    healthy plant 65

B. rex 62, 63
  botrytis 63
  healthy plant 62
  propagation 62
  varieties 62-63
B. tuberhybrid 63
  starved 64
Begonia Vine (Cissus discolor) 84-85
Begoniaceae:
  Begonia 62-65
Beloperone guttata 66-67
  B. g. Lutea 66
  feeding 67
  healthy plant 66
  leaf of starved plant 67
  light and position 67
  pests and diseases 67
  pot-bound plant 67
  propagation 66
  seasonal care 67
  soil 67
  temperature range 67
  watering 67
Biennial 184
Billbergia 72
  B. nutans 72
  healthy plant 70
Bipinnate 185
Bird's Nest Fern (Asplenium nidus avis) 108, 108
Bishop's Hood Cactus (Astrophytum myriostigma) 76
Black leg 53, 67, 148, 154
Black spot 123
Blacking Plant (Hibiscus rosa-sinensis) 15, 126-127
Blechnum 110, 110
Bloom 184
Boston Fern (Nephrolepis exaltata) 111
Botrytis 23, 24
  prime cause of 24
  susceptible plants 24
Bougainvillea 68-69
  B. buttiana 69
  B. glabra 69
  B. g. 'Harrisii' 69
  B. g. 'Sanderana Variegata' 69
  diseased leaves 69
  feeding 69
  healthy plant 68
  light and position 69
  pests and diseases 69
  propagation 68
  seasonal care 69
  soil 69
  temperature range 69
  varieties and purchasing 69
  watering 69
Boundary Plant (Yucca) 182
Bract 184
Brassaia actinophylla see Schefflera
Bromeliaceae:
  Aechmea 46-47
  Bromeliads 70-73
Bromeliads 70-73, 184
  Aechmea 46-47
  Ananas bractatus variegatus 72

A. comosus 72
Billbergia 72
B. nutans 72
Cryptanthus 71, *71*, 72
C. acaulis 72
C. bromelioides 71
Tillandsia 72
Vriesea 72
V. splendens 72
displaying *70-71*
feeding 73
healthy *Billbergia 70*
healthy *Neoregelia carolinae 'Tricolor' 72*
light and position 73
pests and diseases *72, 73*
plant care *72*
raising new plants 70
seasonal care 73
soil 73
temperature range 73
varieties and purchasing 72
watering 73
Bulb 184
Burmese Fishtail Palm *(Caryota)* 144
Busy Lizzie *(Impatiens)* 130-131
Button Fern *(Pellaea rotundifolia)* 110, *110*
Buying houseplants 12-18, 26-27
  as present 26
  azaleas 27
  care on reaching home 16-18
  checking condition of foliage 12
  flowering plants 12, 27
  general appearance (store care) 14, *14*
  healthy hibiscus *15*
  inspecting for pests 12, 26-27
  large plant in small pot 14
  limp leaves 14
  Poinsettias 12, 14, 27
  useful hints 26
  wrapping for journey home 27

C

Cactaceae:
  Cacti and succulents 74-78
Cacti and succulents 74-78
  Astrophytum 76, *77*
  Cleistocactus strausii 76
  desert cacti 74
  Echeveria gibbiflora 77
  E. glauca 75
  E. setosa 75
  Echinocereus 76, *77*
  E. pectinatus 76
  Epiphyllum 76, *77*
  Euphorbia pseudocactus 76
  feeding 75
  forest cacti 74
  Hamatocactus setispinus 76, *77*
  healthy *Opuntia 74*
  light and position *75*
  Lithops 76, *77*
  Notocactus leninghausii 76

pests and diseases 78, *78*
propagation 74
seasonal care 75
soil 75
succulents 74
temperature range 75
Trichocereus spachianus 77
varieties and purchasing 76
watering 75
watering problems *78*
Zygocactus truncatus 77
Calamondin Orange *(Citrus mitis)* 86-87
Calathea 135
  C. makoyana 135, 136
  C. zebrina 136
  feeding 137
  light and position 137
  pests and diseases 136
  problems *136-137*
  seasonal care 137
  soil 137
  temperature range 137
  varieties and purchasing 136
  watering 137
Campanula isophylla 79
  C. i. 'Alba' 79
  C. i. 'Mayi' 79
  feeding 79
  healthy plant *79*
  light and position 79
  pests and diseases 79
  raising new plants 79
  seasonal care 79
  soil 79
  temperature range *79*
  varieties and purchasing 79
  watering 79
Campanulaceae:
  Campanula isophylla 79
Cape Primrose *(Streptocarpus)* 179
Capillary action 184
Care of plants 26-35
  cleaning 30-31
  containers 29
  feeding 30
  frequent inspection 26
  hanging baskets or pots 29-30
  humidity 29, *29,* 36
  positioning 27-28, *27*
  propagation 34, *35*
  pruning 33, *33*
  spraying foliage 20, 36
  staking 32, *32*
  watering 28-29
Caryota 144, *144*
Cast Iron Plant *(Aspidistra lurida)* 58-59
Caterpillars 95
Cathedral Windows *(Maranta)* 134, 136-137
Chamaedorea 144, *144*
Chamaedorea elegans see *Neanthe bella*
Chamaerops humilis 143
Chaplet flower *(Stephanotis floribunda)* 178
Chenille Plant *(Acalypha hispida)* 44-45

Chinese Evergreen *(Aglaonema)* 48
Chinese Rose *(Hibiscus rosa-sinensis)* 15, 126-127
Chlorophytum comosum 80-81
  C. c. Variegatum 80
  feeding 80
  healthy plant *81*
  light and position 80
  pests and diseases 80, *81*
  raising new plants 80
  seasonal care 80
  soil 80
  temperature range 80
  varieties and purchasing 80
  watering 80
Chlorosis 184
Christmas Cactus *(Zygocactus truncatus)* 77
Christmas Cherry *(Solanum capsicastrum)* 174
Christmas Star *(Euphorbia pulcherrima)* 104-105
Christmas Tree Plant *(Araucaria)* 56-57
Chrysalidocarpus 144, *145*
Cineraria 82-83
  feeding 83
  healthy plants *82*
  light and position 83
  pests and diseases 83
  S. c. cineraria grandiflora 82
  S. c. cineraria nana 82
  seasonal care 83
  soil 83
  temperature range 83
  unhealthy leaves *83*
  unhealthy plant *82*
  varieties and purchasing 82
  watering 83
Cissus 84-85
  C. antarctica 84
  C. discolor 84
  C. rhombifolia (see also *Rhoicissus)* 84
  feeding 85
  healthy *C. discolor 84*
  light and position 85
  pests and diseases 84
  propagation 84
  seasonal care 85
  soil 85
  temperature range 85
  unhealthy leaves *85*
  varieties and purchasing 84
  watering 85
Citrus mitis 86-87
  feeding 86
  healthy plant *86*
  light and position 86
  pests and diseases 87, *87*
  seasonal care 86
  soil 86
  temperature range 86
  varieties 87
  watering 86
Cleaning plants 30-31
  leaf cleaning chemicals 30-31
  hairy leaved 31, *31*
  using soapy water 31, *31*
Cleistocactus strausii 76

Clivia miniata 88-89
C. m. 'Variegata' 88
  feeding 88
  healthy plant *88*
  light and position 88
  pests and diseases 89
  propagation 88
  seasonal care 88
  soil 88
  temperature range 88
  unhealthy plant *89*
  varieties and purchasing 88
  watering 88
Codiaeum 90-91
  C. craigii 90
  C. 'Eugene Drapps' 90
  C. holufiana 90, *90*
  C. 'Mrs Iceton' 90
  C. reidii 90
  damaged leaves *91*
  feeding 91
  foliage variation *90*
  light and position 91
  pests and diseases 91
  raising new plants 90
  seasonal care 91
  soil 91
  store care of *14*
  temperature range 91
  varieties and purchasing 90
  watering 91
Collinia elegans see *Neanthe bella*
Columnea 92-3
  C. banksii 93
  C. gloriosa 93
  C. microphylla 93
  feeding 93
  healthy plant *92*
  light and position 93
  pests and diseases 93, *93*
  seasonal care 93
  soil 93
  temperature range 93
  varieties and purchasing 93
  watering 93
  Commelinaceae:
    Tradescantia 181
    Zebrina pendula 183
Compositae:
  Cineraria 82-83
Compost 184
Conservatory 184
Containers, decorative 29
  hanging pots 29-30
Corm 184
Crassulaceae:
  Kalanchoe beharensis 132-133
Creeper 184
Creeping/Climbing Fig *(Ficus pumila)* 114, *117, 119*
Crocks 184
Croton *(Codiaeum)* 14, 90-91
Crown 184
  Cryptanthus 71, *71,* 72
  C. acaulis 72
  C. bromelioides 71
Cultivar 184
Cutting *(see also Propagation)* 184
Cyclamen mite 95, 165

Cyclamen persicum 94-95
  feeding 95
  healthy plant *94*
  light and position 95
  pests and diseases 95, *95*
  seasonal care 95
  soil 95
  temperature range 95
  varieties and purchasing 94
  watering 95
Cyperaceae:
  Cyperus 96-97
Cyperus 96-97
  C. alternifolius 96, *96*
  C.a. 'Albo Variegata' 96, *96*
  C. diffusus 96
  feeding 97
  healthy plant *96*
  light and position 97
  pests and diseases 97, *97*
  raising new plants 96
  seasonal care 97
  soil 97
  temperature range 97
  varieties and purchasing 96
  watering 97
Cyrtomium falcatum 110, *110*

D

Davallia 110, *111*
Deciduous plant 184
Desert Privet *(Peperomia magnoliifolia)* 150-151
Devil's Ivy *(Scindapsus)* 171
Diagnosis chart, instant *40-41*
Diazinon see *Pests and diseases 20-25*
Dichloran see *Pests and diseases 20-25*
Dieffenbachia 98-101
  aphids *100*
  D. amoena 99
  D. amoena 'Tropic Snow' 98
  D. bausei 99
  D. bowmannii 99
  D. camilla 99, *99*
  D. exotica 99, *99*
  D. imperialis 99
  D. maculata 99
  feeding 101
  leaf scorch *100*
  leaves dying naturally *100*
  light and position 101
  overwatering *100*
  physical damage *100*
  raising new plants 98
  seasonal care 101
  soil 101
  stem rot *101*
  temperature range 101
  varieties and purchasing 99
  watering 101
Diseases see *Pests and diseases 20-25*
Display see *Positioning*
Disulfoton see *Pests and diseases 20-25*
Division 184
Dizygotheca elegantissima see *Aralia elegantissima*

Dormant period 184
Dracaena 102-103
  D. deremensis 102
  D. godseffiana 102
  D. marginata 'Tricolor' 102, *102*
  D. souvenir de Schriever 102, *102*
  D. terminalis 102, *102*
  feeding 103
  healthy and damaged leaves *103*
  healthy plant *102*
  light and position 103
  pests and diseases 103
  propagation 102
  seasonal care 103
  soil 103
  temperature range 103
  varieties and purchasing 102, *102*
  wateriing 103
Dumb Cane *(Dieffenbachia)* 98-101

E

Earth Star *(Cryptanthus)* 71, *71*, 72
Earthworms in pots 17, *21*
Echeveria:
  E. gibbiflora 77
  E. glauca 75
  E. setosa 75
Echinocereus 76, 77
  E. pectinatus 76
Egyptian Paper Plant *(Cyperus)* 96-97
Endosulfan see *Pests and diseases 20-25*
Epiphyllum 76, 77
Epiphyte 184
Equipment for plant care *24-25*
Ericaceae:
  Azalea indica 60-61
Euphorbia pseudocactus 76
  E. p. lyttonia 76
Euphorbia pulcherrima 104-105
  buying 12, 14, 27
  feeding 105
  healthy plant *104*
  light and position 105
  pests and diseases 105
  raising new plants 104
  seasonal care 105
  soil 105
  temperature range 105
  unhealthy leaves *105*
  watering 105
Euphorbiaceae:
  Acalypha hispida 44-45
  Codiaeum 90-91
  Euphorbia pulcherrima 104-105
Evergreen 184
Exotic 184

F

Falling Stars *(Campanula isophylla)* 79
False Aralia *(Aralia elegantissima)* 54-55
False Castor Oil Plant *(Fatsia)* 106-107
Fan Plant *(Begonia rex)* 62-65
Fatshedera see *Fatsia japonica*
Fatsia japonica (Fatshedera lizei) 106-107
  feeding 107
  healthy plant *106*
  leaf problems *107*
  light and position 107
  pests and diseases 107
  propagation 106
  seasonal care 107
  soil 107
  temperature range 107
  varieties and purchasing 106
  watering 107
Feeding plants 30
  on-purchase 16-17, 30
  plant food tablet 30
  types of food 30, *31*
  under-nourished plant *30*
Felt Bush/Plant *Kalanchoe beharensis)* 132-133
Ferns 108-113
  Adiantum capillus-veneris 108-109, *111*
  Asplenium nidus avis 108, *108*
  Blechnum 110, *110*
  coarse foliage 108
  commonest varieties *110-111*
  Cyrtomium falcatum 110, *110*
  Davallia 110, *111*
  feeding 109
  fine foliage 108
  general care 112
  light and position 109
  Microlepia speluncia 111
  Nephrolepis exaltata 111
  Pellaea 110, *110*
  pests and diseases 112
  Phyllitis 110, *110*
  Platycerium alcicorne 108, 110, *111*
  Polypodium 110, *110*
  Pteris 110, *111*
  seasonal care 109
  soil 109
  temperature range 109
  three common problems *113*
  unhealthy and healthy *113*
  varieties and purchasing 110
  watering 109
Fertilizer 16, 30
  high nitrogen content 16, 30
  high potash content 16, 30
  types *31*
Ficus 114-119
  common problems *119*
  F. benghalensis 114
  F. 'Europa' 114, *116*
  F. retusa 114
  F. rubiginosa 114

F. sagittata 114
  feeding 114-115
  light and position 114-115
  pests and diseases 118, *118*
  seasonal care 114-115
  soil 114-115
  temperature range 114-115
  varieties and purchasing 114
  watering 114-115
F. benjamina 114
  conditions and care of 115
  healthy plant *117*
  pests and diseases *118*
  propagation 114
F. lyrata 114
  healthy plant *117*
  leaf damage *119*
  mealy bug *118*
F. pumila 114
  healthy plant *117*
  underwatering *119*
F. robusta 114
  conditions and care of 115
  healthy plant *116*
  overwatering *119*
  propagation 114
  pruning 33
Fiddle Leaf Fig *(Ficus lyrata)* 114 *117, 118, 119*
Finger Aralia *(Aralia elegantissima)* 54-55
Fittonia 120
  F. argyroneura 120
  F. a. 'Nana' 120
  F. verschaffeltii 120
  feeding 120
  healthy plant *120*
  light and position 120
  pests and diseases 120, *120*
  propagation 120
  seasonal care 120
  soil 120
  temperature range 120
  watering 120
Flaming Sword *(Vriesea splendens)* 72
Flamingo Flower *(Anthurium)* 50-51
Floradora *(Stephanotis floribunda)* 178
Floret 184
Florida Beauty *(Dracaena)* 102-103
Florists' Azalea *(Azalea indica)* 60-61
Florists' Cineraria *(Senecio cruentus cineraria)* 82-83
Florists' Cyclamen *(Cyclamen persicum)* 94-95
Florists' Gloxinia *(Sinningia)* 172-173
Foliage plant 184
Foliar feed 16, 30, 184
Fountain Plant *(Dracaena)* 102-103
Friendship Plant *(Billbergia nutans)* 72
Friendship Plant *(Pilea involucrata)* 156-157
Frond 184
Fungicide 184

Fungicides, use of see
   Pests and diseases 20-25
Fungus 184
Fungus gnat see *Sciarid fly*

G

Genus 184
Geraniaceae
   Pelargonium 147-149
Geranium *(Pelargonium)* 147-149
German House Lime
   (Sparmannia africana) 175
Germination 184
Gesneriaceae:
   Columnea 92-93
   Saintpaulia 164-165
   Sinningia 172-173
   Streptocarpus 179
Gloxinia *(Sinningia)* 172-173
Goat's Head Cactus
   (Astrophytum capricorne) 76
Golden Candles *(Pachystachys
   lutea)* 141
Golden Hunter's Robe
   (Scindapsus) 171
Goldfish Plant *(Columnea)* 92-93
Grafting 184
Grape Ivy *(Rhoicissus)* 84,
   162-163
Green Cliffbrake *(Pellaea viridis)*
   110
Green Rays *(Heptapleurum)*
   124-125
Greenfly *21, 24*
Grevillea robusta 121
   feeding 121
   healthy plant *121*
   light and position 121
   pests and diseases 121
   seasonal care 121
   soil 121
   temperature range 121
   watering 121
Growing shoot 184

H

Habit 184
Half-hardy plant 184
Hamatocactus setispinus 76, 77
Hanging baskets or pots 29-30
Hardy plant 184
Hart's Tongue Fern *(Phyllitis)* 110,
   110
Heartleaf Philodendron
   (Philodendron) 152-155
Hedgehog Cactus
   (Echinocereus) 76, 77
Hedera 122-123
   feeding 123
   H. canariensis 122, *122*
   H. helix 122
   H. h. 'Chicago' 122
   H. h. 'Glacier' 122
   H. h. 'Little Diamond' 122
   H. h. 'Sagittaefolia' 122
   H. ivalace 122
   healthy plant *122*
   light and position 123

pests and diseases 123
propagation 122
seasonal care 123
soil 123
temperature range 123
unhealthy plant *123*
varieties and purchasing 122
watering 123
Heptapleurum 124-125
   feeding 125
   H. arboricola 124, *124*
   H. a. 'Geisha Girl' 124
   H. a. 'Hong Kong' 124
   H. a. Variegata 124, *124*
   healthy plant *124*
   light and position 125
   pests and diseases 125
   propagation 124
   seasonal care 125
   soil 125
   stem rot *125*
   temperature range 125
   varieties and purchasing 124
   watering 125
Herringbone Plant *(Fittonia)* 120
Herringbone Plant *(Maranta)*
   134, 136-137
Hibiscus rosa-sinensis 126-127
   aphids *127*
   buying healthy plant *15*
   dehydrated plant *127*
   feeding 127
   H. r-s. 'Cooperi' 126
   H. schizopetalus 126
   'Hawaiian hybrids' 126
   healthy leaves *126*
   healthy plant *126*
   light and position 127
   seasonal care 127
   soil 127
   temperature range 127
   varieties and purchasing 126
   watering 127
Holly Fern *(Cyrtomium falcatum)*
   110, *110*
Honeydew 184
Hormone rooting powder *35*
House Lime, German
   (Sparmannia africana) 175
House Pine *(Araucaria)* 56-57
Howea see *Kentia*
Humidifier 1843
Humidity, provision of 29, *29*, 36
   spraying foliage 36
   surrounding with moisture-
      retaining material 36
Humus 184
Hurricane Plantt *(Monstera
   deliciosa)* 138-139
Hybrid 184
Hydrangea macrophylla 128-129
   feeding 129
   healthy plant *128*
   light and position 129
   pests and diseases 129
   seasonal care 129
   soil 129
   temperature range 129
   underwatering *129*
   varieties and purchasing 128
   watering 129
Hydroculture 184

I

Impatiens 130-131
   feeding 131
   healthy plant *130*
   I. 'Arabesque' 130
   I. 'New Guinea' hybrids 130
   I. petersiana 130
   I. 'Red Magic' 130
   I. wallerana 130
   light and position 131
   pests and diseases 131
   propagation 130
   seasonal care 131
   soil 131
   temperature range 131
   unhealthy plants *131*
   varieties and purchasing 130
   watering 131
Inch Plant *(Tradescantia)* 181
Inch Plant *(Zebrina pendula)* 183
Indian Laurel *(Ficus retusa)* 114
Inflorescence 184
Inorganic fertilizer 184
Insecticide 184
Insecticides, use of see *Pests
   and diseases 20-25*
Italian Bellflower *(Campanula
   isophylla)* 79
Ivy *(Hedera)* 122-123
Ivy Tree *(Fatsia)* 106-107

J

Japanese Aralia *(Fatsia)* 106-107
Japanese Kurume *(Azalea
   obtusum)* 60
Jasmine, Madagascar
   (Stephanotis floribunda) 178
Jerusalem Cherry *(Solanum
   pseudocapsicum)* 174
Joseph's Coat *(Codiaeum)* 14,
   90-91

K

Kaffir Lily *(Clivia miniata)* 88-89
Kalanchoe beharensis 132-133
   damaged leaves *132*
   feeding 132
   healthy plant *133*
   light and position 133
   pests and diseases 132
   propagation 132
   seasonal care 132
   soil 132
   temperature range 132
   watering 132
Kangaroo Vine *(Cissus
   antarctica)* 84-85
Kentia:
   K. belmoreana 142, 144
   K. forsteriana 142, *142*, *143*,
      144
Kentia Palm *(Kentia forsteriana)*
   142, *142*, *143*, 144

L

Lateral shoot 184
Leaf cleaning oils 16, 30-31
   effects of direct sunlight or
      cold 16
   removing excess 16
Leaf cutting 184
Leaf miner *83*
Leaf mould 184
Leaflet 184
Leggy plant 184
Leopard Lily *(Dieffenbachia)*
   98-100
Light requirement of various
   plants *36-37*
Lilliaceae:
   Aspidistra lurida 58-59
   Chlorophytum comosum
      80-81
   Sansevieria 166-167
Lindane see *Pests and diseases
   20-25*
Lithops 76, 77
Little Fantasy *(Peperomia)*
   150-151
Little Lady Palm *(Rhapis)* 144
Little Snakeskin Plant *(Fittonia)*
   120
Living Stones *(Lithops)* 76, *77*
Loam 184
Lobster Plant *(Euphorbia
   pulcherrima)* 104-105
Lollipop Plant *(Pachystachys
   lutea)* 141

M

Madagascar Jasmine
   (Stephanotis floribunda) 178
Maidenhair ferns *(Adiantum)* 111
Malathion see *Pests and
   diseases 20-25*
Malvaceae:
   Hibiscus rosa-sinensis
      126-127
Maranta 134
   feeding 137
   light and position 137
   *M. leuconeura Erythrophylla
      (M. l. Tricolor)* 134, 136
   M. l. Kerchoveana 134,
      134, 136
   pests and diseases 136
   problems *136-137*
   seasonal care 137
   soil 137
   temperature range 137
   varieties and purchasing 136
   watering 137
Marantaceae:
   Calathea, Maranta and
      Stromanthe 134-137
Margin 185
Mealy bug *23, 24*
Mexican Breadfruit Plant
   (Monstera deliciosa) 138-139
Mexican Flame Leaf *(Euphorbia
   pulcherrima)* 104-105

Microcoelum 144, *144*
Microlepia speluncia 111
Midrib 185
Mildew *23,* 24
Mock Orange, Houseblooming
(*Pittosporum*) 158-159
Monstera deliciosa 138-139
aerial roots 138
damaged leaf *139*
feeding 139
healthy plant *138*
light and position 139
purchasing 139
seasonal care 139
soil 139
temperature range 139
underwatered plant *139*
watering 139
Moon Valley (*Pilea mollis*) 157
Moraceae:
Ficus 114-119
Mosaic Plant (*Fittonia*) 120
Moss-covered support, to make
32
Mother of Thousands (*Saxifraga
sarmentosa*) 168-169
Mother-in-Law's Tongue
(*Sansevieria trifasciata
'Laurentii'*) 166-167
Mouth of flower 185
Musa 140
feeding 140
healthy plant *140*
light and position 140
M. cavendishii 140
M. ensete Rubra 140
pests and diseases 140
raising new plants 140
seasonal care 140
soil 140
temperature range 140
varieties and purchasing 140
watering 140
Musaceae:
Musa 140

*Neanthe bella (Chamaedorea
elegans)* 142, *142*
problems *143*
propagation *145*
Neoregelia carolinae 'Tricolor' 72
Nephrolepis exaltata 111
Node 185
Norfolk Island Pine/Plant
(*Araucaria*) 56-57
Notocactus leninghausii 76
Nyctaginaceae:
Bougainvillea 68-69

Octopus Tree (*Schefflera*) 170
Offset 185
Oils for leaves see *Leaf cleaning
chemicals*
Opposite leaves 185
Opuntia 74
Organic matter 185

Overwatering 29
root rot 18, *18*

P

Pachystachys lutea 141
feeding 141
healthy plant *141*
light and position 141
pests and diseases 141
purchasing 141
seasonal care 141
soil 141
temperature range 141
watering 141
Painted Drop-tongue
(*Aglaonema*) 48
Painted Net Leaf (*Fittonia*) 120
Painter's Palette (*Anthurium*)
50-51
Palmae:
Palms 142-145
Palmate leaf 185
Palms 142-145
Caryota 144, *144*
Chamaedorea 144, *144*
Chamaerops humilis 143
Chrysalidocarpus 144, *145*
feeding 142
healthy plants *142*
Kentia belmoreana 142, 144
K. forsteriana 142, *142,* 144
light and position 142
Microcoelum 144, *144*
Neanthe bella (*Chamaedorea
elegans*) 142, *142*
palmate frond *144*
pests and diseases 144
Phoenix 144, *144*
pinnate frond *144*
problems *143*
propagation (*Neanthe bella*)
145
Rhapis 144, *145*
seasonal care 142
sensitivity to chemicals *143*
soil 142
temperature range 142
Trachycarpus 144, *144*
varieties and purchasing 144,
144-145
watering 142
Panda Plant (*Philodendron
bipennifolium*) 153
Paper Flower/Vine
(*Bougainvillea*) 68-69
Parasol Plant (*Heptapleurum*)
124-125
Parchment-bark (*Pittosporum*)
158-159
Parlour Ivy (*Philodendron*)
152-155
Parlour Palm (*Neanthe bella*) 142,
142, 143, 145
Passiflora 146
feeding 146
healthy plant *146*
light and position 146
P. caerulea 146
pests and diseases 146
seasonal care 146

soil 146
temperature range 146
varieties and purchasing 146
watering 146
Passifloraceae:
Passiflora 146
Passion Flower (*Passiflora*) 146
Patience Plant/Patient Lucy
(*Impatiens*) 130-131
Peace Lily (*Spathiphyllum*)
176-177
Peacock Plant (*Calathea
makoyana*) *135,* 136
Peat 185
Pelargonium 147-149
feeding 148
healthy plant *147*
light and position 148
P. domesticum 147
P. zonale 147
pests and diseases 148, *148,
149*
propagation 147
seasonal care 148
soil 148
temperature range 148
varieties and purchasing 147
watering 148
Pellaea rotundifolia 110, *110*
Pellaea viridis 110
Peperomia 150-151
feeding 150
light and position 150
P. hederifolia 151
P. lanceolata 151
P. magnoliifolia 'Variegata' 150,
151
P. obtusifolia 151
P. orba 'Princess Astrid' 151
P. scandens 'Variegata' 151
pests and diseases 151, *151*
propagation 150
seasonal care 150
soil 150
temperature range 150
varieties and purchasing 151
watering 150
Perennial 185
Pesticides see *Pests and
diseases 20-25*
Pests and diseases 20-25
aphids *21,* 24
black leg 53, 67, 148, 154
black spot 123
botrytis *23,* 24
caterpillars *95*
control in the nursery 22
cyclamen mite *95,* 165
earthworms 17, *21*
instant diagnosis chart *40-41*
leaf miner *83*
mealy bug *23,* 24
mildew *23,* 24
red spider mite 20, *20,* 22
root mealy bug *21,* 24
rust 148
scale insect *22,* 25
sciarid fly *20,* 22
slug *72,* 154, *155*
sooty mould 25, 87, *155,* 158
stem rot *101, 125,* 131, 167
symphalids (springtails) *21,* 24

thrips 22, *23,* 24
vine weevil 95, 148, 161, 167
virus infection 148
white fly *22,* 24-25
Petiole 185
pH balance 185
Philippine Medusa (*Acalypha
hispida*) 44-45
Philodendron 152-155
aerial roots 152
feeding 154
light and position 154
P. bipennifolium 153
P. bipinnatifidum 153
P. hastatum 152, 153
P. imbe 153
P. pedatum 153
P. 'Red Emerald' 152, 153
P. scandens 153, *153*
P. wendlandii 153
pests and diseases 154,
154-155
propagation 152
seasonal care 154
soil 154
temperature range 154
varieties and purchasing 153
watering 154
Phoenix 144, *144*
Photosynthesis 185
Phyllitis 110, *110*
Pickaback/Pick-a-back
Plant/Piggy-back Plant
(*Tolmiea menziesii*) 180
Pigtail Plant (*Anthurium*) 50-51
Pilea 156-157
feeding 156
light and position 156
P. cadierei 156, 157
P. involucrata 157
P. mollis 157
P. muscosa 157
P. spruceana 157
pests and diseases 157, *157*
propagation 156
seasonal care 156
soil 156
temperature range 156
varieties and purchasing 157
watering 156
Pinching out 185
Pineapple Plant (*Ananas
comosus*) 72
Pinnate leaf 185
Piperaceae:
Peperomia 150-151
Pirimiphos-methyl see *Pests
and diseases 20-25*
Pittosporaceae:
Pittosporum 158-159
feeding 158
healthy plant *159*
light and position 158
P. eugenioides 158
P. garnetti 158
P. tenuifolium 158, *159*
pests and diseases 158
seasonal care 158
soil 158
temperature range 158
unhealthy leaves *158*
varieties 158
watering 158

Plantlet 185
Platycerium alcicorne 108, 110, *111*
Poinsettia *(Euphorbia pulcherrima)* 104-105
Polypodiaceae: Ferns 108-113
Polypodium aureum 110, *110*
Positioning plants 27-28, 36-39
  bathroom *27*
  delicate 28
  flowering 27
  good plants for pedestal 36, 38
  green foliaged 27-28
  groups in wall or floor planters 38
  hallway *38*
  large 28
  light requirements *36-37*
    measuring light intensity *36*
  near radiators 18
  variegated 27
Pot-bound 185
Pothos Vine *(Scindapsus)* 171
Pots, decorative 29
  hanging types 29-30
Potting on 19, 185
  after purchase 17
  after-care of plants 19
  best time for 19
  checking if necessary 19
  drainage 19
  pot sizes 19
  top-dressing 17,19
Prawn Plant *(Beloperone guttata)* 66-67
Prayer Plant *(Maranta)* 134, 136-137
Primula 160-161
  feeding 161
  healthy plant *160*
  light and position 161
  P. acaulis 160
  P. malacoides 160
  P. obconica 160
  pests and diseases 161, *161*
  seasonal care 161
  soil 161
  temperature range 161
  watering 161
Primulaceae:
  Cyclamen persicum 94-95
  Primula 160-161
Problems – instant diagnosis chart *40-41*
Propagation 34, 185
  hormone rooting powder *35*
  leaf cuttings 35
  planting cuttings and seeds 34
  sealed unit to prevent transpiration *34, 35*
  separating plants *33*
  taking cuttings *34, 35*
  temperature 34
Propagators, types of *34*
Proteaceae:
  Grevillea robusta 121
Pruning 33, *33*, 185
  Rubber Plant 33
Pteris 110, 111

Q

Queen's Tears *(Billbergia nutans)* 72

R

Rabbit Tracks *(Maranta)* 134, 136-137
Rainbow Star *(Cryptanthus bromelioides)* 71
Red spider mite 20, *20*, 22
  bad infestation 20
  control of 20, 22
  signs of 20
  susceptible plants 20
Redhot Cat-tail *(Acalypha hispida)* 44-45
Repotting (see also *Potting)* 19, 185
Resting period 185
Rhapis 144, *145*
Rhizome 185
Rhoicissus 84, 162,163
  feeding 163
  healthy leaves *163*
  healthy plant *162*
  light and position 163
  pests and diseases 162, *162*
  R. rhomboidea 162
  R. r. 'Ellendanica' 162
  raising new plants 162
  scorched leaf *163*
  seasonal care 163
  soil 163
  temperature range 163
  varieties and purchasing 162
  watering 163
Ribbon Plant *(Chlorophytum comosum)* 80-81
Rootball 185
Root mealy bug *21, 24*
  detection of 24
Root rot 18, *18*
  to remedy 18
Rose of China *(Hibiscus rosa-sinensis)* 15, 126-127
Rosette 185
Roving Sailor *(Saxifraga sarmentosa)* 168-169
Rubber Plant *(Ficus robusta)* 33, 114, 115, *116, 119*
Runner 185
Rust 148
Rusty Fig *(Ficus rubiginosa)* 114
Rutaceae:
  Citrus mitis 86-87

S

Saffron Spike *(Aphelandra)* 52-53
St Bernard's Lily *(Chlorophytum comosum)* 80-81
Saintpaulia 164-165
  feeding 165
  healthy plant *164*
  light and position 165
  pests and diseases 165, *165*
  propagation 34
  seasonal care 165
  soil 165
  temperature range 165
  varieties and purchasing 164
  watering 165
Sansevieria 166-167
  dry leaf *167*
  feeding 167
  healthy plant *166*
  light and position 167
  pests and diseases 167
  propagation 166
  S. cylindrica 166
  S. liberica 166
  S. trifasciata 166
  S. t. 'Golden Hahnii' 166
  S. t. 'Hahnii' 166
  S. t. 'Laurentii' 166, *166*
  S. t. 'Moonshine' 166
  S. t. 'Silver Hahnii' 166
  S. zeylanica 166
  seasonal care 167
  soil 167
  temperature range 167
  varieties and purchasing 166
  watering 167
Saxifraga sarmentosa 168-169
  feeding 168
  healthy leaf *169*
  healthy plant *168*
  light and position 168
  pests and diseases 169
  propagation 168
  seasonal care 168
  soil 168
  temperature range 168
  unhealthy plant *169*
  varieties and purchasing 169
  watering 168
Saxifragaceae:
  Hydrangea macrophylla 128-129
  Saxifraga sarmentosa (S. stolonifera) 168-169
  Tolmiea menziesii 180
Scale insect *22, 25*
  removal of 25
  signs of 25
  susceptible plants 25
Schefflera 170
  feeding 170
  healthy plant *170*
  light and position 170
  pests and diseases 170
  raising new plants 170
  seasonal care 170
  soil 170
  temperature range 170
  varieties and purchasing 170
  watering 170
Sciarid fly *20, 22*
Scindapsus 171
  feeding 171
  light and position 171
  pests and diseases 171
  propagation 171
  S. aureus 171, *171*
  S. a. 'Marble Queen' 171, *171*
  seasonal care 171
  soil 171
  temperature range 171
  varieties 171
  watering 171
Seeds, growing from see *Propagation*
Senecio cruentus cineraria (Cineraria) 82-83
Sentry Palm *(Kentia belmoreana)* 142, 144
Sharp sand 185
Shooting Star *(Cyclamen persicum)* 94-95
Shrimp Plant *(Beloperone guttata)* 66-67
Shrub 185
Silhouette Plant *(Dracaena)* 102-103
Silk/Silk-bark Oak *(Grevillea robusta)* 121
Silver Torch *(Cleistocactus strausii)* 76
Silver Tree *(Pilea spruceana) 157*
Silver Spear *(Aglaonema)* 48
Sinningia 172-173
  feeding 173
  light and position 173
  pests and diseases *172-173, 173*
  seasonal care 173
  soil 173
  temperature range 173
  varieties 172
  watering 173
Slender Lady Palm *(Rhapis)* 144
Slugs *72*, 154, *155*
Snakeskin Plant, Little *(Fittonia)* 120
Soil 17
Solanaceae:
  Solanum capsicastrum 174
Solanum capsicastrum 174
  feeding 174
  light and position 174
  pests and diseases 174
  S. pseudocapsicum 174
  seasonal care 174
  soil 174
  temperature range 174
  varieties and purchasing 174
  watering 174
Solomon Islands Vine *(Scindapsus)* 171
Sooty mould 25, 87, *155, 158*
Spadix 185
Spanish Bayonet *(Yucca aloifolia)* 182
Sparmannia africana 175
  feeding 175
  healthy plant *175*
  light and position 175
  pests and diseases 175
  propagation 175
  seasonal care 175
  soil 175
  temperature range 175
  varieties and purchasing 175
  watering 175
Spathe 185
Spathiphyllum 176-177
  feeding 177
  healthy plant *176*
  light and position 177

propagation 176
S. 'Mauna Loa' 176, *176*
S. wallisii 176
seasonal care 177
soil 177
temperature range 177
unhealthy leaf *177*
varieties and purchasing 176
watering 177
Species 185
Speedy Jenny *(Tradescantia)* 181
Sphagnum moss 185
Spider Plant *(Aralia elegantissima)* 54-55
Spider Plant *(Chlorophytum comosum)* 80-81
Spineless Yucca *(Yucca elephantipes)* 182
Splitleaf Plant *(Monstera deliciosa)* 138-139
Spore 185
Sport 185
Spraying foliage, benefits 20, 36
Springtails (symphalids) *21,* 24
Stagshorn Fern *(Platycerium alcicorne)* 108, 110, *111*
Staking plants 32 *32*
making moss-covered support 32
trellis 32, *32*
types of stake *32*
Star of Bethlehem *(Campanula isophylla)* 79
Starfish Plant *(Cryptanthus acaulis)* 72
Stem rot *101, 125,* 131, 167
Stephanotis floribunda 178
feeding 178
healthy plant *178*
light and position 178
pests and diseases 178
raising new plants 178
seasonal care 178
soil 178
temperature range 178
varieties and purchasing 178
watering 178
Strawberry Cactus *(Hamatocactus setispinus)* 76, *77*
Streptocarpus 179
feeding 179
light and position 179
pests and diseases 179
raising new plants 179, *179*
S. 'Concorde Hybrid' 179
S. 'Constant Nymph' 179
seasonal care 179
soil 179
temperature range 179
varieties and purchasing 179
watering 179
Strike 185
Striped Dracaena *(Dracaena)* 102-103
Stromanthe amabilis 135, *135,* 136
feeding 137
light and position 137
pests and diseases 136
problems *136-137*
purchasing 136

seasonal care 137
soil 137
temperature range 137
watering 137
Succulent (see also *Cacti and succulents*) 185
Sweetheart Plant *(Philodendron scandens)* 152-155
Swiss Cheese Plant *(Monstera deliciosa)* 138-139
Symphalids *21,* 24
Systemic insecticide 185

T

Tailflower *(Anthurium)* 50-51
Tendril 185
Terrestrial plant 185
Thrips 22, *23,* 24
Thunder flies see *Thrips*
Tiliaceae:
Sparmannia africana 175
Tilllandsia 72, 73
Tolmiea menziesii 180
feeding 180
healthy plant *180*
light and position 180
pests and diseases 180
seasonal care 180
soil 180
temperature range 180
varieties and purchasing 180
watering 180
top-dressing 17, 19, 185
Touch-me-not *(Impatiens)* 130-131
Trachycarpus 144, *144*
Tradescantia 181
feeding 181
healthy plant *181*
light and position 181
related plants 181
pests and diseases 181
propagation 181
seasonal care 181
soil 181
T. albiflora 'Albovittata' 181
T.a. 'Tricolor' 181
T. fluminensis 181
T. f. 'Quicksilver' 181
temperature range 181
varieties 181
watering 181
Transpiration 185
Tree Ivy *(Fatsia)* 106-107
Trichocereus spachianus 77
Tuber 185

U

Umbrella Plant/Palm/Sedge *(Cyperus)* 96-97
Umbrella Tree *(Schefflera)* 170
Urn Plant *(Aechmea)* 46-47
Urticaceae:
Pilea 156-157

V

Variegated plants 185
Variety 185
Vein 185
Velvet Plant/Velvet-leaf *(Kalanchoe beharensis)* 132-133
Venus Hair *(Adiantum capillus-veneris) 108-109, 111*
Vine weevil 95, 148, 161, 167
Virus infection 148
Vitaceae:
Cissus 84-85
Rhoicissus 162-163
Vriesea 72
V. splendens 72

W

Wandering Sailor/Jew *(Tradescantia)* 181
Wandering Sailor/Jew *(Zebrina pendula)* 183
Watering 17-18, 28-29
azalea 16, *16*
capillary 17-18
on purchase 16
reviving parched plant *28*
technique 28
testing if needed 28
Watermelon Plant *(Pilea cadierei)* 156-157
Wax Flower *(Stephanotis floribunda)* 178
Weeping Fig *(Ficus benjamina)* 114, 115, *117, 118*
White fly *22,* 24-25
White Sails *(Spathiphyllum)* 176-177
White Torch Cactus *(Trichocereus spachianus) 77*
Whorl 185
Windmill Palm *(Trachycarpus)* 144, *144*
Window Plant *(Monstera deliciosa)* 138-139
Wine Palm *(Caryota)* 144
Worms in pots 17, *21*

Y

Yellow Palm *(Chrysalidocarpus)* 144
Youth on Age *(Tolmiea menziesii)* 180
Yucca elephantipes 182
feeding 182
healthy plant *182*
light and position 182
pests and diseases 182
seasonal care 182
soil 182
temperature range 182
varieties and purchasing 182
watering 182
Y. aloifolia 182

Z

Zebra Plant *(Aphelandra)* 52-53
Zebra Plant *(Calathea zebrina)* 136
Zebrina pendula 183
feeding 183
healthy plant *183*
light and position 183
pests and diseases 183
raising new plants 183
seasonal care 183
soil 183
temperature range 183
varieties and purchasing 183
watering 183
Z. p. 'Discolor' 183
Z. p. purpusii 183
Z. p. Quadricolor 183
Zimmerlinden *(Sparmannia africana)* 175
Zygocactus truncatus 77